# The Eloquence of a Stutterer

## (Volume 2)

## Arul Lourdu

Title : **The Eloquence of a Stutterer**
**(Volume 2)**

Author : Arul Lourdu

Subject : Spirituality

First Edition : April, 2022

Pages : 336 ( xxiv +312)

Publication : © The Author

Price : Rs. 300/- , Euro 30,00

ISBN: 978-3-9818465-3-9
Herz – Jesu Verlag

Printed at : Modern Reflections, Chennai - 600 014

# DEDICATION

The Volumes are dedicated to my beloved parents whose names (Arul Lourdu) I bear for their gift of life and faith!

# FOREWORD

**Most Rev. Dr. George Antonysamy**

Archbishop of Madras and Mylapore

MS/ABS/21/17                    Chennai, 24<sup>th</sup> March 2021

"He who does not know the Scripture, does not know God" said St. Joerome. The Word of God is the Proclamation of the Gospel is one of the three essential ministries of the ordained. With the Apostolic Letter in the form of a Motu proprio *"Aperuit illis"* issued on 30<sup>th</sup> September 2019. Pope Francis has instituted 'The Sunday of the Word of God' to be held every year on the third Sunday of Ordinary Time, intending it to be a day dedicated to the celebration, reflection and dissemination of the Word. This special call of the Holy Father is to emphasise those who proclaim the Word of God in the assembly – priests, deacons and lectors to "explain and enable all to understand Sacred Scripture" and to "make it accessible to their communities", carrying out this ministry "with special dedication, treasuring the means proposed by the Church".

*"Indeed, the word of God is living and active, sharper than any two-edged sword, piercing until it divides soul from spirit, joints from marrow; it is able to judge the thoughts and intentions of the heart,"* (Heb 4:12) The Word of God is truly alive in the lives of the people. It becomes meaningful and real in our daily circumstances. It is for this reason. Pope Francis exhorts all priests to be in touch with their faithful in

v

order to be totally aware of their joys and sorrows. He calls it as, 'knowing the smell of the sheep, While the Word of God is ever creative and transformative, in application it is unique and special to each one's pattern of life. Therefore, as pastors those entrusted with the vocation to preach the Word are invited to apply it to concrete life situations, so as to enable God's message abundantly-fruitful.

I have known Rev. Fr. Arul Lourdu for many years and I am glad to know he has given reflections and insights on the Word of God, corresponding to the circumstances of his ministry in Germany. I have seen his videos in German and liked it and congratulate his tireless work on evangelization for the past ten years. However, his translated work in English, I am sure, would appeal to all people in seeking God's will through the spoken Word. While congratulating him for his contribution, I invite you to make use of these reflections, to come closer to God, listen to Him with an open heart like Mary of Bethany, and put them to practice. In this way, we would be able to glorify God, not only in Word, but also in deed.

With assurance of wishes and prayers, I remain In Christ Our Lord,

+ hugy auriny

**+George Antonysamy**
**Archbishop of Madras-Mylapore**

Archbishop's House, # 41, Son Thome High Road, Chennai 600 004
☏ +91 - 44 - 2464 1102 / 2464 0833  📠 + 91 - 44 - 2464 1999  ✉ Email: abpmmsec@gmail.com

# FELICITATION

**Hans D. Reinwald**
Mayor of Leimen
Germany

Greetings from Mayor Hans Reinwald on the 500th jubilee!

Dear readers,

Since 2011, Father Arul Lourdu has been regularly proclaiming "The Spiritual Word for Sunday". For this purpose, in addition to the classic church service, he has chosen the Internet as a medium, which is progressive and modern then and now. For the consistency in the Proclamation he received the Honorary Doctorate from an Indian university. He has retained this consistency – mean while he has proclaimed the "spiritual word" in 500 episodes. It's a proud anniversary on which I can congratulate him personally-together with the local council and the city administration.

Fr. Arul Lourdu not only preaches the word of God as a pastor, his speeches are those of a person who is there for his fellow men and cares for them.

Fr. Arul Lourdu is not afraid to express his personal opinion in addition to the Spiritual Word. In the short video messages, he sometimes has to deliberately generalize and shorten facts. This can trigger discussions, but this is a desired stylistic device so that the audience, believers and non-believers, deal with the content and the issues addressed in the sense of a living church. Fr. Arul Lourdu is a good shepherd. With his videos he offers his viewers support and thanks to this format he is also there for people who cannot attend the worship service in person. As a good shepherd, I got to know Fr. Arul Lourdu in many personal conversations, as a person who is not afraid of discussion, always striving for compromises and is interested in consensus-oriented solutions. His pleasant personality and way of speaking to people are the key to people listening and seeing him for 500 episodes. Dear Pastor Lourdu, I hope that you will be able to produce many more episodes and that your digital community will remain loyal to you for a long time to come.

Yours sincerely,

Stay healthy

**Hans D. Reinwald.**

# FELICITATION

**Georg Kletti**
Mayor of Sandhausen
Germany

Greetings for the 500th jubilee from Mayor Georg Kletti!

Greetings for the 500th edition of the video column "The Spiritual Word for Sunday" by Arul Lourdu, pastor of the major pastoral care Unit Leimen – Nussloch - Sandhausen of the Catholic Church.

My heartfelt congratulations on this extraordinary anniversary should begin with a quote: "Because the more modern technologies create ever more intensive connections and the digital world expands its limits, the more the priest will be challenged to deal with it in pastoral care and to increase his own commitment to put the media at the service of the Word."

This was said on Sunday, May 16h, 2010, a good one and a half years before the first broadcast of the "Spiritual Word" on October 9th, 2021, at that time for Thanksgiving. The quote, however, does not come from Father Arul Lourdu, which is with a view to what was to follow could well be obvious, but from Pope Benedict XVI. More precisely: from his "Message for the 44th World Day of Social Communication", entitled "The priest and pastoral care in the digital world-the new media in service of the Word".

In addition, the head of the Roman Catholic Church stated that the "channels of communication opened up by technological achievements have already become indispensable instruments" and that the digital world provides means that "offer almost unlimited possibilities for communication". However, priests are required to be "able to be present in the digital world in constant fidelity to the biblical message".

All in all, Pope Benedict XVI highlighted, the priest could "make known the life of the Church through modern means of communication and help the people of today to discover the face of Christ". Even more than the hand of the media technician, as a man of God, the priest should let his heart shine through to "be in contact with the digital world in order not only to give a soul to one's own pastoral work, but also to the uninterrupted communication stream of the Internet".

Ten years later, on January 26th, 2020, there was also a message from Pope Francis for Media Sunday. Under the title "Man is a narrator" he came to the following conclusion: "Often the 'looms' of communication do not produce constructive stories that hold social ties and cultural fabric together, but destructive and provocative stories that wear and tear the fragile threads of living together."

"In an age," continues Pope Francis, "in which the art of forgery is becoming more and more sophisticated and has reached an unbelievable level (deep fake), we need wisdom in order to receive and produce beautiful, true and good stories. We need courage, to reject the false and vicious stories. And we need patience and discernment to rediscover those stories that will help us not to lose the thread in the midst of the turmoil of our time."

It is precisely such a beautiful, true and good story that Father Arul Lourdu is telling for the 500th time. Whereby he always adheres to the following requirement: "You can preach about what you want, but never preach for more than forty minutes." And just as this quote comes from Martin Luther, the next comes from the German-American computer scientist and computer critic Joseph Weizenbaum: "The internet is a big dung heap, in which you can also find small treasures and pearls." Nothing other than a little treasure and a pearl is certainly the "Spiritual Word" in Friedrich Uthe's Internet newspaper, and not just for me.

**Georg Kletti**

# FELICITATION

**Joachim Förster**

Mayor of Nussloch

Germany

"Digital pioneer" - Greeting from Nussloch's Mayor Joachim Förster!

A special format was created 500 weeks ago. A format that teaches, strengthens and sometimes makes you smile. A progressive format brought to life by two gentlemen who already understood 10 years ago how important the provision of digital Content would be for us one day.

Today, in the year 2021, in which we are dependent on digital exchange, you are both pioneers. In this uncertain time you bring stability with which you strengthen our community.

I congratulate you both, Father Lourdu and Mr. Uthe, on your anniversary and thank you for your engagement and commitment over the past few years, but above all for the contribution you have made to our community.

I hope all readers will continue to enjoy these two formats.

Yours Sincerely,

**Joachim Förster.**

# FELICITATION

**Norbert Knopf**
Member of State Assembly
St. Leon - Rot
Germany

Greetings to the 500th jubilee from Member of the State Assembly Norbert Knopf

The Spiritual Word for Sunday-a theological series of contributions on spiritual, social and cultural topics-has been giving viewers reflection every week for the past 10 years.

To celebrate the 500th announcement to four Father Arul Lourdu in the local Online Magazine Leimenblog. de, these 500 impulses have now been collected and published in this book. In his blog column, Fr. Lourdu also gives support to people who cannot attend Church services regularly. At the same time, he shows how the church, especially in hectic times, in which cohesion and contact seem more important than ever, is able to bring its message to the public consciousness. Every week a new point of view is conveyed, which is helpful for all people in the irrespective phase of life, stimulates reflection and gives hope. Regardless of whether people are Christians or have any Church affiliation.

Our city Leimen is very fortunate to have two very committed parishioners, Father Arul Lourdu and Mr. Friedrich-Wilhelm Uthe, editor-in-chief of the online daily newspaper in our region, who have put together this book on the occasion of this anniversary and in honour of His Holiness Pope Francis, They have produced this wonderful book. We are very grateful to both of them.

I hope you enjoy reading this book!

Your Member,

**Norbert Knopf.**

# FELICITATION

**Friedrich-Wilhelm Uthe**
Publisher
Internet newspaper
Leimen-Lokal
Germany

My Catholic Jour Fixe: 500 Spiritual Words with Pastor Lourdu

Attending Sunday worship was, at least in the past, one of the firmly anchored customs in the life of a faithful Christian. New German would probably be called "Jour Fixe" today. But as times have changed, only a fraction of all German Christians now regularly attend church services.

In order to maintain and strengthen the loosely bonded relationship of many (also) Catholic Christians to the Church, Pastor Lourdu has been speaking his Spiritual Word not from the pulpit but into the video camera for exactly 500 weeks. So that it is always available as a YouTube video and can give a spiritual, Christian, Catholic impulse to reflect and believe without having to attend a Church worship at a certain time.

The Spiritual Word has been recorded and published by the regional internet newspaper Leimen-Lokal.de for the last 500 weeks. This is because the church is still not only physically but also sociologically present in the middle of the "village" and because its Christian values and beliefs have a profound influence on the general framework of occidental values.

The Spiritual Word as a Christian-moral weekly impulse helps to adjust and stabilize this framework of values and beliefs!

In both Christians and agnostics! That is what makes it so valuable. That is why I am particularly pleased that the previous Spiritual Words have now also been translated into English and are therefore become understandable for an even larger circle of readers and viewers.

The Spiritual Word of Pastor Lourdu has been a "Jour Fixe" for me for 500 weeks, just like attending Sunday worships in the past of many Christians. I therefore wish the readers of this book many good reflections after reading the impulses of Pastor Arul Lourdu.

**Friedrich-Wilhelm Uthe**

# FELICITATION

"The Eloquence of a Stutterer"-by the will and grace of God I was entrusted with the wonderful opportunity of editing this book, "The Eloquence of a Stutterer" consisting of 500 precious stones like pearls, rubies and diamonds each sparkling and twinkling with their own radiant beams and illuminating light and beauty to enlighten the hearts and minds of the reader without an iota of doubt.

This book contains 54 chapters, the topics arranged in alphabetical order. The whole contents were the reflections rendered by Rev. Fr. Arul Lourdu, a Pastor of our origin. He settled himself as a German citizen in Germany, pasturing the people of God of five parishes under his care and guidance. These reflections were given by him without any gap in between for 500 consecutive weeks through You Tube to his people to nurture them in their spiritual life and also to strengthen them in their faith in Christ. This is indeed a great service, untiringly rendered for the sake of the people. The rendering of the reflections shows the pastor's experience.

As I was editing each reflection, I was more and more edified and enlightened on various vistas of Catholic faith. On reading this book one can get good information about the topic concerned. For example if anyone wants to know about Mother Mary, ample information is available like Mother Mary's life, about her name, the dogmatic proclamations promulgated down the centuries about her etc. Atleast some important information can be obtained from such short notes.

Each reflection is done in such a way that they convey the main thrust of the message they want to convey. That is the beauty of each reflection. Each reflection is unique in itself. This book is like a small encyclopedia.

I profusely thank from the bottom of my heart Rev. Fr. Arul Lourdu, Germany, who without even seeing or knowing me came forward to entrust me this work with confidence. My whole hearted thanks go to Rev. Fr. (Dr) John Peter, HOD Social Works Department of Mar Gregorious College, Chennai for suggesting my name and thus paved way for getting the onerous task of editing the book "The Eloquence of a Stutterer" by me and also for his corrections and suggestions in this book, for which he spared his valuable time in the midst of his multifarious activities. I thank Ms. Janet Rekha Chennai, for her cooperation and coordination and for the hardwork she had done in translating the German sermons into English. On the top of all I prostrate before the Trinitarian God with folded hands for giving me this rarest and life time opportunity of laying my hand and do my bit by way of editing of this book "The Eloquence of a Stutterer" which is gifted as a souvenir by Rev Fr. Arul Lourdu to our Supreme Pontiff Pope Francis in the year AD 2021.

May this book be successful. I hope Rev Fr. Arul Lourdu will publish more and more valuable videos as well as spiritual books in the years to come.

**Lourdhu Mary**
Chennai

# Welcome!

# A Warm Welcome to You!

*"He has taken me to his cellar, and his banner over me is love. Feed me with raisin cakes, restore me with apples, for I am sick with love."* (Sg 2:4-5)

A hearty welcome to you to my two volumes of the "The Eloquence of a Stutterer" my beloved readers. It is an invitation to enjoy a tasty banquet! As you begin to turn the pages of this book, you would be astonished to see a lot of bowls, vessels, mugs and tumblers spread here and there filled with a variety of food and drinks - the food for soul, the spiritual food, to fill your hearts and minds and quench your thirst for the Lord!

In the forthcoming pages, under fifty three different topics, you can enjoy five hundred interesting thought provoking, reflective messages. Under the fifty main topics, there are a number of reflections related to the main topic. There are also seasonal messages which can be used to ponder during different festival seasons in the Church. For example there are messages pertaining to the season of Advent - a season of waiting for the Coming of the Lord - the Second Coming of Christ. There are meditative messages for the season of Lent which also include a full reflection on the 14 Stations of Cross, a popular devotion in the Catholic Church. The book enables you to create Desert space in your heart to welcome the Lord and be with him - a home away from home - away from the routine odds in the house, office and other hectic schedules of the day, making you busy all the time, providing no space for the Lord. It helps you to find the small break ups, brokenness here and there which may require mending and repair within our heart and soul.

Most of the narratives are scriptural, the scripture explained in a variety of dimensions to suit the minds and time of the users. The messages contain Biblical thoughts and explanations, anecdotes, small stories, incidents from lives of people, lessons from nature, a little bit of politics from the political arena, religious issues etc. As special guests, a few Saints are there who share their life stories, so that the readers can be inspired by their lives and take them as their role models to change their life patterns and to walk along a path leading to sainthood.

It is not a book which gives only a stiff and serious reading. There is a lighter side too. It is like a Comedy Corner. A few jokes pertaining to the major religions - Christianity, Judaism, Buddhism, Hinduism and Islam adorn the book, bringing laughter on your face. It is sure for certain even a person vowed not to laugh cannot control his/her laughter, in spite of strong resistance.

Thus this book is a grand banquet - a buffet. A number of varieties of dishes are set in all the pages of this book spread before you. Now it is your turn to go round - pick whatever you want here and now. If you wish you can have all at one time, you can go ahead. It is not the food for a stomach to cause health issues or allergies because of overeating or for consuming prohibited items. It is spiritual nourishment. No restrictions here. Taste it. Relish it. Cherish it. This banquet is not like the usual banquets you know. Enjoy and come back. The dishes don't get over just on that single occasion. This banquet is right in your hands, on your table, in your book shelf. When ever you feel hunger and thirst for the Word of the Lord with in you, open the book, taste any dish of your choice that is found in any of the pages in the book - read it, chew it, again and again and enjoy number of rounds.

Life being dynamic, aspires to grow and evolve as ever. One of the God-given and gifted qualities of human beings is language and the ability to articulate things fluently, which in my opinion involves the quintessential role of both mind and soul.

Born as the youngest child of a loving couple in a delightful family of six children, I had the privilege of having been raised in a very spiritual path and enjoyed the serendipity of nature-surrounded and simplicity nestled in a typical village called Thiruvarangam in Ramanathapuram district of Tamil Nadu.

My horrific encounter with an unfortunate fire accident in my early childhood and the resultant traumatic experience left me virtually 'speechless'. Yes, I lost my ability to speak cohesively. Thus being a stutterer at the very formative age of my childhood, I found stammering a constant companion of mine that took a toll in the early part of my life for an agonizing three decades and more. There were numerous occasions where I felt very humiliated in front of my classmates and others as I became a laughing stock due to my inability to strike conversations fluently. Gradually I stopped raising my voice in public for the fear of getting ashamed and insulted.

Yet there used to be some noble souls, helpful people in the form of teachers, priests and seminarians who helped me with their advice to go for an ergo therapy and to practise spiritual exercises. I underwent a lot of such practices during this time with the hope to overcome this accident-inflicted speech deformity.

Ironically and to the surprise of everyone, I was made the class leader from my 9th Grade onwards in the school. Then an inhibition crept onto me as I found it extremely difficult to address and represent student related issues at several forums. I experienced an excruciating mental anguish, pain and the yearnings to overcome this daunting hindrance of stammering and stuttering. I often thought of the words of Isaiah: "Then I said: 'Woe is me! I am lost, for I am a man of unclean lips and I live among a people of unclean lips, and my eyes have seen the King, Yahweh Sabaoth" (Is 6:5).

After graduating in Chemistry followed by a break of a year, the divine call for priesthood inspired me to take up this holy path. However, I could not be rest assured whether I could ever overcome the speech hindrance which I had been grappling with for years. All the same I did not know, with this disorder, if I would ever be able to preach the Word of God in sermons.

The Society of the Divine Word (SVD) came to my rescue to alleviate my problems. Through my several spiritual discourses and studies in Philosophy, Anthropology and Theology I could feel the uttermost need to be healed with the miraculous hands of Jesus.

Through constant intercessions and allowing the healing hands of Jesus I came out of this impediment by and by. I then left the congregation of SVD and joined the archdiocese of Freiburg, Germany in 1999. The challenge continued to be present as I had to preach in another foreign language. Also here I was blessed with great help from many and on 18th May 2003, I could say a complete YES to the Lord to send me to HIS people. After having served as an assistant parish priest in two parishes, I was appointed parish priest in the year 2008 in Leimen - in the beginning for three parishes. In the year 2011, I was given in addition a charge of two more parishes by my archbishop.

At this juncture, Mr. Friedrich-Wilhelm Uthe started his internet newspaper in this region, situated in Leimen. It was quite an innovative idea to start a digital newspaper. He approached me and asked me whether I could offer spiritual thoughts for his viewers and readers once a week, via YouTube. So we started to organize every week and were clueless about how long the program would last.

We have completed successfully our mission for ten years without any gap. It was a journey of spiritual nourishment for 500 weeks with 500 sermons accentuating Catholic liturgy, Biblical verses and socio-economic as well as political Issues.

The city of Leimen wanted to highlight this contribution for all the citizens and has organized with the Nuncio of Germany that a delegation would visit the Pope to present this project that such a contribution belongs to the pioneering work of evangelization through digital media. The idea of publishing these 500 sermons in English to offer it as a token of love to the Holy Father came up. This thanks giving initiative of mine to the Almighty stands testimony to the fact how a stutterer whose life has been transformed in an elevated and enhanced manner to glorify the ways and words of the Lord, whose miraculous intervention in being with whom I came in contact brought about life-changing experiences.

"The Eloquence of a Stutterer" is the expression of my reflection on my life, where God's hand formed me to take his Word to the humanity of varied languages. I am very grateful and ever indebted to this vocation of His choice. In this book which is written in English consists of the reflections conveyed through YouTube on various topics related to the Catholic way of worship, the dogmas and doctrines, the theology and Biblical explanations, the important feasts of the Church and their importance and their origin, the veneration to Mother Mary, the promulgated dogmas about the Blessed Virgin Mary, about the saints, which include information about the life of a few important Saints and Martyrs of the Catholic Church like St. Augustine, St. John Maria Vianney and St. Thomas Moore., about the seven Sacraments of the Catholic Church as well as on prayer, repentance and sins. All this has found a place in this book which will enable any reader to read, reflect, search and find according to their needs, moods and circumstances. This endeavour would not have been possible without the contributions of many including Mr. Friedrich-Wilhelm Uthe, an Agnostic, who has the openness to all variations of thought patterns and high regards for the Catholic Church. Our project continues even after these 500 weeks. Mr. Hans Reinwald, the Mayor of the city Leimen and a good political partner appreciates my service here. He could organize the religious trip to Rome to have a private audience with the Holy Father. I also thank sincerely Mr. Georg Kletti, Mayor of Sandhausen, Mr. Joachim Foerster, Mayor of Nussloch and Mr. Norbert Knopf, the member of the State Assembly for their words of felicitation.

Mrs. Marika Raab from Germany and Ms.Janet Rekha residing in Chennai - India have taken the responsibility of translation from German to English. Mr. Petros Eckert, Mr. Henning Polzer, Nicole Senger, Sr. Maria Jansi CIC, A. Malar and Fr. Dr. Vincent Chinnadurai have done their part and contributed for the cause of this book. Mrs. Lourdhu Mary, a Lay Preacher in the Archdiocese of Madras-Mylapore has edited the whole book marvelously, categorizing the topics in alphabetical order. Fr. Dr. John Peter, HOD of the Department of Social Works, of Mar Gregorious College, Chennai, India has rendered the corrections and suggestions in this book. Also thanks to Mr. Rex and Birgit Ulrich-Reinisch, Fr. Dr. Joemics, Prof. S. Vincent and Mr. Arockiasamy for their corrections and valuable insights. All these people have made rich contribution towards editing this compendium of sermons adeptly and presenting the thoughts eloquently in well-knit written form. I am greatly privileged to receive the unstinting support and constant guidance of Archbishop Dr. George Antonysamy in

Chennai. To all of them, I am indebted a lot and thus would like to extend my heartfelt gratitude for their great service. I owe my thanks to my elder brother, Rev. Prof. Dr. Anandam Lourdu who has been an integral part of my life journey. I thank the staff of Maviga press, Madurai for the DTP work and Modern Reflections, Chennai for printing the two volumes of this book. May this book "The Eloquence of a Stutterer" unlock many a heart around the world and the Word of God may spread and reach far and wide ubiquitously to the hearts of the entire human race!

With abundance of love and prayers,

**Arul Lourdu.**

# Contents

# 1. ABBA – FATHER

*"Here is my servant whom I uphold, my chosen one in which my soul delights, I have sent my Spirit upon him he will bring fair judgment to the nations"* *(Is 42:1).*

## Abba experience of Jesus

Almost all religions that exist in the world, whether major or minor, begin with a God experience, an encounter or vision with their particular deity or with a god who is named according to their tradition and culture. Christianity also began with the Abba experience of Jesus. Jesus made his Abba experience at the time of his Baptism in the river Jordan, when he was baptized by John the Baptist. Jesus experienced the unconditional love of his Father who sent him to the earth to fulfill his will of redeeming humanity which fell down due to the sin of the first parents Adam and Eve (Gen 3:15). At the time of Baptism the heaven opened and the Holy Spirit descended on him in a physical form, like a dove. A voice came down from heaven: "You are my son today I have fathered you" (Lk 3:21-22).

Mathew and Mark have reference to Is. 42, which says: "This is my son, the beloved, my favour rests on him" (Mt 3:16-17, Mk 1:11). Luke took the reference from Psalms (Ps 2:7-8) - which portrays Jesus as the King/Messiah enthroned at the baptism to establish the rule of God in the world. The Abba experience sustained Jesus throughout his ministry on earth. Jesus called the Heavenly Father as Abba - as his Father. It does not mean mere familiarity with that Person but it implies a personal and unique experience of God. There is no direct reference as Jesus experience in the New Testament. Jesus is addressing God as Father in words like and for 17 times in "My father", "Our Father", "Your father" the "Sermon on the Mount" section alone in the Gospel according to Mathew Chapters 5-7. In the Old Testament God revealed Himself to Moses and people of Israel as Yahweh. The correct pronunciation of the word Yahweh is YHWH - without a vowel word as in the case of Islamic Rahim - when the real word is RHM, again a vowel less word. But the people of Israel refrained from calling God by his name but wanted to uphold His Divinity. The Israelites were even frightened to hear the Lord speaking to them. They wanted Moses to hear everything from the Lord and convey it to them (Ex 20:18-19). Though God of the Old Testament in many instances and places revealed his fatherly (Dt 32:6, Ps 68:5-6, 103:13, Is 64:7-8) and motherly (Is 49:15) sides through the prophets and kings, the Israel people were uncomfortable to call their God as their Father. God who is referred to as Father appears in the Old Testament only fourteen times, often just indirectly, whereas in the New Testament the Aramaic term appears 140 times. Jesus shared and passed on this great experience to his followers, his disciples, and through them, we inherit and enjoy the same experience.

## Returning to Father's Home

On the day of Ascension, Jesus was returning to His Father's House. It is a great experience to imagine of Jesus returning back to the Father, after a period of 33 years of human life on earth with all its ups and downs, passion, his ignominious death on the cross and his resurrection, after further fourty days of staying on earth and meeting his disciples again. He enters into glory, to sit on the right side of the Father. Word of Eternal Word, Light from Eternal Light- Jesus was always with His Father, but for a short while he accepted human flesh and became man for our sake. Now as a victor he makes his entry into the Eternal World to join His Father. John's Gospel says: "I am ascending to my Father and your Father: to my God and your God" (Jn 20:17). This Father is also our Father. Pope Benedict once said in a very good way: "By calling God Abba, Father, we, the mortal people, may too call God Abba - Father". An improbably great gift that Jesus gave to us. How can we call and feel God the Father? We should never forget that we have a Heavenly Father who is always there for us and also stays with us all through our lives.

## 2. Acceptance / Accepting

*"Yahweh, bless his worthiness, and accept the actions he performs" (Dt 33:11).*

### Are you an Outsider

Are you accepted at home? Are you satisfied in your country? Or are you a person who thinks differently, who does not agree with the majority who have new ideas? Are you a lateral thinker? An outsider? For most people, "drawer thinking" is normal. Whoever is like us is accepted. Anyone who thinks the same as we are, is accepted as one among us. Those who are different feel uncomfortable or are rejected.

This is what happened to Jesus in his home village of Nazareth. For the common Jews who already were suppressed and oppressed and threatened by the so-called religious authorities, in the name of Law, Jesus became a saviour, a consoler and liberator. This was a block and hindrance to those who earned name, fame, respect and wealth in the society. So Jesus was been rejected not only in Nazareth but in Galilee, Capernaum and wherever he went on preaching and healing.

Though Jesus referred to the prophecy of prophet Isaiah 11:1-5 "A shoot will spring from the stock of Jesse, a new shoot will grow from his roots. On him will rest the spirit of Yahweh, the spirit of wisdom and insight, the spirit of counsel and power, the spirit of knowledge and fear of Yahweh: his inspiration will lie in fearing Yahweh. His judgement will not be by appearances. his verdict not given on hearsay. He will judge the weak with integrity and give fair sentence for the humblest in the land. He will strike the country with the rod of his mouth and with the breath of his lips bring death to the wicked. Uprightness will be the belt around his waist, and constancy the belt about his hips."And in Is 53:4 "Yet ours were the sufferings he was bearing, ours the sorrows he was carrying, while we thought of him as someone being punished and struck with affliction by God" and spoke to the people after curing the sick as in Mt 8:16-17.People simply rejected him. People saw his family background and his profession as a carpenter. What is he telling us? He is only the son of the carpenter! Mt 13:15. He felt uncomfortable. The saying that a prophet is not welcome in one's own country became reality. We too live in a comfortable zone, with our old-fashioned ideologies, we do not want to have any change, and we don't accept anything new. Without weighing the pros and cons of what is being said and being done, we abruptly turn away. What do we learn from this? We don't have to be afraid. But we have to be careful. If we see anything separates from God, we need not accept this. Then we rightly refuse. To feel uncomfortable, for the sake of God, is always better!

**Release Blockages**

Everyone wants to move forward, yet there are a few stumbling blocks on the way. Physically speaking, when the energy of the body is exhausted, or immunity power comes down, or some virus infects the body, then the routine gets blocked and sicknesses and diseases are the result. Spiritually speaking, when there are some disappointments, sadness, news of irreparable losses knocking at our door, anxieties, worries of questionable future, our faith gets shaken and sometimes shattered. In the event of a very valuable relationship gets broken and no appropriate solution seems to be possible in the near future, despair, anguish and fear grips our hearts and minds resulting in a blockage in spirituality. Not able to accept the whole situation, sometimes people get angry on their own selves. They are not able to accept neither the reality nor their own selves. Consequently they blame God, oneself and the people around. These situations prevent people from uniting together, come as one community. This happens in all fields of life including political and economic fields. If we have nobody with us, to accompany us spiritually, we cannot overcome these blockades and the struggles within ourselves.

To handle the crisis we have an excellent example in the Gospel. It is none other than Peter, the prime disciple of Jesus. He was a fisherman by profession, an expert in fishing, knowing the pros and cons of his job. One day after the death and resurrection of Jesus he was losing all hope. He wanted to turn back to his original profession to earn a living. Another six disciples also joined him. They set down and all through the night they could not catch a single fish. It was dawn already. The Risen Lord, who did not know anything about fishing during he was living in the human form, commanded Peter to cast his net on a different direction, to a place of the sea unknown to Peter. Peter trusted Jesus and obeyed, and as the blockade of his life was gone, he caught more fish than ever before. (Jn 21: 1- 8). Not only Peter's blockages removed but his entire life had an upside down turn. He was commanded by Jesus to feed his lambs (Jn 21:15). This command also applies to our lives. Especially when we are blocked, we should go further, break new ground, we should pursue other ways and use other means. Sometimes get the guidance of elders or trustworthy friends and relatives and try new things. On the top of everything, trust in the Lord, accept whatever He has in store for each of us. Jesus walks with us when he says, "Go out." And if we trust him and do so, then success is guaranteed.

## Black or White Painting

You certainly know this expression. It means the existence of two extremes: light or dark, day or night, left or right, good or evil. There is nothing in between. People who see everything only like this feel life very difficult. But there are also different shade of grey in between white and black. There are dawns and dusks, there is a middle ground in between a right and a left way. If rigorously hanging on only to the extremes, life may be rather irksome. To make life easier, one has to be flexible. Many millions of people think like this and they are actually quite satisfied. They stay in the middle may be a little more to the right or to the left, but they stay on a middle course. But when it comes to moral living, a matter of mind and of the heart, however, there is no middle course. You can't just be a little good or a little bad. Either you are good, with all of your heart, or you are not. Just being a little friendly to some people, but not to others, is not possible. Just loving some and not loving others is not possible. Either I do something with my heart or I don't. At this point you need to weigh up the things for the benefit. Not for the body and worldly benefits, but to recognize, whether they are worthy for entering the Kingdom at the end of life. Chose and accept the right thing. God knows our heart, He can judge whether we are really good. In the last Book of the Bible - in the Book of Revelations there is a verse which tells the fate of such indifferent men. "But since you are neither hot nor cold, but only lukewarm, I will spit you out of my mouth" (Rev 3:16). In society or in politics you have to find a consensus to arrive at a concrete decision. Clinging on to extremes or simply exactly staying in the middle is often not the ideal way. If through my inward journey into my mind and soul, I discover that I am emotionless in my way dealing with God or that I am unclear about my relationship with God, then it is not acceptable to God. Do I really enjoy life, can I really love? Am I with all my heart accepting God and my fellow beings wholeheartedly?

## We are made for Heaven

A similar lesson is taught to us through St. Paul. In his letters both to the Galatians and to Colossians he had given his teachings in tune with the above. "But formerly when you did not know God, you were kept in slavery to things which are not really gods at all; whereas now that you have come to recognize God - or rather, be recognized by God - how can you turn back again to those powerless and bankrupt elements whose slaves you now want to be all over again?" (Gal 4:8-9) "If you have really died with Christ, to the principles of this world, why do you still let rules dictate you, as though you were still living in the world?" (Col 2:20) We are not created for the earth, but for heaven.

## Seem or Be

How often do we show ourselves to the outside world differently from what we really are? How often do we overplay our true feelings? Are we really there when we are there? Are we showing our true face? We might think that this making is often very clever to give a different impression of ourselves. It is not always correct. There are so many people who live with two faces. But this is day in, day out a struggle. When am I and when I am not? Do I show when I'm happy? Do I show when I'm sad? Do I show whether I am angry or happy? And if I do so, when? When not? Christianity says: We do not have to pretend what we are not. We are invited to get away from the "shame" and live in "being". God is there to help us. Even if we sometimes align our behaviour with the "shame", we may always return to "being" and be as we really are.

In the New Testament Jesus vehemently condemns the hypocrisy of the Chief priests, the Scribes and the Pharisees. In order to gain familiarity they pretended as though they were pious, devoted to God, adherers of commandment without making any mistakes. They were living with two faces - never shown their real face to the society. But Jesus sensed all their double standards and the way they oppressed people. Because Jesus tore off their masks, they were slowly losing people's trust, popularity and support. (Mt 23:11-36)

## Off to the Desert

A desert is a place which most people may not like to go. There is nothing in the desert. It's not like a big beautiful city where there's everything we like and need. There are no shops, eateries, entertainment, doctors, free time activities. No big events or festivals are organized in such a place. But we don't want to dwell in remote tiny villages either, where no modern comforts and facilities are readily available. Because of this, big events are held in big and famous cities. But small villages with lots of cultivable lands, ponds and lakes are definitely needed, without them we could not get anything to eat - the food the basic need for life. Desert and wilderness are also needed. They are part of creation. They are part of the eco - system of nature. They are created with a definite purpose.

Biblically speaking the desert plays an important role in the lives of many great figures in the Bible. Moses, the Israel people (Exodus), prophets like Elijah (1kgs 19:4) lived in the desert. In the New Testament, John the Baptist was dwelling in the wilderness (Mt 3:1), and Jesus has been in the desert for forty days (Mt 4:1). He conciously sought solitude, He walked away from the people and from his everyday life. The desert does not distract you. In silence, you are alone with yourself. One recognizes his longings, looks into his heart, thinks about his view of life and thereby accepts his destiny, accepts what is in store for him. The view becomes clearer. One can see one's mission and goal in life. Jesus went into the desert to find his identity. Why did he come into the world? He found out the will of the Father and accepted the same wholeheartedly and he began his mission after his return. The knowledge that he is the son of God makes him great. Accepting his destiny makes him greater.

Let us also, at some point of time in our lives, especially during the lent, create a desert within ourselves, meditate and find out our destiny, the role we have to play in the world, the will of God for us and accept them fully and let us be clear about what we live for, for whom, and to whom we are to go.

## Allow Fascination

Do you find nothing interesting or fascinating in your life? We have lots of channels to get fascinated in life. Some may like to look at nature. For this we need not take a long tour of the world searching for natural scenes. A gaze from the terrace upwards - to see the clear Milky Way, the starry sky could make a person reminiscent. Some may turn to entertainment - hearing music or movies or reading good books of their taste and choice. We humans were created not to be bored, but to be fascinated. Nevertheless, we are often so bored. Why? We have so much in our lives: devices that make our lives easier, radio, TV, internet. We live in an abundance of things and employment opportunities. And yet we are bored, because we have forgotten the right view of the world. Of all things having children is the best. Let us see the world through the eyes of a child. The child does not know what boredom is. It is fascinated over very trivial things. It is bubbling with happiness even on seeing a small blade of grass, a tiny new leaf, a caterpillar, a butterfly, a sparrow, a small kitten. Or it becomes happy on receiving a toy, a candy to eat, a colourful simple dress. A child always discovers something new and derives happiness and fascinating.

That is why Jesus also taught us to become like little children. Jesus said: "Let the little children alone, and do not stop them from coming to me; for it is to such as these that the kingdom of Heaven belongs".(Mt 19:14)

## Seeing life's positive side

During 1960s there had been upheavals, rebellions, criticism resulting in chaos and pandemonium all over Germany. But that has gone and we are now in 2020. Even today, it seems too many people, who had undergone such traumatic experiences, live in a the shadow of those nightmares things. They don't think for one moment that God had been journeying with them and safeguarded them up to this age for realizing they are alive. They have a beautiful life before them which they do not want to live with a joyful heart. They want to bury their faces in the yester year's sorrows only. This sickens them as well as those around them. They don't want to see the tremendous developments that took place over the years. And those people who refuse to develop are always just whining they can't see anything good. They think that the world around them is totally bad and no one is there to do good things. Everything is bad for them. This is like a heart rhythm disorder in our society. Why do they always have to complain about everything?

In everything they find something bad. These people have not understood life's positive side. Also they are not having any deep faith in the God who from the moment of their birth is living in their midst.

For such people God spoke through the prophet Isaiah. He gives lots of assurances and new hopes which will surely boost the shrunken hearts and minds with the past memories.

"I, the God of Israel, shall not abandon them. I shall open up rivers on barren heights and water-holes down in the ravines; I shall turn the desert into a lake and dry ground into springs of water. I shall plant the desert with cedar trees" (Is 41: 17-19)

"Fresh things I (Yahweh God) now reveal, before they appear I tell you of them" (Is 42:9)

## Those who are not against us are for us!

Have you ever watched a game of children? There's a group of kids playing together. There will be some other children. Sometimes you can hear one or the other child saying to the new one, "Hey, you don't belong to this game!" You don't belong to this game! That means you don't belong to this group that's just together and playing. This is very common when children play together, especially in the schoolyard, when the students are together. You don't belong to this game!

Especially these days, we often hear about the Chancellor's election: who is the candidate for Chancellor of one party or another? We have quite a long time before elections in our country. You will hear very often: "Hey, you don't belong to us! You are not ours" – even in your own party or in the pool of the various parties. You don't belong to us! We can hear more and more words that speak of exclusion than words that promote togetherness.

In the Gospel (Mk 9:38-48) Jesus says, "Anyone who is not against us is for us (cf. Mk 9:40). Those who are not against us are for us. What does Jesus mean by this? The disciples

13

want to exclude people who do not belong to their group. But Jesus says, no, let the others be as they are. Please do not exclude! Whoever is not against us is for us.

The Second Vatican Council made it very clear that there is an invisible work of God in the other religions, in particular in the document *Gaudium et spes* (GS 92). The other religions, as well as other worldview groups, also have "seeds of truth". Can we let go so that we can deal calmly with other people, with other worldview groups and other religions? That is actually the message of Jesus Christ. But one thing is still important. Jesus says: Be tolerant to others, but be consistent in one's own group! You can't act at will, but practice what you've learned! "And if your eye should be your downfall, tear it out" (Mk 9:46 f). So far Jesus deals with the consequence in his own group! Preserving one's own, living one's own life properly, but still being open to the other worldviews, to the other religions, This is the message of Our Lord Jesus Christ.

## Accepting Self and Others

Each person is unique in himself/herself. Not all are the same in physique, colour, shape, height, so also in mental stability. Some may be highly intelligent, quick grasping power, and some may be little slow in understanding and grasping. But each person is blessed with some kind of talent or other ability and every person who comes to this world is with a definite message to share by his/her words, deeds and thoughts. That is the plan of God. No one is created and sent to the world in vain. So everyone should come forward to accept others as they are. If anyone starts comparing and complaining about themselves, they are wasting their lives and fail the beauty with which they are created by God. So the first step is to accept what we are. This includes also the gender and sexuality. Some may not be comfortable about their gender. Mostly women may grumble for being a woman. It should not be so. Each of us is to respect and accept our sexuality and try to print our foot prints on the surface of earth as models, as examples irrespective of gender in their own ways. Some people are unhappy with their appearance, the physical built up. It is not necessary to feel so. One should be content with what they are, what they have and prove themselves worthy of living on this earth. We have lots of examples in the field of politics, arts, and film industries. For some of them, whatever is seen negative, the colour, and the height become the positive ones and they show case their talents and they climb heights in their field and become popular. In the Bible also we have examples. David, who was sent to tend the flock among all other brothers, was the one became suitable to be anointed to be the king of Israel (1Sam16:1-13). Zacchaeus who was climbing the tree to see Jesus because he was not having enough height to see Jesus standing on the ground in the midst of the crowd, was called by Jesus specially and earned the salvation for himself and his family (Lk 19:1-10).

Some people as they grow old may not accept their old age. But the scripture praises the old age: "White hairs are a crown of honour, they are found in the ways of uprightness." (Pro 16:31).

So accept as it is whatever and whoever; however you are and live a virtuous living which can earn the wholehearted appreciation of God your creator.

So also everyone should come forward to accept others as they are. Each person is individual. Not all are alike and not everyone would be as per our expectation. But one should have a broad mind and heart to accept persons as they are, including their physical appearance and try to see the goodness, their talents and character in them and try to appreciate them. If they have anything wanting for fulfilling certain tasks, then they should be suitably advised and taught in a way that does not hurt the feelings of others, especially pointing out their lacunae or the milieu they come from etc.

This is a good way for a smooth and harmonious living in a world with innumerable differences.

# 3. COMMANDMENTS / LAWS

*"You lay down your precepts to be carefully kept. May my ways be steady in doing your will" (Ps 119:4-5).*

## Commandments and laws

In the Jewish tradition there are 613 commandments or mitzvot as they were called in the Torah. They are the commandments followed by the people who lived in the 3rd century BC. When Rabbi Simlai mentioned them in a sermon recorded in the Talmud Makkot. These included positive commandments (to perform an action - Mitzvot Aseh) and "Negative Commandments" to abstain from certain actions (Mitzvot lo Taasse). These 613 commandments cover many topics including instructions about eating, the punishment of crimes, worshiping God, etc. Jews agreed to obey these rules after they were given to Moses as a part of the covenant. Obeying these laws is a core part of Jewish identity for Jews. The Pharisees, scribes, and Jews believed that keeping commandments and laws was the only means of salvation.

The Mitzvot can be read as a sequential list in the Mishnah Torah, written by Moses Maimonides. Maimonides was a Jewish philosopher who contributed to the Jewish nderstanding and interpretation of the Torah.

## The Ten Commandments

The Ten Commandments, also known as the Decalogue, are a collection of biblical principles relating to ethics and worship that play a fundamental role in Judaism and Christianity. The text of the Ten Commandments is found in Ex 20: 2-17 and Deut 5: 6-21.

The Ten Commandments were given to Moses on Mount Sinai. Of the 10 commandments, the first three deal with God and worship and keeping the Sabbath. The remaining seven commandments deal with family and society.

## The pure Heart

We Germans have many customs and laws. We do a lot because it's just written on paper. We have laws and rules for everything. I stand at the traffic light and know that no car is coming from the left or the right, from the front or from the rear. But because the light is red, I stop. A French or an Indian will likely think and act differently about it. But it is good that we stop at the traffic lights to avoid certain undesirable things that might otherwise happen. So there are many rules and laws in our life.

The people of Israel received a package from God, a "package of commandments" the Ten Commandments - The Decalogue. During his ministry, Jesus proclaimed new standards that were even higher than the old ones, than the Ten Commandments given through Moses (Mt 5:20-48, 15:1-9). The commandments and laws were good in themselves. On a Sabbath day, because of their hunger, the disciples of Jesus picked the ears of wheat in the cornfields. The scribes and Pharisees criticized the disciples for breaking the law (Mt 12:1-14). For this, Jesus cited an Old Testament precedent (1 Sam 21: 2-7) and gave them a new dimension for the Sabbath. He points out how the Jews easily withdrew from the tradition of their parents by saying that they had already made an offering (Mt 15:1-9). He also referred to washing hands before eating and washing the dishes (Mt 15:10-20).

The Pharisees had spoken out against eating with unclean hands. But Jesus moves on to the larger question of the actual contamination of certain foods (Mt 15:11). For Jesus the statutes of men are subordinate to morality, which is the only purity that really matters (Ac 10:9-16, 28, Rm 14:14). He explains that only bad thoughts, fornication, robbery, murder, adultery, greed, malice, deception, debauchery,envy, slander, arrogance and irrationality (cf.Mk 7:21 f.) defile people and not what someone eats.

## Wealth And Greed

"What must I do to inherit eternal life?" – A question posed to Jesus by a young rich man (cf. Mk 10:17-30). I was standing in front of a building that hit the headlines five months ago. There were people playing in an illegal game hell, driven by greed. They all were arrested. This shows how people live with greed to get rich by any means.What do I have to do to win eternal life? A young man asked Jesus. And Jesus answered him: You know all the commandments. - Then the young man lists every commandment he obeys promptly. They were six in total. He said: "Master, I have kept all these since my earliest days." Jesus answered: yes, you did everything well. But one thing is still missing. "What is it"? The young man was eager to know what was missing in his life. Jesus said: Go and sell everything you have, and then come again and follow me. Then you will gain eternal life. - But the young man's face fell down because he was not ready to part with the enormous wealth he had.Wealth and money should never bind and grasp us in this way. Money captivates people's hearts. If we have greed in us and want to collect everything, unscrupulously accumulate wealth, it hardens our hearts and there is a very large gap between us and our God. Where money and wealth play the role of God and are worshiped, God, who created us and cares for us, no longer has a place and must go. The Bible is not against making or collecting money, but attitudes towards how we deal with money and wealth are important. In order to inherit eternal life, money and wealth should never become a barrier in our life, but should be a guide to show us the way into eternity. If we are blessed with abundant riches, it is for sharing with others, the poor and needy. That would increase our wages in the eternal world.

## Stone her!

She broke something! She did not stop at the red light! She evaded taxes. So can I stone her? Stone? Is that normal in our society? But I ask you, don't we stone people? Ask yourself: stoning? You can say no. But the stones wouldn't. In reality, we stone many people in our daily life. You may remember the Pope's visit. As soon as he arrived, the Pope was stoned - with verbal stones and gesticulated stones on specific topics. That has become normal in our society. We stone people when we accuse them of something. There is the word 'reproach' in the English and also in the German language, which conveys the meanings of a very strong reprimand, shame, etc., which are tantamount to stoning a person. Whether in the political sphere or in our neighbourhood, sometimes even against our own family members, relatives and friends, our work colleagues or against our subordinates. The idea of stoning sometimes crosses the line and people tend to stone anything without first weighing the problem the stone is being thrown against.

We know a similar story from the Bible. It happened in the life of Jesus. Jesus went to the Mount of Olives and came into the temple area. When they saw Jesus, many people came to him and he started preaching to them. Pharisees and scribes brought with them a woman who they accused of catching them committing adultery. They also established the

Mosaic Law that the perpetrator should be stoned to death for such crimes. They wanted to stone her. The law written in the book of Leviticus calls for both men and women who have committed adultery to be killed by stoning (Lev 10: 8; Dt 22:22). Their aim were not to punish the woman. But they wanted to prove a mistake to Jesus. In case he declared that she should be treated according to the law, they had planned to accuse him of being a rabbi who preached love, mercy, forgiveness and mercy but would mercilessly kill the woman by stoning. But if Jesus said that she should be released without any penalty, then they would accuse him of breaking the Law of Moses. Even though they shouted loudly, Jesus didn't care. He simply leaned over and wrote something in the sand with his fingers. Nobody knew what he was writing, but to their horror, he pronounced a liberating judgment on the woman. His words were clear: "Whoever is without sin among you, let him be the first to throw a stone at them" (cf. John 8:7). He made no mention of the fact that they had sinned too. Jesus was very careful when handing out harsh words. He knew the people who stood there. Although outwardly they appeared pious, law-abiding, gentle, dignified, their inner thoughts and moods were full of filth. So when they heard the words of Jesus, they left one by one, starting with the elders! Who should be stoned now?

## Is God Righteous?

This weekend is a special weekend for Leimen: More than 100 people from Baden and the entire Archdiocese of Freiburg come together who are physically and / or mentally handicapped. When you see the plight of the disabled, one might wonder why God created people with disabilities. We also had a leader in German history who wanted to destroy the sick and the disabled. He put 150,000 disabled people in gas chambers and killed them because he wanted to create a new world without disabilities. He thought that if all disabled people had died, the country would become "clean" without disability. But even after the murder of so many people, there are still many disabled people in Germany, this is reality. And these people come to Leimen. They want to be with us as a pastoral entity. They want to play with us, dance with us, sing and pray with us and even celebrate the Eucharist, the divine service, with us.

This Sunday, the Gospel presents us with the theme of God's righteousness. Jesus tells about a unjust judge, but he wants to help a poor widow because she harasses him by repeatedly coming to him and demanding judgment from him. (cf. Lk18:3). The God of Christians is the one who gives justice to every individual person. For God every person is important. Therefore, the Christian Church takes Jesus' mission seriously to support disabled people. The theme of this weekend's meeting is: "Believe you're a treasure!". The church and we all want to say to the disabled people: Yes, you are a treasure, even if you are disabled. A treasure of God. You are precious.

In the Gospel of John we hear two wonderful messages. The first is about a man who was motionless for 38 years and was healed by Jesus. Immediately he jumped up and went away, taking with him the mat on which he had been lying all these years (Jn 5:1-15). The next was also a disabled person - a man who was blind from birth. Jesus made himto see. (Jn 9:1-7). Both individuals, who were considered disabled by the rest of society, became able immediately after meeting Jesus. They saw the glory of God. On this weekend we want to experience as a community what joy we can experience in the company of these disabled people.

We seem physically fit in every way. But we are all disabled in some way. If we do not see the glory of God or if we do not meet the disabled, sick and needy and want to share their pain, we become blind. Even after hearing the words of God calling for repentance and opening a new chapter in our lives, when there is no change in us, we can be called deaf. If we don't become the voice of the voiceless in society, we are stupid. If our legs don't like to get out to reach those in need, to help someone in need, we are lame. While we have all of these disabilities, who are we to point the finger at the other person who is only physically disabled. God is close to all of us.

## Is God Just?

If all the suffering in the world is allowed, is God just? In a way, is the Lord really right when he says, "Where does all this come from - the suffering? I got a bit of a cold today. I cough sometimes. Why do I have to cough at all? To be in pain at all? Surely I need to be able to live normally? If I just have to suffer, why is there a benevolent God in heaven? Is he just watching me suffer from heaven. If there is no goodness, healing, and salvation, then why do I need a god? But I would say that in the midst of suffering you can experience God's love and compassion, feel the existence of God. If I suffer, if I am torn as a person in my experiences, if I have to fight myself physically, mentally and morally, then I have to be saved - I need someone. That someone is God. I need healing, otherwise I just can't live. This means, that if I want something better in my life that is always present in my everyday life, then I need God. When I am sad, I need joy. This means, when I am weak, when I am sick and when I can no longer cope with everything on my own, then I need someone who can be by my side to free me. That is exactly the logic of belief. Now I have visited an 81-year-old woman and she told me the following:

"I experienced a lot in the war and later. I come from Hungary. And father, without my belief in God I would not have made it all." Alone in suffering we can feel God all the more. There is a new book by Heiner Wilmer "God is not nice". As a pastor, I too have to suffer a lot. If I have to suffer a lot as a pastor, what about others? May I say that God is not nice? Am I entitled to say that? I don't know the reasons for all of the suffering or I cannot understand them in this life, but I know that there is an answer to all of our sufferings. But we can feel certain things because of suffering. Suffering definitely makes sense. We cannot move forward without suffering. It gives us the strength to endure, conquer and march forward. But very often in our world suffering does not just fall from heaven, but comes from within, from one's own family, from one's surroundings, mainly through selfish motives. We cause a lot of suffering to humans and nature through our callous way of life. You can't blame anyone else for that. It's our sole fault. If we did it differently, then we could really help each other, if we stand together in suffering, then God is there. God is not somewhere in heaven, but here with us, in your heart, in my heart, in your family and in my church and in our world. For the suffering people, the life of Job is a concrete example. He always praised God even in the midst of all his loss, pain, and worry (Job 1:21). He never cursed God and complained that he was not a nice God. (Job 2:10) But he praised and thanked him and that was rewarded in the end. He received many blessings (Job 42:10-17).

## Laws

Do you know how many laws there are in Germany? There are 2,197 federal laws with 46,777 individual ordinances, 3,131 ordinances with 39,197 individual ordinances. In addition, there are the national laws and regulations of the

European Union. When we have so many laws, how can we really live? Do we even need these many laws?

However, strict laws are required in certain situations. When a lot of people are together there is always a mess because everyone thinks independently. A society can only live together successfully if there are laws, rules and regulations that all people must adhere to. But whether we need so many laws is a good question. It is interesting that religions also have their own laws. The Catholic Church in particular has its own "canon law" with laws and ordinances ("Corpus Iuris Canonici" - corpus of canon law).

On this Sunday Jesus says in the Gospel: I did not come to abolish the law, but to keep it (cf. Mt 5:17). I see a big difference between a religion and a state: A state needs laws. A state also enacts criminal regulations for non-compliance with the law. If I don't obey the law, I'll be punished. So I have to be ready to take it all on. I only obey the law to avoid punishment.

For example, when I stand in front of a red light and then think I'll just keep driving, when there is no traffic, but I stop anyway because I'm scared of being caught by the police and losing my driver's license. So I'm afraid of punishment. And that's why I endure the law. But the words of Jesus are different. He was very strong in mediating and in his views on adherence to the laws and prophets. He also gives certain modifications to the existing laws. But he makes them stricter than the old ones. For example, he said: "You have heard how it was said to our ancestors, You shall not kill; and if anyone does kill he must answer for it before the court. But I say this to you, anyone who is angry with a brother will answer for it before the Sanhedrin." (Mt 5:21-22). That is to be condemned. You don't have to go as far as killing, but it would be enough to think about punishing feelings such as anger and hatred towards others that are carried in your head and heart. This definitely shows that the Old Testament laws and rules were much simpler than those spelled out by Jesus. But that is the greatest law. If someone strictly adheres to the words of Jesus, then that person would be absolutely clean of body, mind and soul. Another wonderful example is the taking of oaths. Old Testament law allowed people to take oaths, but only forbade the false oath. But Jesus immediately says that no one should take oaths - no one can swear by heaven, because that is God's throne, nor by the earth, which is also his footstool, nor by Jerusalem, because it is the city of the great king. "Do not swear by your own head either, since You cannot turn a single hair white or black. All you need say "Yes" if you mean yes, "No" if you mean no; anything more than this comes from the Evil One" (Mt 5:33-37). Isn't it a very strong law given to the Old Testament people? If you and I followed the rules prescribed by Jesus above, we would not need the 150,000 laws that we have in Europe. We could live freely. The church must also learn to move away from laws and regulations and to stay with "God of the heart".

## Eye to Eye

"An eye for an eye" is a Mosaic law (Ex 21:24, Lev 24:20, Dt 19:21). But Jesus speaks something very different from the old law. He says: "You have heard how it was said: Eye for eye and tooth for tooth. But I say this to you: offer no resistance to the wicked. On the contrary, if anyone hits you on the right cheek, offer him the other as well"(Mt 5:38-39). "You have heard how it was said, You will love your neighbour and hate your enemy. But I say this to you, love your enemies and pray for those who persecute you" (cf. Mt 5:43-44). - Is that normal? Are these words applicable in practice? That is Christian philosophy and Christian teaching. However, this teaching comes not only from Christianity, but also from Judaism. I chose three sentences from the three readings. In the first reading, Leviticus 19, God says: "Be holy, for I, Yahweh your God, am holy" (Lev 19:2)". In the second reading Paul writes to the church in Corinth: "Do you not realise that you are a temple of God with the Spirit of God living in you?" (1 Cor 3:16). In the Gospel, Jesus says: "You must therefore be perfect, just as your heavenly Father is perfect"(Mt 5:48). We are more than we usually think of ourselves, as individuals, as nations or as politicians. We are actually called to be holy. We are called to be the temple of God and we are invited to be perfect like our Heavenly Father. This is the philosophy of God. We are completely different and, above all, much more than we appear to be. The reason is the life of Jesus. He crosses all boundaries. Just through love we could win and conquer everything. But we humans usually don't do this. We pass numerous laws and implement them.

We always have reasons for hating other people. But do we even have any reasons to love them? Especially the people we don't like? Especially the people who hate us? Do we have any reason to love these people in particular?

But we have a definite reason. Because we are God's children, we are loved by God beyond all measures. And if we want to be as holy as our loving God, then we have to live the words of Jesus our Lord. We are the temples of God, and because of this fact, we are to keep our heart and soul without blemish, pure, and make it as an abode of our God. "You may be children of your Father in heaven, for he causes his sun to rise on the bad as well as the good, and sends down rain to fall on the upright and the wicked alike" (Mt 5:45).

27

## Do we need Politics?

Do we need politics? It is a valid question to be asked, but the answers we may get would be different. Over the last two thousand years, the world has experienced different political currents: monarchies, communism, dictatorship etc. Most countries are governed by democracy these days.We have seen various political currents come and go for thousands of years, but the question still remains. Although the effects may be for and against the will of the common people, politics is necessary for a decent life. A group of people who has a common goal needs rules. It also needs a direction, a way. In order for the whole people to be properly led, it needs politics. While different political directions have lost their influence, people still need politics. Politics is good and important in the New Testament. Jesus was openly asked by the Pharisees and Herodians about certain political questions about paying taxes to Caesar. Herodians were the supporters of the Herodian dynasty. They were the most suitable persons to report to the Roman authorities. They hoped that Jesus would say something against Caesar. They said: "Master, we know that you are an honest man and teach the way of God in all honesty, and that you are not afraid of anyone, because human rank means nothing to you. Give us your opinion, then. Is it permissible to pay taxes to Caesar or not?' But Jesus was aware of their malice and replied, 'You hypocrites! Why are you putting me to the test? Show me the money you pay the tax with.' They handed him a denarius, and he said, 'Whose portrait is this? Whose title?' They replied, 'Caesar's.' Then he said to them, 'Very well, pay Caesar what belongs to Caesar - and God what belongs to God.' When they heard this they were amazed; they left him alone and went away." (Mt 22:16-22).

Jesus gave them a very fitting answer. He said that they never expected. In practice, the Jews recognized the authority and virtues of the Roman government, which this coin symbolizes. Hence, it was a matter of course for them, and also their duty, to pay taxes to the government and as a sign of their obedience, too. In fact, they took it from their personal property, as long as the tax did not conflict with the superior authority of God. Jesus did not contradict the politics of the time, although the Romans ruled the Jews. Jesus added: Give God what is his. You see in these situations Jesus always put politics in the shadow of God. We experience this in the time before and during the crucifixion, when Pilate explained to him: As you know, I have the power to redeem you, but also to crucify you. To which Jesus answered him: "You would have no power over me at all if it had not been given you from above"(Jn 19:11).A wonderful answer. This means that God is above everything. Also above politics. God is above any worldly power. And this God lives in our hearts. If I am convinced that God is my personal God, my personal property, it means that no one, not even politics, can destroy my faith. When religion plays politics, it is no longer a religion. If the Church only is politics, then the Church has lost its point of view. This is why we need politics. But we need God much more! For I have come from God, I live with God, and I return to God.

## To stand on one Leg

Can you stand on one leg for a long time? People with only one leg struggle to keep their balance. For this, the body usually needs two legs. It is said that our ancestors had four legs (the hands we now use were our legs). At some point we started walking on two legs. So we know that we humans cannot really stand on one leg. We need two legs to stand stable and to keep our balance. Stability is needed not only for physical fitness, but also for spiritual harmony. Once the Pharisees came to Jesus and asked him: "Master, which is the greatest commandment of the law?" (Mt 22:36).The question was posed to Jesus just in order to trap him. Normally they were well aware of the greatest and the least commandments. Jews have classified the laws into the most important and into the least important. So the question is not about gaining knowledge or clearing doubts, but simply setting a trap and criticizing Jesus if he gives a wrong answer. But Jesus gave a very perfect answer. He said that the first and most important commandment is the love of God, which can be found in the book of Deuteronomy and which every Jew should confess daily - the "Schema Israel" (Dt 6.5), and Jesus commands about the commandment to love one's neighbor in Lv 19:18.If human life is to succeed, it needs two commandments, namely love of God and love of one's neighbor. If God is integrated into life and we allow Him to work in and through our life, then our life will be led in accordance with the will of God and this life would be a life that pleases God and one's neighbor. Love of God is much easier than love of neighbor. It is easier for anyone to sit in the church or in any place of worship for hours, or at home, chanting the name of God and participate in the worships and may have the satisfaction of Loving God. But that is not the real love of God. Love of God should reflect in the day-to- day life of the person, for example by loving fellow human beings and lending helping hands to those in need, being considerate, showing love and compassion - These are the qualities of the commandment of love of neighbor. There are also people who live only for themselves and who do not give God any space in their lives. They may even be humanistic and take care of other people, but they cannot find their own center and they do not feel where God dwells in themselves. Our human life only can succeed if we stand on two legs, presenting the two commandments of God, namely the love of God and the love of neighbor, the golden rule conveyed by Jesus himself.

## Out of Chaos into Harmony

During peak hours in places where lots of business houses, offices, shopping complexes are situated, a chaotic traffic is a common scenario in India. There will be numerous vehicles on the road almost touching very other vehicle blowing horns, there will be pedestrian crossing, and small vehicles intervening between two big only. Traffic regulations, are rarely followed, no one bothers about the traffic signal lights, and in most places there is no traffic police to regulate the traffic - it is really chaotic. This is very typical in India. But here the situation is entirely different. In Germany there are strict traffic rules and proper signal lights and it is in the psyche of the people to adhere to the traffic rules without fail. Now imagine for a moment all the traffic lights suddenly would stop working. Or that there would be no more road signs. What would the traffic look like then?

There would be lot of confusion and problems everywhere. If this has such an extremely chaotic effect on the world of traffic, how does the confusion affect our own lives? We humans sometimes break down from unstructured behaviour and distraction. We have often lost our orientation and don't even know where we are going, where our life ends or where our life began. What is really important and what is unimportant? We make a lot of mistakes in our life, not just as an individual, but also as a society. We know the sad history of our country of the Thirty Years War, in which millions of people lost their lives, which led to complete disorientation everywhere. There was no longer any human dignity or respect.

There is a story about the time after this Thirty Years War. A hiker asked a woman whether the "old god" was still there. The woman replied: "Yes, the old god is still there." - This means that the old order that we had as a society can be restored because God is still there. When we experience chaos in life and feel that nothing can be restored, we feel exhausted and begin to believe that our life path has come to a standstill. That it can't go on anymore. But we don't have to give up hope. Our God is a loving God who longs for us. If we approach him with contrite hearts, he will show us the right light in the midst of the darkness. Once we have seen the light and recognized it, we can find the right path and safely get to our destination.

## The categorical Imperative

Usually people want to live as they like and at the same time they want to claim everything the state can offer them. If this takes longer, every citizen should make his contribution to the wellfare of the state. We are a community that works tirelessly and where everyone does their part. Immanuel Kant (1724-1804) said: "Only act according to the maxim according to which you can; at the same time it should become a general law". Or as the vernacular saying goes: "What you do not want someone to do to you, don't do that to anyone else". The same philosophy is found in the New Testament in a reversed form. "So always treat others as you would like them to treat you; that is the Law and the Prophets."(Mt 7:12). This is marked as the Golden Rule of Jesus. Prophet Amos said (Amos 6:4-7): While one section of people enjoy all comforts and live in luxuries, it is their moral responsibility to take care of those in want. Those who are struggling to make both ends meet should be taken into consideration and all that is needed should be done to them also to enjoy a life of comfort and fulfillment. Another important thing to think about is to stay away from fraud, manipulation and exploitation. Such things only deprive the common people of the satisfaction of their basic needs. The prophet Amos warned the swindlers and exploiters (Amos 8:4-7): "Listen to this, you who crush the needy and reduce the oppressed to nothing, you who say, 'When will New Moon be over so that we can sell our corn, and Sabbath, so that we can market our wheat?'" Then we can fraudulently manipulate the scales to make the bushel measure smaller and the shekel weight larger. We can buy the weak for silver and the poor for a pair of sandals, and even get a price for sweeping the wheat. Yahweh swore by the pride of Jacob: I will never forget what they did. I will not the earth tremble and all who live on it mourn when everything rises together like the Nile in Egypt; it swells and then sinks like the Egyptian Nile.

## Wealth and Poverty

This weekend we hear again Amos, in the Old Testament who denounces society in clear terms: some have everything, while some have nothing left.

This great injustice is prevalent all over the world. It is not for nothing that the gap between the rich and the poor is widening and the middle class is slowly disappearing. More and more people are dependent on government services because they are either unemployed or underemployed and do not receive a salary that corresponds to their job. It is a paradox. The state can only do good when there are right rules and laws, and individuals / families can do well when there is justice, including on the economic side. It cannot be that a few earn so disproportionately and have everything in abundance to lead a smoother life. But on the other hand, many have to live on the subsistence level. It's a question of conscience -and human love. I come from India, where the situation is the same. On the one hand there is absolute poverty and on the other there is glittering, lavish luxury spending. At this point we should think about making the rules and laws so that there is equality and more balance. Justice should be done to all citizens of the country. In the book of Amos we find: "Disaster for those so comfortable in Zion and for those so confident on the hill of Samaria!" "Lying on ivory beds and sprawling on their divans, they dine on lambs from the flock, and stall- fattened veal; they bawl to the sound of the lyre and, like David, they invent musical instruments; they drink wine by the bowlful, and lard themselves with the finest oils, but for the ruin of Joseph they care nothing. That is why they will now go into captivity, heading the column of captives. The sprawlers' revelry is over." (Amos 6:1, 4-7).

## Nature and Faith

It's autumn again. And this year, too, nature has given us plenty of gifts. The harvest of vegetables and fruits is abundant everywhere. Nature shows us again and again how valuable it is to us, because the most important basic human needs such as food, clothing and shelter are covered by nature alone. In Europe, nature falls asleep in winter, so to speak. But before it takes a break, before it falls asleep, it gives us so much. It makes our life self-sufficient. Isn't that a wonderful act of concern and consideration from nature? Although it needs rest, it does not wither. It keeps its life. The growth is silent, but it is happening. The growth of nature is important to our lives because it helps to stay healthy, safe and protected. This is a great gift from God. We should learn from nature. Although it wants to rest, it doesn't just give up its routine. We should also take care of our fellow human beings and also of all living beings. We should never forget to feed the suffering brothers who go to bed with an empty stomach before falling asleep ourselves after endless and extravagant meals. The law of nature should make us think about whether we too can imitate the care and prudence of nature. But we also have a soul. When we need strength for the soul, we find this "nourishment" in faith. When we look at nature and see how wonderfully it grows in silence, it teaches us a great doctrine of faith. It is a reminder that it is God who sustains us, and as He sustains our lives, so can our faiths grow. The God who gives us food for our body also gives us strength for the soul. That is double nourishment. Isn't that wonderful? Jesus gave a beautiful parable of the seed that grows by itself (Mk 5: 26-29).

## Many Thanks

Thanksgiving is the culmination of the quest of the soul in the school of faith. We have to thank others again and again in everyday life, because most of our needs are fulfilled by others. And also because someone comes to our aid in emergencies and emergency situations. But giving thanks in faith means even more.

In the Gospel we find a narrative in which ten lepers had raised their voices and followed Jesus for getting cured of their leprosy, a disease which was seen as unclean and which separated them from the rest of the society. Seeing their faith, Jesus cured them by his words, and as they walked away, they found themselves cleaned of their disease.Among the ten, one was a Samaritan, who was considered as an untouchable by the Jewish community, and he was not allowed to mingle with them. This man, who got cured, wanted to thank the Lord. So he returned to Jesus and thanked him from the bottom of his heart. When Jesus saw him, he said: "Were not all ten made clean? The other nine, where are they? It seems that no one has come back to give praise to God, except this foreigner.'

And he said to the man, 'Stand up and go on your way. Your faith has saved you." (Lk 17:17-19).

This man believed in the authority of Jesus. When he returned to thank Jesus, he received another reward, which was confirmation that his faith had saved him and that he was allowed to live in joy.

This story is comparable to the situation today. About 20% of Christians do not go to church. They say they don't need it, and they prefer to pray at home or in nature. The word Eucharist comes from the Greek word *"Eucharistia"* and means thanksgiving. When Christians say thank you, they receive the reward from God, the promise that He loves them. It's worth coming to church and celebrating together and saying thank you.

## Sunday Service is Sunday care

How important is God to you? How important is Sunday to you? It is called "Sunday duty", especially in the Catholic Church. And not everyone likes it. We have to go to church every Sunday. It is the rule or command of the church. We are liberated people. We don't all have to meet all our obligations. But I would rather call Sunday service "Sunday care". We say "personal care, car care" and caring also means taking care of elderly people in need. So care is a good thing. We work all week, rushing from one appointment to the next, walking from pillar to post, we have many obligations, a lot to do, and hardly any time to rest. Sunday is there to rest completely, to recover, to draw new energy and enthusiasm in order to master the challenges of the coming days of the week. The Sabbat is also important for the Jews. Refreshment is necessary not only for the body but also for the soul. During the weekdays with our busy schedule, we do not have enough time to think about God and allow ourselves some time to pray. Sunday is a perfect day to refresh our souls. It is also the time when we as parish priests can gather under one roof and pray for one another as one family in the presence of God. Sunday mass should therefore not be seen as a kind of duty, but welcomed with joy. We also get the opportunity to meet our friends and share joys and sorrows with them. Here the Sunday service becomes Sunday care. When we question each other and hear of their joys and sorrows, we express our care, our oneness with them. This is Sunday care. We can also thank the Lord for watching, caring for, and protecting us all week. When we hear the Word of God, He speaks to us. When we pray, we speak to God. When we receive Holy Communion, we receive our spiritual nourishment - our spiritual nourishment to nourish our souls. So Sunday care has a lot to do with God. He wants us to rest, relax, and prepare for the week ahead.

## You will Not!!!

Moses received the Ten Commandments on Mount Sinai. These are still practiced today by Christians and Jews. But do we even need these commandments? The Ten Commandments are not necessarily warnings or threats of punishment, but rather they help us to lead for a life that can lead to success. They are built both horizontally, i.e. towards God, and vertically, i.e. towards people. They form the shape of a cross. God tells us through these commandments that He has chosen us. He wants to shape our life. He says that He is our God and we should only worship Him and not pay homage to other gods. The relationship between individuals and God should be real and right. His name should not be pronounced in vain. Nobody should swear by His name. Shabbat / Sunday is reserved for God. These three form a common section. They are about God. The rest are commandments that apply to individuals, families, and societies.

The 4th commandment is about honoring parents. It relates to family life and shows respect to the elders at home and in society.

The 5th commandment asks us not to kill - it doesn't just stop with literal meaning. The murder of people with guns. But anyone who brings a person or persons to the brink of suicide or who destroys the name, fame and dignity of a person or persons or institutions and causes shame and depression or frustration is also breaking this law.

The 6th commandment is against adultery. This is a sin that not only corrupts the soul but also taints the body, which is the abode of the Holy Spirit.

The 7th commandment forebids to stealing. You should be satisfied with everything you have. One should always make a living from one's own hard work and not at the expense of others.

The 8th commandment relates to giving false testimony against another person. This causes severe agony for the person concerned.

The 9th commandment is about wanting another man's wife. This act leads to conflict and turmoil in families and also in society.

The 10th commandment expects us not to covet the property of other people.

If everyone keeps these commandments, life in the private and social sphere will be a success. They form the basic truths and basic rules and regulations for a real life.

We know the text as "You shall not", but in the original text it actually says "You will" - you will not have a god next to me, you will not kill, you will ... Because it is an inherent quality of man to act and live like this. This shouldn't scare us off in any way, but rather it should help us to lead a successful life that would then be feasible or everyone.

## The New Commandment of Jesus

Before he left for his father's house, Jesus gave a long farewell speech to his disciples before the institution of the Eucharist (Jn 13:13-17). At that time he commanded his disciples: "I give you a new commandment: love one another; you must love one another just as I have loved you. It is by your love for one another, that everyone will recognise you as my disciples" (Jn 13:34-35). When he said I am giving you a new commandment, those words equated Jesus with Yahweh. The disciples should represent Jesus through their loving cooperation with one another through their words, deeds and deeds. And not just among them, the 12, but goes beyond that. The love of Christ should be experienced by all people with whom the disciples may come in contact during evangelization. He also wants them to become a replica of Jesus through their lives and for people to easily recognize them as His own disciples through their love - like the love that Jesus poured out on the disciples. In short, the disciples were asked to share the love they experienced for Jesus. Jesus also carried out his command by saying: "This is my commandment: love one another, as I have loved you. No one can have greater love than to lay down his life for his friends." (Jn 15:12-13).

## The Book of Books - The Bible

There is justice in every country, in every village, in every community. People cannot live without laws, even if many do not like them. The Old Testament in the Bible contains over

613 laws in the first five books of the Bible. And these laws were wonderfully kept because people said that these were not the laws that were made by humans, but that they were given by God. God's laws are fulfilling. Something that can be vital to us. And we Christians use not only the laws of the Old Testament, but the laws of the New Testament as well. In all 73 books of the Bible we find a whole series of laws and rules for a perfect life. The word bible means a collection of books, it is the book of books. And in that Bible, in the book of books, there are 73 books, forty-six in the Old Testament and 27 in the New Testament. The Old Testament is about how God intervened in the history of the people of Israel (Torah, Historical Books, Prophets - major and minor, Wisdom literature and Deutro - Canonical books). It was a love story between God and man.

If you want to read about laws and different directions, you will find them in the book Sirach, which deals with almost all aspects of everyday human life. The depth of suffering and patience, of faith in God can be learned from the book of Job. There are 150 psalms. Dealing with many classified topics. They are good prayer books.

They were used by the Jews as prayer books and each Jew was taught to recite the Psalms daily during their prayer time. The Old Testament is just great. Although we can find words that express violence, anger or death, annihilation, etc., they also all teach us many lessons that we can learn and correct our daily lives. The New Testament is the book about Jesus. The life of Jesus is written down in four books, the Gospels. The writers are known as evangelists. They are Matthew, Luke, Mark and John. Of the four, Matthew and John were Jesus' disciples. The fifth book, Acts of the Apostles, was written by Luke the Evangelist and tells the story of the birth and growth of the early Church. This is followed by letters from various apostles.

Paul, who is known as the thirteenth disciple of Jesus and the second founder of Christianity (the first Founder is Jesus), has written thirteen letters to various Churches he had founded. It is a great thing that about 50% of the New Testament comprise of Paul's letters only. There is the letter to Hebrews. There are seven Catholic Letters (as they are known) written by James (1), by Peter (2), by John (3) and by Jude (1). And the Bible finally ends with the Revelation of John, in which a new vision of a New World is presented.

It begins with Genesis, starting with the creation of the world, ending with the Revelation of John, which reveals how this world is brought to perfection - it is a wonderful book. It is an apocryphal book. In this sense, it is the law for all Christians. The Bible can be read as many times as one wishes to read. Each time fresh lessons can be derived from this book of perennial wisdom.

In other words, God always gives us strength through his words and his commandments and leads us to a life in which we bear witness for him. The Bible is therefore referred to as the book that reads me and you. It's not just that we read it, but that it reads and also shows us where we are in life, what and how we live. That is why all people in the Catholic Church say: The Bible is the word of the living God. That means: the life-giving God speaks to you and to me.

# 4. CORONA VIRUS - COVID 19

*"It is not those that are well who need the doctor,*
*but he sick" (Lk 5:31).*

## Pray

The whole world has been affected by the corona virus, including Germany. It has already spread all over the world. Everyone was in a panic. Big lockdowns were announced and the whole country looked deserted. The market places, the entertainment areas were all closed, no traffic; nobody walked on the street. There was a deep feeling of stillness and immobility.

We also need to follow guidelines in our community to prevent contagion. We must ensure distance, we are not allowed to shake hands, we have to disinfect everything. In this hopeless, helpless and pathetic situation, all hearts ask one question: Where will help come from in this fearsome circumstance?

The Scripture has the answer. "Help comes only from the Lord." Ps 121:1-2 says: "I lift up my eyes to the mountains; where is my help to come from? My help comes from Yahweh who made heaven and earth. "Our politicians, regardless of nationality, have the responsibility of giving due thought about the importance of the world and how precious is the human life instead of merely thinking about themselves. The virus affects everyone, worldwide.

We should all pray for each other especially during this pandemic. Our God is merciful and looks upon us with compassion, and he will definitely bring us out of this danger.

That is why I stand in front of the Heart of Jesus statue in the Catholic Church in Leimen. When we are despondent, when we need hope, Jesus shows us his heart. He invites us to find solace there and unload all our burdens in Him. We find his soothing words in Mt 11:28-29.

## Accepting Suffering and having Trust in God

A polish philosopher once said that people are fleeing from suffering in panic. People are like that. People want to be safe, to have a corner in the world where they are well, where they have no worries. The question is: where can such a corner be found? Wherever we go, there will be pains and perils, problems and anxieties in life. Changing places would not wipe out the problems totally.

Jesus sees it differently. When he was on Mount Tabor, he was glorified there, during transfiguration (Mt 17:1-8). But he climbed down from the mountain to face the reality of life. He was arrested treated barbarically and killed. However, he did not escape this reality and suffering. He was aware of His passion and pain, but he accepted it because this was the will of His Father who sent him. On the Mount of Olives, however, he also had a moment of agony, as a human person.

He too was afraid of the sufferings, which we clearly find in the Gospels. Luke gives a graphic description of the Mount Olive episode: "He then left to make his way as usual to the Mount of Olives, with the disciples following. When he reached the place he said to them, 'Pray not to be put to the test.' Then he withdrew from them, about a stone's throw away, and knelt down and prayed. 'Father,' he said, 'if you are willing, take this cup away from me. Nevertheless, let your will be done, not mine.' Then an angel appeared to him, coming from heaven to give him strength. In his anguish he prayed even more earnestly, and his sweat fell to the ground like great drops of blood." (Lk 22:39-44).Perhaps we also need suffering and pain to gain confidence and trust in God.

## Self-isolation - but not from God

The whole world has been hit by a virus. Regardless of country, regardless of rich or poor, regardless of region or religion, everyone is affected. The virus kept everyone under control. We were afraid. We asked ourselves: what would happen to my family, my community, my country? There was a total lockdown. That means, there were no public events, no private celebrations, Schools and Colleges, the stores of markets, shops, restaurants, theatres,entertainment venues, including churches, were closed. We had to stay at home, we couldn't meet friends and relatives. All social contacts had to be avoided in order to contain the spread of the virus. Nobody can live as an island permanently. That's impossible. We are social beings and we have to look after our fellow human being in the Christian sense.

Despite all these restrictions, we had complete freedom in another sense. We were now free to deal with ourselves want to task This time could be used to make a journey inward to ourselves and to get to know our real life. To find out if it is consistent with the values of Christ. To discover what essentially it takes to correct your life. To find out what is really important in life, etc. Another important aspect was the family. There was enough time to spend with family that our presence would keep spouses and children happy. There was also no social distancing or restriction between my God and me. During the pandemic, people who believed in God could quietly chat with him, devote a lot of time to him, and travel with him while he led them.

## White Sunday blessings for the Great Pastoral Unity

The Sunday after Easter is an important Sunday for the Catholic Church, especially in Germany. Why is it called White Sunday? Because on this Sunday hundreds of children go to first communion. Due to the corona restrictions, this could not be celebrated with the children, so it was postponed to a later date.

10/7/97 in Texas. The door to death row opens. "Mr. Nobels, what is your last meal?" A standard question commonly asked of those sentenced to death. And shortly before the person is brought to the gallows, he was asked about his last wish before death. Like all those sentenced to death, Jonathan W. Nobels is allowed to put together his menu before the execution. Ten years earlier he had murdered two women. He wished for Holy Communion as the last meal. His plate, like everything else, was photographed as evidence. Instead of steak and salmon, instead of vegetables and fried foods, there was a small white host in the middle of the white plate. What made Jonathan W. Nobels want this menu at the end of his life? What did he want to taste while others ordered their favorite food at the end of their life? What did he expect from it? A force that would help him face death? Did he feel abandoned by the world because of his terrible act and was he looking for consolation? Did he long for forgiveness after destroying his own life with a double murder? Did he hope to find in this host that which no meal in the world could give him, a future that went beyond this world? Forsaken by the world, Jonathan W. Nobels believed in this little piece of bread to find the message that God had not forsaken him. God's love applies to him on death row too. This does not bring the murdered person to life and does not play down the terrible act. God loves the victims, but He also loves the perpetrators. Jonathan

46

accepts this love of God as a perpetrator, as a glorious meal. He wants to have spiritual nourishment in the last moment of his life on earth and also to die in God's presence and with God in him in peace of mind - God remains in him. Does this Holy Communion actually offer comfort on death row or is it just consolation? - Jonathan can no longer answer this question, so we have to look for an answer ourselves.

"The Lord bless you, for he will stay with you, for the Word has become flesh. May the Lord be in your hearts, strengthen you, be gracious to you, and give you his peace. In the name of Almighty God, the Father, the Son, and the Holy Spirit. Amen".

## See and Recognize

The effects of a tiny virus that we can't actually see have brought us and our lives under its control. A virus has crippled the whole world, we don't know how to detect it, and it can take months / years to find drugs or a vaccine against it. We see people suffer, we experience the effects of the virus, but at the same time no one has seen the virus enter someone else's body. It is a phenomenon indeed.

This is what happened to the disciples of Emmaus. Luke's Gospel says that their eyes were open, but they could not see or recognize Jesus, even though he stood before them. They didn't even recognize him when he explained the scripture, the prophecies that were uttered about Him. But they could recognize only when He broke the Bread. It was at that moment, Jesus brought light into their blind eyes so that they could see Him (Lk 24:13-35).

This also applies to us. Even if we have eyes, we still need eyesight to see certain things clearly in life. But seeing doesn't necessarily mean recognition, because that's more than seeing. We are invited, especially in these days when we are confronted with this virus, to recognize what is important in life, namely the presence of God in our midst. During these quiet days, we have the opportunity to see and recognize something new about our own lives, our families, our relationships. Let's see what we haven't seen before, because everyday life and the hustle and bustle have kept us from doing it. You may also see something new in Church that you have never seen before. Yes, that is also possible.

**Jesus the Real Bio:**

The word "Bio", means "organic," and it has been on everyone's lips lately. For years, shops have been offering more and more organic products with huge discounts. "Bio" comes from the Greek and means "life". But life does not come from organic products alone or from a vegetarian or vegan diet. Jesus promises that HE is life, He gives us life.

There are different religions in the world like Hinduism, Buddhism, Islam, Judaism etc. But no religion can replace Jesus. That's why I loved becoming a priest. Today I am happy and grateful for the 12 years that I have been able to work here as a pastor. I am very pleased to be able to accompany you as a pastor during this time of the pandemic. I was allowed to be a companion to many people and have experienced a lot of good things. It is so nice to have Jesus with us in good times and bad, but we would not have seen this day without His care and protection. I have a great bond with Jesus because he is not just one of many different gods in this world, but because only He is the way, the truth and the life (Jn 14:6). Despite all the uncertainty, with all our fears and worries, we must not forget one thing: without Jesus our life is only half a life. Only he can give us the fullness of life here in this world and in eternity.

## Walk with Christ - the Way, the Goal

Everyone should have a goal in their life, and in order to achieve that goal there should be a specific and correct path for it. People should persevere to achieve this goal. This is important and normal for worldly life. In the life of every person, the goals and paths change in different phases. Students would like to achieve their goal by successfully completing the chosen course of study or the chosen field of study. After education, the next goal would be to find a job and make a living. Until they get a suitable job that will bring them both income and spiritual satisfaction, they must pursue their goal.

Then settle into family life, start a family, raise children, and so on. That is normal. But certain people are gifted with special talents that will bring them out and they strive to reach the maximum and earn names and fame. It can be used in the world of sports, music, dance, art, science, writing, and other crafts. But all Christians in common have to achieve a goal and a way. Yes, Jesus - He should be our goal and He is the way to achieve. Jesus said: "I am the Way; I am Truth and Life. No one can come to the Father except through me"(Jn 14:6). To achieve the goal, we first must find the goal - Jesus - and believe in him and walk on his ways. Of course, Jesus will enable us to achieve the goal. We humans always want to plan and know where we want to go, when we will arrive and what exactly the destination looks like. But Jesus says we don't need any of that. We just have to trust him, walk with him, and then with him and through him we will reach the right goal, because he himself is the way.

## Vaccine - for the Poor too

Can we still be really happy during this time? I have come to bring good news to the poor. To the poor? Good news? How can we bring joy into people's lives at this time, especially the poor in this Corona time? The message of Jesus gives us great confidence and increases our enthusiasm. At the beginning of his ministry, he enters the synagogue on a Sabbath day, opens the scroll, and reads the passage from the prophet Isaiah that reveals the purpose of his coming to earth. "The spirit of the Lord is on me, for he has anointed me to bring the good news to the afflicted" (Lk4:18).

The fear of corona could come to an end if a suitable vaccine is invented and given to all people. This would bring a sigh of relief to humanity under the influence of fear and apprehension. A vaccine has been found in some place. But the behavior of some developed countries-causes disappointment and distress. They want to keep all or some of the vaccines just for themselves. The poor and underdeveloped countries go away empty-handed. Countries that do this say they are Christian countries. Is that the attitude towards being a Christian? But all human persons have a right to survive and to live on this planet earth. We are created by one single God. If there is such discrimination, then how can the poor have joy in their heart and in their mind which can be reflected on their countenance?

Christ taught us to love the poor and needy, and He gave every help for their well-being. So we all have a responsibility to help people in poor countries. Can we take everything away from them and keep it to ourselves just because we have enough money? All the knowledge, all the technology - do we keep it all to ourselves? Can this world live without the other countries? If the poor people read our Bible and compared it to our attitudes, our selfish ways, wouldn't these people question the authenticity of our Christian life?

I therefore urge all politicians to remember this. If we really want to celebrate Christmas and really want to take Jesus Christ into our midst, if we really want to invite Jesus into our homes and hearts, then we should think carefully about how to deal with these difficult situations. Christians can only truly be Christians and accept Christ in their hearts if they bring the good news to the poor.

**From Meat to Meat**

Lately fear has prevailed everywhere, because there are more and more people infected by the dreadful diseases. You never would have thought that the situation would get so serious in a country like Germany, or in the USA. Not only that, almost all countries around the world are infected, There are very few exceptions. One wonders how one can go on living under these harsh circumstances. The virus is strange: it is transmitted from person to person, i.e. from meat to meat. "The Word became flesh, he lived among us" (Jn 1:14). God's Spirit became flesh in Jesus Christ so that resurrection could take place. In the book of Ezekiel we read: "The hand of Yahweh was on me; he carried me away by the spirit of Yahweh and set me down in the middle of the valley, a valley full of bones. He made me walk up and down and all around among them. There were vast quantities of these bones on the floor of the valley; and they were completely dry. He said to me, 'Son of man, can these bones live?' I said, 'You know, Lord Yahweh.' He said, 'Prophesy over these bones. Say, "Dry bones, hear the word of Yahweh. The Lord Yahweh says this to these bones: I am now going to make breath enter you, and you will live." (Ez 37:1-5). These words certainly give us great strength. God gives us a promise that He will pour His Spirit into us so that we may come to life. Even if we sit in our homes like in a tomb, God gives us His Spirit so that we can come to life. Now it is

51

important to persevere in the hope that it will not all be in vain. Perhaps this time is the most precious time of our lives, not to live in fear, but to experience that God gives us strength and hope.

## What wants to come comes! Chance!

What wants to come comes. Do you believe in coincidences? Corona has taken our security away from us. Suddenly there was a virus. We know it was coming from somewhere, but we had no idea that something like this was going to happen in 2020. And at first we even thought that it could stay somewhere in China or some other country, but it would never come to us. But suddenly it was there! And then we started looking into it. Then we thought it couldn't be that bad. But it wasn't like that. Over 30,000 people are now infected. Here. in this dire situation, our confidence wants. Nobody knows whether we can even celebrate Christmas or other festivals in the church calendar. Even if allowed to celebrate, there would be a lot of restrictions, social distancing, etc. that can spoil the mood. Now that such a strange situation has arisen, we don't know when it will return to normal. The Hindus and Buddhists would say: Everything happens for the sake of karma. It's the way they believe and see things.

# 5. DECISIONS / CHOICES

*"You did not choose me, no, I chose you" (Jn 15:16).*

**We are created as free Beings**

God created man as free beings. God is not like a ringmaster in the circus show, who controls the animals under his care, who obey the whims and fantasies of the master. But our God has given us full freedom to choose life as we please. But the decisions are not always made for the benefit of people. Sometimes they turn out to be wrong and harm others due to wrong decisions made about other people. Therefore, from childhood, parents, elders in the family, teachers in schools, priests, nuns, parishioners, and other spiritual leaders warn people about wrong decisions and guide them to make the right choice. Wrong decisions and wrong decisions not only ruin health, wealth and reputation. They can destroy the dignity of a person or a family, but they also ruin spirituality. For example, a bad habit like alcoholism would be a threat to the person himself and to all those associated with him. Those who have made wrong decisions are prone to succumbing to temptation and sin. Sin drives the person out of the presence of God. The gap between man and God increases as long as he remains in the same sin and has no intention of changing. Hence the need for repentance - to change the wrong path chosen.

## The Scripture says in Sir 15:11-20

*"Do not say, 'The Lord was responsible for my sinning,' for he does not do what he hates."*

*"Do not say, 'It was he who led me astray,' for he has no use for a sinner."*

*"The Lord hates all that is foul, and no one who fears him will love it either."*

*"He himself made human beings in the beginning, and then left them free to make their own decisions."*

*"If you choose, you will keep the commandments and so be faithful to his will."*

*"He has set fire and water before you; put out your hand to whichever you prefer."*

*"A human being has life and death before him; whichever he prefers will be given him."*

*"For vast is the wisdom of the Lord; he is almighty and all- seeing."*

*"His eyes are on those who fear him, he notes every human action."*

*"He never commanded anyone to be godless, he has given no one permission to sin."*

## God's will be done

Today "wishes" are the subject of reflection. Every living being has one or more wishes in its everyday life. There is no one who has absolutely no desire. People on earth have many wishes that they would like to have fulfilled, not only for themselves, but also for generations to come - for their own children, children's children and for the many generations to come. A sincere wish for the benefit of yourself and others, for the benefit of society and the world as a whole, should hopefully be fulfilled. The desires should come from the heart of the person concerned. Christmas is the fulfillment of the wishes of the whole world. All of humanity is expressing its wish for the coming of the Messiah, the Redeemer of the world. The people of Israel repeatedly expressed this longing before the birth of Jesus: "When will the Messiah come? When will the Savior come?" People who suffered from slavery, oppression and all kinds of obstacles and who were humiliated in society, longed to be freed from all of these problems. So it wasn't a normal wish, but an existential one. The Christians shouted "Maranatha!" 2,000 years ago, again and again, which means "Come, Lord!" Because they recognized that everything they had here in this world was wonderful and beautiful, but the world cannot live without God. In 2 Sam 7: 1-16, King David, who lived in his own palace, wanted to bring the ark of the covenant - that was the presence of God in the tent - into the palace to have his God with him. But God informed him through the prophet Nathan that the Lord lived among the Israelites when they were wanderers after escaping their slavery in Egypt. He never asked for a house to dwell. He also informed that it was God who made David a mighty emperor who was a mere shepherd. He always accompanied him. Lastly he informed that it would not be David but his son building a house for the Lord. Here David had a wish to build a Temple for the Lord. It was a very good and sincere wish. But the Lord had a different plan. David's wish would be fulfilled through his son King Solomon. That happened in course of time. The Bible and the secular history talk of the reign of Solomon and about the mighty temple he built in Jerusalem. Mary might would have wished to have a beautiful family, too – a husband and a few children. But then God's will was revealed that she should give virgin birth to a child, who is Jesus, the Messiah and the Redeemer of the world.

Even though we may have different decisions, desires and choices, the Lord's will would surpass all of them and that would win the prime place. If we say yes to the will of God, then our life will be harmonious and joyful.

## Decisions are made

Every day we make many decisions: whether you have to have breakfast this morning or strap yourself in the car, whether you should go to bed early today or may visit your friend for a short while. So there are big and small decisions every day, every moment in our life. We consciously or unconsciously make many decisions. Some decisions shape our lives. These decisions are mostly made from our past experience or with a view to the future. But very often our decisions shape our future. In the Book of Joshua, we find him asking the Israelites to make a decision (cf. Jos 24:1-2.15-17.18): Joshua, as the successor to Moses, has accompanied the people, the people of Israel. Moses, unfortunately, could no longer see the promised land. Joshua accompanied the people. But he had grown old and wanted to make a will with the people of Israel. There is a problem: the Israelites are slowly looking for other gods as well. They worshipped not only Yahweh, but also gods worshipped by their neighbours around them in places of their stay. Joshua said, "Today you must make up your minds whom you do mean to serve" (cf. Jos 24:15). He did not say: You must believe in Yahweh, but look at the situation and talk about what the past was like, what history was like, how Yahweh God, helped them, the people of Israel. He wanted them to look back and decide! He did not say: You can make a decision at some point, but they should decide then and there. The decision should be for or against Yahweh. He declared that he had chosen Yahweh. But the people were to have their own choice. There was no compulsion.

This question also arises for us Christians. The Orthodox, Protestant and Catholic churches are suffering from the fact that it looks like people have forsaken their God and many are still on the verge of leaving the churches. Today the question arises: do we choose this God? This God, Jesus Christ, who has been very consciously with us and our country for over 2000 years. Our ancestors lived from this faith! For Christians, one thing is clear - being a Christian, being born to Christian parents has never been your own choice. It is the choice of Jesus who chose you (Jn 15:16). Now it is up to you to say yes to Jesus and stay with Him or leave Him and run away - both options are before us. It is up to you to decide.

**All or nothing**

Today the churches and the faith are not doing so well. There are different names for Christians: Submarine Christians, these are those who only show up 1-2 times a year, maybe at Easter or Christmas, but do not practice the Christian faith properly. Some Christians attend Church in times of need. It is jokingly said that these Christians come to church for "Matching-Hatching- Dispatching": (to get married, to be baptized and in the coffin to get the last blessing). Jesus tackles such ideas with uncomfortable words. He says either you follow him or you don't. There is no middle ground or a back door. You have to make a decision, for or against him. He compares this decision with the considerations of a builder, who has to calculate exactly the costs before the construction project, to see, whether he has enough resources to mobilize to complete the construction (Lk 14:25- 33). This is how all Christians should be: decisive. In some churches adult Baptism is administered.

In the Catholic Church, children are baptized in the hope that parents and godparents will help the child to become a determined Christian. We must choose Jesus.Without him there is no Christianity. Perhaps the church suffers today for want of determined Christians and staunch believers.

Many people went to Jesus and he said to them: "Anyone who comes to me without hating father, mother, wife, children, brothers, sisters, yes and his own life too, cannot be my disciple. No one who does not carry his cross and come after me can be my disciple. 'And indeed, which of you here, intending to build a tower, would not first sit down and work out the cost to see if he had enough to complete it? Otherwise, if he laid the foundation and then found himself unable to finish the work, anyone who saw it would start making fun of him, saying, "Here is someone who started to build and was unable to finish." Or again, what king marching to war against another king would not first sit down and consider whether with ten thousand men he could stand up to the other who was advancing against him with twenty thousand? If not, then while the other king was still a long way off, he would send envoys to sue for peace" (Lk 14:26-32).

## Yes is Yes and No is No

Countless decisions are made in one day, small and big. This starts with deciding when to get up to start the day. What clothes is to wear for the office or other work places, food choices - what and where to eat, who to eat with and so on. The word decision goes back to the knighthood in the Middle Ages. If there was peace or no struggle, the sword was safely in the SCABBARD / SHEATH. But when an enemy was in sight, the knight had to quickly pull the sword out of the sheath, "de-divorce" it, so that he could defend himself. Today there are no knights, but we still have to make countless decisions.

Jesus says, "Your yes shall be yes, your 'no' shall be no. Not perhaps, or something in between, but clearly yes or no. But in order to be able to say yes or no, you have to think carefully beforehand." Take time for making the decision. Also the Talmud, in the Old Testament and religions such as Buddhism, it is warns people against ill-considered decisions: "Watch out for your thoughts, for they become words. Pay attention to your words, for they will be actions. Pay attention to your actions, because they become habits. Pay attention to your habits, because they become your character. Pay attention to your character, for he will be your destiny". If I am clear in my deliberations, I will make good and correct decisions.

## Do you hear me? Do you see me?

I'm standing in a park. Do you hear me? Do you see me well? Can you hear me, but also understand me? You can see me, but can you also recognize me? Now we are going to think about what Jesus said relating to this Jesus said, "You hear me, but you do not know me. You don't understand and see what's behind the meaning. You have ears, but you don't hear properly. You have eyes, but you don't see right. Perhaps life is an opportunity for us humans to learn to see and hear properly. We take in as many impressions as a sponge every day. Our world is so wonderful, with the wonderful sky, nature and everything it can give us. We perceive many things, but not many things. It is not for nothing that we say: we only hear or see what we want. Why do we only hear or see what we want? For example, there is always an argument and we say: I'm always right, YOU are always wrong. I only see what YOU did wrong. Jesus encourages us, to broaden our perspective, to change direction, to continue to walk new paths unceasingly.

In the case of differences,disputes, relationships, nderstanding of people, the ideologies in which we are arrested, our allegations, prejudices about people, their faith, their religion, etc. Life is as great as heaven, as the whole earth. I am just a small person in this big picture and should be willing to change my perspectives. Jesus can help us to see and hear properly, giving us hope for a better life.

## God's Thoughts on Choice

The Bundestag election is close. Have you thought about who they will vote for this Sunday? Before I ask you, I would like to ask what the goals, ideas are for the politicians and parties that want to govern us. This is important because the values and thoughts of politicians will determine our lives after the election. But people's thoughts are very different from the thoughts of God.

When I think, "I want to do everything the way I want it, I'm important, I just see my advantage, I have to do well," then I'm a long way from God's thoughts. When I think, "All bad or evil people must be punished or destroyed," I am far from God's thoughts. Jesus told a parable to explain this point. This parable in in Matthew's gospel 20:1-16. In Palestine, the owners of the vineyard used to engage lots of laborers for the harvest because soon after the harvest the rains would start. So before the onset of autumn, they would finish the harvest. On seeing the volume of work to be carried out they would hire the laborers even at the last hour. But the owners usually pay the laborers as per the hours they worked. But the owner of the vineyard in Jesus' parable was very generous. He hired the workers in the morning and he goes out for many spells and brings in labourers to work in his garden. The last set of workers worked only for an hour. The owner before hiring the laborers fixed a rate per day and the laborers agree to work for that wage since it was genuine and sufficient for them for the day. They saw that many were brought to work late in the evening. Those who came in the morning thought they would be paid more than people who came late. But this owner paid the same amount at the end of the day to those who worked from morning to evening and those who only worked an hour that day. They all got irritated and mumbled. The owner gave a very honest answer: "My friend, I am not being unjust to you; did we not agree on one denarius? Take your earnings and go. I choose to pay the lastcomer as much as I pay you. Have I no right to do what I like with my own?" (Mt 20:13-15). The person who was only brought in in the evening was ready to work in the morning and earn a daily wage to support his family. But nobody hired him. He had been waiting to get work. So he decided to wait until he got a job. He should be paid in full to meet his daily needs. If he were paid for just an hour, he would starve to death. So Jesus teaches us not to jump to conclusions from the decisions of others. We have to weigh the pros and cons. We have to fit into the other person's shoe and think and then come to the conclusion. They can rule us, but their thoughts should be like the thoughts of God. Equal "wages" for everyone: every citizen is important, every person is important, regardless of state or culture. Especially the poor, the sick, the oppressed and the persecuted. See that in the above parable there is justice, equality, brotherhood, forgiveness, reconciliation, and peace. These are the thoughts of God. If they could live this reconciliation and this penance, we would be very happy. So let's try to pray that the politicians will have these thoughts of God within them.

## What do you live for?

What is determination? This is about decisions. We make a lot of decisions every day, important and less important, big and small. We decide on one thing, and the moment this decision is made, our energy is released, we bundle our resources and use all our creativity to put this decision into practice. Choices and determination are important for success. But a lot of people make wrong decisions. They overestimate themselves and implement everything immediately without taking time to think and decide. Long-term success cannot be achieved without concrete decisions and thorough planning. Their life remains in imbalance. Take an example from Jesus. Right from the start of his ministry, he focused on spreading the kingdom of God. He invited the people and said,"The time is fulfilled, and the kingdom of God is close at hand. Repent, and believe the gospel" (Mk 1:15). He was ready to do anything for it. Although he was criticized, he did not give up because he was firm in his decision to obey the will of the Father while constantly moving towards the goal. He spent a lot of time praying and talking to the Father in quiet and lonely places (Mk 6:46). This made him full of energy, but he used this energy to kindle the fire of God in men. For Jesus, the kingdom of God was more important than anything else. More important than ideologies that make people small and oppressive, more important than property, position and wealth, more important than prestige and power. The kingdom of God is near. That's what Jesus burns for. What is your soul burning for? What do you live for?

## Are you a Human or a Consumer?

It's always about optimization, it's about performance in our society. Everything is subject to the compulsion to be as efficient as possible, with the highest yield, with the highest performance. Even at school it is about performance. You no longer learn for yourself and have fun doing it, you learn for your future profession, for industry, for optimization. So it's no wonder that so many people, including our children, suffer from burnout or psychological problems as a result of constant stress, especially if they do not meet the requirements optimization. It is bad that as an individual I am only used or abused for this purpose. I should be able to live the way I want. Christ set us free to be free! Even if I make mistakes, I should be able to learn from them in order to do better next time, to develop myself further, to learn from my experiences. But perfection is expected of me. When Paul came to the church in Corinth, he said:"I came among you in weakness, in fear and great trembling"(1 Cor 2:3). Christianity is a religion that sees people not as puppets, but as the image and likeness of God.

Christianity is not just about paying church taxes or obeying do's and don'ts, it encourages us to live the way we want to, with all our weaknesses and strengths. That is why there is the sacrament of Confession. If I did something wrong but regret it, God is always ready to forgive me.

## Money or Rescue

It is true that we cannot live without money. But it's also not so good to have huge amounts of money, to be able to buy anything, to do anything, to experience anything you want. A well-filled account gives us security. The human idea of being rich is very good. But Jesus says exactly the opposite. He said: "It is easier for a camel to pass through the eye of a needle than for someone rich to enter the Kingdom of Heaven" (Mt 19:24). What does that mean? The church shouldn't have any money? Must the church be poor? Many accuse the church of being very rich. But; the church as an institution needs money, just like any other institution. In my pastoral care unit in Leimen-Nußloch-Sandhausen there are almost 140 employees, 6 institutions and 27 buildings. I need money for social projects, for paying salaries and for maintenance, etc. Jesus says, "It is good what you have in this world". But compared to what we get from God, it is secondary. Money and possessions must never come first. The church must learn that when it comes to our salvation, it should only prioritize rather than increase its own resources. The church must give up everything when it comes to working for the salvation of people. Money is not the most important thing. God should be the most important place in our lives.

## I Warn You

Actually, we do not like to be constantly warned about something, about bad things that could happen, or when we are judged for something that we do wrong in the eyes of others, whether in school, in family, in the circle of friends, in partnership. According to Duden, the word warning means: "Point out a danger, or strongly advise someone not to do anything with reference to possible unpleasant consequences". The other day, a father told me that his daughter was smoking and that he had warned her of the possible bad consequences to her health, but then left her to decide for herself whether or not continue the habit of smoking, because she had the freedom to decide for herself. There are several reasons why warnings are issued. We are all flawed people, no one can always do everything right or foresee ahead of time the consequences. My doctor also warns me of the negative consequences of my behavior, which may be harmful to my health in the long run. Getting warned in such things are good and helpful. But if a warning is made out of jealousy or evil intention, or to expose someone, it does not help. God warns us again and again, out of love for us. The prophets keep on warning people to remain mindful of our words and deeds. Prophet Ezekiel says: "Son of man, speak to the people of your country. Say to them, When I send the sword against the people of that country, take one of their number and post him as a watchman; if he sees the sword coming against the country, he must sound his horn to warn the people. If someone hears the sound of the horn but pays no attention and the sword overtakes him and destroys him, he shall have been responsible for his own death. He has heard the sound of the horn and paid no attention; his death will be his own responsibility. But the life of someone who pays attention will be secure. If, however, the watchman has seen the sword coming but has not blown his horn, and so the people are not alerted and the sword overtakes them and destroys a single one of them, that person will indeed die for his guilt, but I shall hold the watchman responsible for his death." 'Son of man I have appointed you as watchman for the House of Israel. When you hear a word from my mouth, warn them from me" (Ez 33:2-7). If my fellow human beings are really important to me, if I love them, then I can't look away. If they did something well, I should praise them. If they do something wrong I have to be honest and warn them. Whether or not they heed the warning is up to them, but I should have to warn them anyway.

## Really Living in today

*"Call me! I will tell you how you will do tomorrow!"* There are many television channels which advertise on fortune telling. Lots of people do approach such people and listen to whatever they say. But it is a big question whether whatever told by such fortune tellers have come true and really happened? But one thing is sure. The people who call are prototypes of many people who want to have a good and better future. Who doesn't want that? We always wish for a better tomorrow only. Such people forget about today, a day given as a gift from God. They are only concerned with the

worries of a future, neglecting the pleasures that are just in front of them today. They refuse, they are incapable of recognizing a beautiful today that awaits to embrace them if they decide to live it fully.

The Gospel according to Luke gives importance to the word TODAY. There are many 'todays' in Luke's Gospel. The Gospel passage (Lk 4:14-21) deals with today. There is a wonderful story of Jesus who came to Nazareth and read the Scripture in a synagogue. He interpreted the written words to read in one sentence as this: "This text is being fulfilled today even while you are listening" (cf. Lk 4:21). Today, it is indeed an important word in the Gospel of Luke. When Jesus was born, the angels proclaim that Today the Savior was born (Lk 2:11). When a paralyzedman was healed, people say, "We have never seen anything like this" (cf. Mk 2:12; Lk 5:26). Jesus said to Zacchaeus: "Today salvation has come to this house, because this man too is a son of Abraham"(cf. Lk 19:9). Zacchaeus' decision to make use of the opportunity of that "TODAY" to see Jesus by hook or crook, and taken pains to climb the tree, bore abundant fruits.

He became the Child of God, a liberated and grace filled person. The good thief on the Cross decided to avail the forgiveness and grace from Jesus and submitted his petition from the Cross to remember him when He comes in Glory. Jesus granted his request and said to him: "Today you will be with me in paradise" (cf. Lk 23:43). So, today! Now!

We also think of many Victims of National Socialism. It was a painful story. For those victims it was terrible day, a black day. But we, the people who live today, might feel the presence of God, today and now in the middle of our life. Always decide to fully live today. Do not worry and don't focus always your attention on tomorrow or to a farthest future of which we still do not know anything. Make the most of the opportunities that come your way today and utilise for a proper shaping of your life. It will automatically pave way for a bright future. Life's happiness, joy or sorrow and mourning are dependent upon how we see things and decide. Decisions are very important and they play a vital role for a good living.

## As big as a Mustard Seed

I must confess or admit: I am ashamed of my faith in Jesus Christ. If your faith is as small as that of the mustard seed, you can say, "You, tree, lift yourself off and go away from here and transplant yourself somewhere else!" the tree is supposed to obey your command." This is what Jesus says (cf. Lk 17:6): "If you had faith like a mustard seed". Embarrassing! Do I have so much faith as a pastor, as a priest? Would I have expected a little more from myself? But my faith is not as great as a mustard seed. And I just can't move a tree. It will not obey me. Can you do that? I don't think so. Do you have as much faith as a mustard seed? Well, we all don't have that. But one thing can perhaps be learned from this parable which is to do small things with great love. Jesus practised this again and again in his life. For him, big things or events were not so important, but small experiences were delightful to Him. That is why he expresses such small things in various Parables. For example the Parables about a small penny or a small coin lost by a woman, or about a sheep lost by the shepherd, or his words: "Look at the birds in the sky" (Mt 6:26). All are unimportant things, but for Jesus these little things are very, very important. And that is why he is willing to be there for these little things and help them like a leper who's really very unimportant to the society. Then Jesus said: "I am willing. Be cleansed" (cf. Mk 1:41). For our God, small things are very important. And what's about us? We also have the temptation to be great, to grow up, to become richer and more popular. But Jesus shows the opposite: if your faith is as great as a mustard seed, then you can say to the tree: "Get off and go somewhere else." – So shall we can ask ourselves if we do little things with great love or big things with little love? But if we want to be on the side of God, then this one sentence is important. Even if we do something small with dedication, joy and love, the reward we get back is boundless blessings. great happiness and an abundance of divine love that overflows the heart. What is your choice?

# 6. DISCIPLES / DISCIPLESHIP / LEADERSHIP

*"So in the same way, none of you can be my disciple without giving up all that he owns" (Lk 14:33).*

## Who is a Disciple?

A disciple is someone who is a pupil or an adherent of the doctrines of another person in any field. It may be in the field of politics, cinema, arts and crafts, spirituality/religion. A disciple is a follower of the person of his choice. In Christianity disciple means the disciples of Christ. Those who were chosen by Jesus to continue his mission after Him. Disciples of Christ are those who were trained and sent by Jesus to preach the Good News to various places during their life time on earth. Not all the people who believe in Jesus need be his disciples. Believers are those who have faith in Jesus, pray to Him and worship Him. They need not go behind Jesus. But a disciple is a person who strictly follows the instructions of Jesus and accomplish whatever is expected of him (Mt 10:5-15, Lk 10:17-20). A believer need not be a disciple; but a disciple has to compulsorily be a believer.

## Looking for Workers

Those who are unemployed seek for a job. Depending upon their life situation, people may take up full time job, some take up part-time jobs. Perhaps many people are of the following view: in Germany we are in a fortunate position. The problem of unemployment is less compared to other countries of Europe. But it seems not to be true. In one field lots of workers are needed. That is the spiritual field.

Now- a-days vocations are coming down. There is a paucity of priests, sisters and those who carry out the Evangelical work for the spread the Kingdom of God. Now you can ask me: What kind of work? For the whole good of the people we need workers. This is what the Gospel tells us.

Jesus' Galilean ministry or mission started immediately after John the Baptist, who was the forerunner of Jesus, was imprisoned. Jesus needed more and more "collaborators" to work with Him. He walked by the Sea of Galilee and found some men and invited them, saying "Come after me. I will make you fishers of men". Accepting his invitation a few followed Jesus, leaving everything behind (Mk 1:14-10). For 2000 years, many millions of people have been addressed to the work of Jesus Christ, including me. I did my studies in chemistry. But I felt the call of Jesus for his work. I obeyed his call and today I am sitting in front of you - that too in a foreign country as a worker for the Lord.

I would like to give you an open invitation to become a worker to spread of the Kingdom of God in our country or elsewhere in the world. You can work for a few hours, or for half a day or for the whole day. Where there is a will, there is a way - so even if you feel you do not have time to spare: if you give a serious thought about the work for which you are being invited, certainly you may find time to spare for this wonderful job. The Church is the institution that has always been running short of employees. It is constantly looking for workers for 2000 years because Jesus Christ lives and works in this Church. The call is for you it is for you to decide. "Come after me" (Mt 4:19).

## Body, Mind And Soul

Religion is always associated with spirit. It is not for nothing that the pastor is called "spiritual". But religious people are not only responsible for the spirit but also for the mind and body of persons. Jesus gives a concrete example for this in the Gospel. (Mt 8:14-15): "And going into Peter's house Jesus found Peter's mother-in-law in bed and feverish. He touched her hand and the fever left her, and she got up and began to serve him." Here in this miracle we can notice a difference. In other miracles there were requests from the sick or the disabled to heal them, or someone asked Jesus to heal on behalf of the sick. Here Jesus acts on his own initiative when entering the house of Peter. He touches her and cures her fever. After her healing she was able to find the courage and strength to wait for Him.

Jesus as the Son of God, who is actually responsible for spiritual wellness also has the concern for the physical wellbeing of the people. He seems to be a wonderful physician. If I simply let this text work in me, then I realize that religion is actually also responsible for the body. Not only the doctors, but also the priests, the pastoral staff, the pastors all are actually responsible for the wellbeing of the body. Only in a healthy body can the mind and soul be healthy. This means that mind, body and soul are connected to one another. So if one part is sick or broken, the other part is affected. After all, we know psychosomatic illnesses in which people feel physically sick even though the soul is actually sick. Religion should offer comprehensive healing, not just for a specific part of the human being. It should be holistic. People who cure physical illnesses should also be spiritual. It would be a shame if we only had atheistic doctors or healers. We need comprehensive healing and care. The body is the temple of God. If God's temple is good, God can enter and dwell in it. For this, the body should also be cared for. Good food, exercise, good

71

rest, and good habits are all musts to maintain a healthy body. When the body is doing well, the mind and spirit also become healthy.

## Inclusion

Inclusion is an important issue. Especially in our times. I hope that you are well and that you will not be left out by anyone. I hope that you don't belong to the group that remark isolated for reasons like illness, physical disability, mental illness, or because you have just ended your relationship. Inclusion is a particularly important issue, especially in our schools. One mother told me that she was still fighting for her disabled son to be educated at school together with other children. But there are also opposing views.

There is a miracle done by Jesus in the Gospel of Mark, curing a leper. "A man suffering from a virulent skin disease (leprosy) came to him and pleaded on his knees saying "If you are willing, you can cleanse me". Feeling sorry for him Jesus stretched out his hand, touched him, and said to him: "I am willing. Be cleansed". And at once, the skin disease left him and he was cleansed. And at once Jesus sternly sent him away and said to him: "Mind you tell no one anything, but go and show yourself to the priest, and make the offering for your cleansing prescribed by Moses as evidence to them.' The man went away, but then started freely proclaiming and telling the story everywhere, so that Jesus could no longer go openly into any town, but stayed outside in deserted places. Even so, people from all around kept coming to him." (Mk 1:44-45).

In Jesus' day, lepers were treated as outcasts and unclean. There were various rules and regulations they had to follow and they were not included in the mainstream of the society. The book of Leviticus Ch '14 contains elaborate laws and commandments regarding leprosy and the resulting cleansing rituals when reported as clean by the priest. But Jesus didn't shut the man out because of his leprosy. He wanted to heal him and allow him to live with other people in society. Jesus even reached out and touched the leper, which was forbidden under the Mosaic Law.

This society has everything and everyone can live well. Nonetheless, there is exclusion, which is quite unthinkable. Why do we exclude others? Because they are aliens or because of their age? Or because of a disability? When I came to Germany from India, I could observe something. I rarely saw people with disabilities on the streets or in the city centers. I could see hardly anyone in need. Then I wondered what the reason for the exclusion could be. I got the answer when I was asked to work among the mentally challenged for a period of three months immediately after completing my priestly training. There I learned that these people had been picked up from their homes.

That means normal society doesn't even know these people. Can a society behave like this? We remember euthanasia in the Hitler program when many hundreds of thousands of people were killed, even if they were Germans. This inhuman ideaology should not be acceptable in a civilized society. We must not exclude people because none of them are responsible for their condition. We should change our society. We should start this from home. Then it should move on to our friends, ward groups, and churches. We need to send out a signal that everyone is really welcome because God is not marginalizing us. As disciples of Jesus, it is our duty to proclaim such inclusion in our societies. The parable of the vineyard (Mt 20:1-15) teaches us this lesson.

## Go in Pairs

A company is founded, a new path is shown and a great institution that is to last until the end of this world begins. Perhaps you are the manager or founder of an institution, club, group or party, or maybe a member of an institution. It is worth learning from Jesus and his methodology the run it.

He called his disciples and wanted them to go into the world in his name and preach the good news as he brought it to them. He gave his disciples certain instructions for performing this ministry that may seem crazy and ridiculous in today's context. He said: "And as you go, proclaim that the kingdom of Heaven is close at hand. Cure the sick, raise the dead, cleanse those suffering from virulent skin-diseases, drive out devils. You received without charge, give without charge. Provide yourselves with no gold or silver, not even with coppers for your purses, with no haversack for the journey or spare tunic or footwear or a staff, for the labourer deserves his keep. 'Whatever town or village you go into, seek out someone worthy and stay with him until you leave. As you enter his house, salute it, and if the house deserves it, may your peace come upon it; if it does not, may your peace come back to you." (Mt 10:7-15)

But one thing was important: that there were two of them. Two people (Lk 10:1), Number twelve means perfection. In other words, the whole world should be filled with these two people. It is interesting that these pairs later returned to Jesus and reported wonderful things, and that everything went as well as Jesus had imagined. This is a great success! No storage bag, no money, no bank account, no second shirt - but always two to be successful. "Better two than one alone, since thus their work is really rewarding. If one should fall, the other helps him up; but what of the person with no one to help him up when he falls? Where one alone would be overcome, two will put up resistance; and a threefold cord is not quickly broken" (Ecc 4:9-10, 12). If two people agree, the whole thing has a great chance of success. It is considered to be is more credible. And this probably also apply to the Good News, which Jesus proclaimed. He was alone. He had the power of God the Father, but we human beings are not like him. That means we are weak. We need another person. And especially in the postmodern era when many people are trying to retreat to their own homes to sit in front of a computer or other device, or some people think they don't need a church and can still believe in God. Or in fearful situations in which people say: I am alone. In this country over 30% live as singles. This means that these people also live alone. And in this post- modern era, I could well imagine the idea of "Take Two". If people would team up with a second person for a good cause, that would be wonderful. And that also applies to the church, which is not allowed to be lonely. The church, too, should always try to be with others.

## You are chosen

I would like to narrate my experience at the Highschool in Sandhausen two weeks ago. There I was invited by the 9th grade who wanted to get to know the special species of our society. Who will become a Pastor today? Or a priest? The conversation was interesting. The students were very curious to know why I became a priest. And even voluntarily renounce family and children. It's a call. Isaiah felt called to be a prophet. Paul was mysteriously called by Jesus on his journey to Tarsus. In the Gospel, Jesus invites people - most of them fishermen - as his disciples to make them fishers of people (Mk 1: 16-20). Why do many people become priests, religious, pastors or volunteers? The answer is that God needs people for His work. We know that God rules the whole world. If we want to experience God concretely, he also needs concrete people who have concrete experiences and can connect their concrete experiences with spirituality. My vocation as a priest is not just about me. Basically, I was chosen to connect God to people through my work. I want to travel with Jesus without anything binding me because God is everything to me. I am totally dependent on Divine Providence. My whole life has been focused on being with Him, but I feel more and more joy in my life because I was chosen, because I was called for His work. Of course, I also make a lot of mistakes, and I'm not perfect either. I unintentionally hurt people sometimes. But despite my limitations, despite my weaknesses, even with my sins, I feel that Jesus is still calling me into this task today. Therefore my calling is not exhausted. I will move on, I will live my calling even more deeply. Every day is a test of my calling. But one thing I know for sure: God will never leave me. He will continue to accompany me. What I am saying about myself here also applies to you and everyone who wants to give their lives for Jesus.

## An Invitation to serve

The next Sunday is the Feast of Christ the King. Jesus speaking on the Last Judgment Day says: "In truth I tell you, in so far as you did this to one of the least of these brothers of mine, you did it to me" (Mt 25:40).To help those in need, we need people. If it is only a small amount. We can do it ourselves with our own resources and efforts. But if many people are to be helped, we need people who hold hands together people who share their resources, and people who are needed to distribute things to those in need. People had to worry about people's health care during certain pandemics like Corona, the bitterest experience we've had. Help can be sought not only at the highest political level, but also privately, in organizations or even with individuals. Today many countries face the problem of refugees. People for political or other serious reasons such as famine, natural disasters and wars migrate from their own country and seek asylum in neighbouring countries. For the most part, they lead miserable lives. Here they sometimes have to live in containers and fight for everything. Nevertheless, they live with the hope that someone will light a lamp in their dark life. That someone could be you and me. Let's bring a glimmer of hope into their life.

In addition, there are many people who in their old age are necessarily dependent on some one in order to be able to lead their everyday lives. Some of them also live in poverty. You even have to fight to survive. Jesus would be very happy to welcome those who volunteer to help these poorest brothers and sisters in society in their dire need. Let our hands and legs always be ready to save people in need. This is the invitation that the King of Kings sends us through his gospel message. Are we ready to accept this invitation?

## Manual

We have different experiences with different executives. Be it the bus driver who brings us to our destination, the paramedic who brings us to the clinic in an emergency, or the train driver or pilot. You will be happy if you accomplish your goal well. When landing, people even clap in the plane. So we are always people who want to move from one place to another and are grateful for the people who guide and accompany us. This also applies to schools. Teachers accompany the children from one class to the next in the school year. Then there are lecturers and professors at the college level who accompany the students to the desired goal. It may be pre-diploma or diploma or postgraduate diploma or doctorate. Later on, these people are able to supervise, moderate or guide in crisis situations. When that happens on a perfect level, we feel good. I am very grateful to the people who helped me achieve this goal.

And so it is on the path of faith, too. We need people who lead us to Jesus. In the Gospel we hear that John the Baptist introduced Jesus to his disciples and that two of his disciples followed Jesus. Andrew was one of the two disciples who, after hearing from John, followed Jesus. He met Simon, his brother, and introduced him to Jesus. (Jn 1:35-37, 40-42). So in every sphere someone is needed to guide an other in this world. Instructions are always required. In the Acts of Apostles we come across another instance. The Ethiopian eunuch was reading the Scripture - a passage from Prophet Isaiah, of which he did not understand anything. Philip was prompted by the Spirit and approached the Ethiopian. He confessed to Philip that he did not understand what he was reading and also asked him: "How could I, unless I have someone to guide me?" (Ac 8:31). The last line speaks about the Baptism of the eunuch. Today many are there longing to know and understand the Word of God. But people to do that work are very few. Hence Jesus said: "The harvest is rich but the labourers are few" (Mt 9:37). Let us become the labourers of harvest. Let us get into the field of Kingdom of God and begin our work for His glory. In worldly matters too, there are many people with good talents to showcase their abilities. But they do not have proper guidance and therefore cannot step into the limelight. For example, many people have great knowledge of medicinal herbs to cure various diseases at a very low cost and with no side effects. But without someone showing them the right way to showcase their talent, nothing happens. Unfortunately, there are always those who do not divulge these secrets and who do not want to pass this knowledge on to future generations or to other simple people. Such people do not do justice to the society in which they were born and raised.

Jesus, the Son of God, was no secret. Andrew led Peter to Jesus because he had found the Messiah in him. He didn't keep it to himself. He said, "Simon come on, I'll show you". That made Peter a great man. We humans also need someone who shows us God. Let us therefore not be afraid to show others Jesus and lead them to him.

## You come with me

We can sit comfortably in the living room, watch TV or have a nice drink and say to each other, "life is beautiful, I enjoy it". But what if someone suddenly comes and says to us: "You - come with me!" When our children are bored, they are happy when friends come and say: "Come on, we'll go out and play." They go with them immediately. If we can do something better outside, we will also leave the cozy house and do whatever pleases our minds and hearts.

There is a very powerful account of the calling of the disciples in the gospel. Peter, James and John were called by Jesus. They were ordinary people who were fishermen and made a living. Suddenly this unknown man (Jesus) stood in front of them and said: "Come after me and I will make you into fishers of people. And at once they left their nets and followed him" (Mk 1:16-20).

What power do you think these words had that made these fishermen leave everything, including their families, parents, property and possessions, and follow this man when he called them. They felt the depth of his calling. Our Western world suffers from the fact that we are slowly losing this dimension of depth, becoming more and more superficial we no longer ask: What makes me special? What's the meaning of my life? How is my approach to God? So that I don't sink into everyday life, but experience a much deeper dimension and thus give my life a meaning. These three men allowed Jesus to give them the dimension of depth. They became people fishermen. They did not keep this experience to themselves, but tried to open other people's eyes to this dimension of depth. If we started again not only to stay on the surface but to go in depth, then we would experience a poignant and happy new dimension of divine depth.

## Should I get married

A good question, especially for the elderly. Should I live alone or should I get married? There are many singles, both in Germany and in many other countries. Many live in partnerships without getting married. But there are still many people who want to get married and stay together until "death do us part". So should we better get married or should we better stay alone? Actually everyone wants the best for themselves. Those who stay alone can do what they want and when they want. Nobody determines my eye or makes me rules. You don't have to be considerate of a partner. But partnership is also nice, because when I come home someone is waiting for me to ask "How was your day?", Who cooks for me, accompanies me and looks after me when I am sick. Marriage is good because I still have someone by my side. I can also have a family, children and grandchildren. with me. I also thought of getting married as a young man. I had studied well, got a suitable job with a good income to support a family. My parents even chose a girl for me to be my wife. But I decided to take a different route and stay alone, from a Christian-biblical point of view, from the point of view of Paul, whose letter deals with one thing:

whether you want to get married or not, it is about serving God (1 Cor 7:32-35).

Whether alone or married, or as a priest: it is always about caring for God. But if I just take myself as the center, that's not good. Then it goes wrong. And that is exactly what it is all about: taking God as the center. And every way of life is good as long as I have God as the center.

## Walking with Christ

In our life we always want to do everything at the same time, multitasking is the keyword today. As you do one more thing, you are already thinking of another that you still want or need to do. That is exhausting. A walk or a hike in nature is all the more beautiful. It brings relaxation and is good for the body. But may be, is it not a little boring on your own? It is better to be with others.

Let us think about the fact that Jesus sent 72 disciples into the world. Jesus sent them ahead in pairs to every city and place he wanted to visit. He felt he couldn't cover a huge area and needed your help (Lk 10: 1-2). They were directed to keep proclaiming that the kingdom of heaven was at hand. They should heal people. He gave them the strength to do whatever he wanted to the people. On their return they shared the wonderful things they had done and everything that had happened during their service.

They were able to heal people, cast out evil spirits, and win many over to the kingdom of God (Lk 10: 17-20). In this sense: We should not only do something for our own soul, but for all people we meet. Because Christ is sending us all over the world.

## As soon as the Leader is gone

We live in a democracy, People participate in making decisions, including the election of the heads of state. This applies not only to our country, but also to the family, the community, the parish or the district. There are leaders everywhere who make decisions for a particular group. People need leaders who stand up for their group, their people. There are different models for selecting executives. By referendum, by election, by arrangement.

It was the same with Moses. He was directed by God to take the lead to free the people from slavery in Egypt. (Ex 3:9-10). It was not easy. There were many problems with Pharaoh, the journey lasted forty years. At various points during the trip, people began to complain. Moses had to watch out how best to deal with them in order to accomplish his mission. Moses went to Mount Sinai and had an encounter with God there. He was given the Ten Commandments and other rules and regulations. Moses stayed there a long time and had be a separated from his people. During his absence they were leaderless, they were headless. They forgot everything. They created their own god. They created a golden calf and began to worship this statue. (Ex 32: 1-21). Being a leader in the name of God is an exciting thing. But managers shouldn't be away from their people for too long either. Because they may not know how the people there, are doing. Perhaps they do not know their present needs and their worries and needs, Moses' story teaches us that if I stay too long on the mountain, too long away from the base, from the people, they lose their bearings. They could take in a "golden calf" in the meantime. How many new parties have emerged in Germany recently? Do they serve our democracy and the people? For the leaders of our state are not vigilant, they are too far away from the base, too long "on top of the mountain". A manager also has to change, learn a lot, and update his or her knowledge of human resource management. Our Pope once said: "If I want to be a leader, I have to know the smell of sheep. If I want to be a leader, I have to know the people who are my base." Can we become such leaders?

## Cross Driver

Are there lateral drivers, lateral thinkers, or do they say yes to everything? In our history there were always people who thought differently from the great masses and who had great influence on the following generations, such as Karl Marx. or a great man in India, Periyar, without whom I would not be here. In India, only the Brahmins were allowed to learn, as here in the Middle Ages only the monks and priests could study. Ordinary people, were the low castes in India, were not allowed to study or even walk freely. But today everyone in India is allowed to go to school and learn, and we owe that to this man. For me, lateral thinkers are people who come from God, as long as their thoughts do not cause anything negative for people. God always said: "For my thoughts are not your thoughts and your ways are not my ways" (Is 55:8). God keeps saying he's different through the parable of vineyard in the Gospel (Mt 20:1-15).

If the owner had only calculated hourly wages and paid a small amount to last- minute workers, it would be of no use to these people and their loved ones. These people would not make ends meet. Their families would suffer. The landowner wanted to be a just person. But from a worldly point of view, the landowner would have been an unjust person. But that's what God is about. His grace is the same for all. Jesus, too, as the image of God, always made the Father present in his thoughts and treated everyone equally. The strong believer who lives righteously and the life long sinner who repents for all his sins and receives the forgiveness and mercy of God are treated equally in the kingdom of heaven. In our democracy we have the freedom to say anything, and that's a good thing. Thinking outside the box must always be close to people. All human beings have the right to live, but not at the expense of others or the disadvantaged or the earth. We have to be there for those who have no voice in society and wait for us to speak for them.

# 7. ETERNITY AND ETERNAL LIFE

*"I know that whatever God does will be forever. To this there is nothing to add, from this there is nothing to subtract, and the way God acts inspires dread" (Ecc 3:14).*

## What is meant by Eternity and Eternal life?

In the sermons, in the scriptures, the words Eternal (Life) (Rest) and Eternity are often heard and read. What do these terms eternity and eternal mean? The word Eternal means "eternal forever with no beginning or end; always existing; incessant, eternal" etc. This word is in contrast with the word temporal. A metaphysical word that exists outside of all temporal relationships. It is unchangeable. Our triune God existed for all eternity. Before the creation of the universe, when nothingness prevailed, the Father, Son and Spirit already existed. They are still active today; they are the guiding force and protector of all humanity and every tiny and powerful living being in the universe. They will be there forever even after the completion of the world. They have no beginning and no end - they rule forever and ever. The word eternity is associated with the word eternal. It also means infinite, duration with no beginning or end. Eternal existence is contrasted with mortal life. We humans and all created beings have mortal bodies, while God alone is immortal. Eternity is the state into which the soul passes when a person dies.

## Know the Eternal Father

Eternal life - what does that mean? Have you ever had an experience where you said: I want to stay here forever? Or may be you have had an experience in which you said: I will never forget this time. I would stop the clock to make the time stand still. Or maybe you have had another experience where you felt you were doing wonderfully well, or you had a similar feeling of happiness. When I think of good things, when I feel wonderful, my face shines like the sun, so I'm glad that I just feel endless joy in my heart. Perhaps this was the first time you had a good experience with a person; maybe you were totally in love with this person. Or may be you have had the pleasure of being rewarded after a great effort. Or you received luck given from outside that you did not expect yourself. These are expressions or periods of eternal life. We are finite people. We have time and space as limitations. The experiences we have had are over. However, we are constantly reminded of the happiness that we have experienced from various life experiences in our daily life. We long for better, good experiences, we long for joy. These are parts of our life in which we wish for eternal life. We have the right to eternal life. The Gospel of John (Jn 17:1-11) contains the prayer of Jesus. In prayer, 17:3 defines the meaning of eternal life. For Jesus, eternal life means that people should know the Eternal Father, who is the true God, and Jesus Christ, the Son whom the Father sent. (Jn 17:3). That means eternal life for Christians, that we should know God the Father and His Son Jesus Christ. We belong to the original reason, we belong to the "original soul". We cannot have eternal life in this world. We belong to the "primal experience" of divinity. We have to go back to where we came from. The entry into eternity would only happen through Jesus Christ, who was God incarnate, who became man for man's sake. He was the Word, the Logos, and He became flesh to do the will of the Father. After his death on the cross, he rose from the dead and ascended to heaven to be with the Father for all eternity. He gives us eternal life by sitting at the right hand of the Father. This does not mean that we cannot have this experience of eternal joy until after we die. We can have a fraction of this life, a taste of it in this life itself. If we limit ourselves to our own strength, if we think that this world is endless, then we are making a grave mistake. We are born for eternal life. We are born for infinity. We are born for the improbably endless joy.

## Are we all going to Heaven?

What happens after life? An important question to which all religions try to answer. The gospel answers this question too. Jesus explains that there are indeed some people who will be judged and will not go to heaven. - This are very hard news. If you look up the Bible and read the reasons why people are judged or rewarded, we don't find much when it comes to faith. It remains to be seen whether or not you can go to heaven if you believe in God. But there is one thing that God personally points out strictly that if you set certain things aside, you will not go to heaven. It's about charity. The entire judgment of Judgment Day would be based only on what answers people give to the six simple questions. (Mt 25:31-46). The Lord will ask "I was hungry did you give food? I was thirsty did you give me drink? I was naked did you clothe me? When I was sick did you take care of me? When I was a stranger did you welcome me in your midst? When I was in prison did you visit me?" If our answers for these six questions in the affirmative, wewould be welcomed into the eternal joy. But if our answers are a big NO to all these 6 questions He would also say a big NO and send to the eternal fire - everlasting punishment.

## Show them the Foretaste of Eternity

In the last few days the media have reported a lot about Pope Francis' speech at the World Food Conference. There the Pope declared that the world had enough food for everyone. In other words, God made sure that all people could be satisfied. But why do 800 million people in this world still have to go hungry? The reason is, their share is taken away from them by other people. You are being robbed. Even if we live in a land where everything is in abundance, God asks us: I have given you everything. So why does a person have to starve to death in Africa, India, Asia or South America? I did not create such a world. And if you live in this rich world and do not share anything with the hungry and thirsty, with the homeless and with refugees, then you will be judged by me forever. A harsh judgment from the king. He doesn't ask me to believe in him. But he demands of me that I am there for the hungry, for the thirsty, for the homeless, for the refugees. The media often reports on the conditions under which refugees have to live in our time and how we treat them. A terrifying experience. In our country, too, people are not given sufficient support. When foreigners come here, they have to face a violent situation. But in spite of everything, our world has got a little better, if not yet optimal. Perhaps through our friendly gestures we can help to satisfy hunger and thirst and to give those in need a foretaste of eternity.

## Don't live for your Belly

Speaking of eternity: We hear something strange from Paul. Paul who tearfully speaks: "They are destined to be lost; their god is the stomach" (Phil 3:19)."Your God is the belly". By the way, in our country there are two different types of belly. First the belly of prosperity, which shows that you enjoy life, which shows how great the prosperity is in our country, and then there is the well-toned six-pack. On the one hand you see the people who prefer to enjoy their life and do not care about their health and on the other hand the people who exercise every day to be slim and look good. If that is indeed the case, I can

understand why Paul corrected this by saying:" Their God is
their stomach". He said: earthly things alone are in their mind.
He meant that many people only meet the short-term needs of
their lives that are personally important to them. They don't
look left or right, they don't care about tomorrow or the day
after, they just meet their own immediate needs. In other words,
they try to do what others think is important. There is nothing
wrong with working for earthly needs. But to forget our eternal
life and goal for this is not fair. Man lives between heaven and
earth. And everything was made to last forever, not for a
limited time. When we are literally fed up with this life, when
we see people who have no home, when we meet people who
live without many basic needs, it is easy to believe that our
home is heavenly. So they live in the hope that one day their
hardships will be over.

But also for the people who are not in such a situation, for the
people who live in a prosperous society, for the people who
do not have to starve or die of thirst, for the people who are not
looking for one as refugees need to travel to a new home, for
those who are not struggling with a serious illness, it might
actually be true when Paul says: Our home is in heaven. Paul
didn't lose hope. He said that we humans were created for
God, for divinity, not just for short-term needs.
Therefore: a well-to-do stomach or a well-toned six-pack is
basically only superficial. We are made for eternity and so we
will be resurrected.

## Will just a few be saved?

That is a question people asked Jesus, and we today also are
asking the same question. Especially in our world, in which
only performance counts, only a few get by, without an
elbow mentality it doesn't seem to work at all. So what do I

have to do to be saved? Jehovah's Witnesses say only 1.44.000 people will be saved, while other sects have precise rules that must be obeyed, as well as other religions that put people into a tight corset of do's and don'ts. Also, many people say they don't care. But Jesus spoke of a narrow door that one has to go through. It is said that life is not just a walk in the park, but that one must strive to achieve something or move forward. In this way, we are not simply given everything. We also have to contribute to it. In religious life we need this willingness to go through this narrow door, even if it is difficult. Just like a mother is in pain during labor. Bringing a child into the world is hard work, but afterwards it is even happier and happier to have given the world a new life (cf. Jn 16:21). So we have to make an effort to get a good result. As Christians, we believe that God gives much more than we expect.

**First will be the Last and Last will be the first**

Lk 13:22-30: "Through towns and villages he went teaching, making his way to Jerusalem. Someone said to him, 'Sir, will there be only a few saved?' He said to them, 'Try your hardest to enter by the narrow door, because, I tell you, many will try to enter and will not succeed. 'Once the master of the house has got up and locked the door, you may find yourself standing outside knocking on the door, saying, "Lord, open to us," but he will answer, "I do not know where you come from." Then you will start saying, "We once ate and drank in your company; you taught in our streets," but he will reply, "I do not know where you come from; away from me, all evil doers!" 'Then there will be weeping and grinding of teeth, when you see Abraham and Isaac and Jacob and all the prophets in the kingdom of God, and yourselves thrown out. And people from east and west, from north and south, will come and sit down at the feast in the kingdom of God. 'Look, there are those now last who will be first, and those now first who will be last".

These words of Jesus emphasize the fact that a great effort is required to enter the kingdom of God. There is an urgency to seize the present opportunity to enter because the narrow door cannot be left open indefinitely. Behind this lies the rejection of Jesus and his message by his Jewish contemporaries, whose table seats in the kingdom of God are taken by the heathen from all over the world. Those who (the Gentiles) are called last will go forward into the kingdom of God as those to whom the invitation to enter was first addressed (the Jews).

## Is this all Life

Life goes on, but not forever in this world. Our life here is finite. After everything you have achieved and experienced, the time to say goodbye comes. This end is called death. Nature shows us again and again that new life arises from death, that it is not the end. Just as a tree loses its leaves in autumn, is bare in winter and looks "dead" when it sheds new leaves in spring, it is alive. Even if something has to "die" or it looks like it to us, there is another life, a life that goes on. The resurrection is to be understood as a life that goes beyond our earthly life. It is not yet visible to us because we are stuck in the world and still exist here. This is a good explanation for me, and philosophers and other religions also say that this earthly life is only one aspect of existence. And every religion has this longing for a different life, a life that goes beyond our earthly life and lasts. I am convinced that we can only find fulfillment in our earthly life with God and that he gives us the certainty that death is not all over.

In the text of Lk 20:28-33 we read: Some Sadducees, those who deny that there is resurrection, came forward and put this question to him saying: "Master, Moses prescribed for us, if a man's married brother dies childless, the man must marry the widow to raise up children for his brother. Well then, there were seven brothers; the first, having married a wife, died childless. The second and then the third married the widow. And the same with all seven, they died leaving no children. Finally the woman herself died. Now, at the resurrection, whose wife will she be, since she had been married to all seven?"(Lk 20:34-40)

## What do you want to be?

We often ask children: What would you like to be in the future? And they answer: I want to be an astronaut or a policeman or a baker or a bricklayer. - At the same time someone asks you whether you have become what you wanted to be? Do you have the job you wanted? Have you built a house yet? Did you buy your dream car? Have you found the spouse you wanted? But is that all you wanted to achieve in life? It's not what you wanted, it's what you want to be. Whatever we may achieve in life, even if we accumulate enormous wealth, or if we have earned names and fame in our own country and state, and are internationally famous, that will come to an end at some point. When man's life comes to an end, the soul goes through eternity. This is explained in the Gospels Lk 21:5-24. Jesus gives us a tip: If we stand firm, remain faithful to Him, stay with Him in the midst of all tribulations, then He gives us eternal life. Then, despite all the hostility, nothing can happen to our souls. - For Christians, the longing and the goal is to attain eternal life. And Jesus helps us to live better not only in this world but also after death. If we stand firm, Jesus gives us eternal life and death loses its horror.

## End times Moods

"We tell you about the lovely Advent, see the first candle burns.

We tell you about a holy time, prepare the way for the Lord. Rejoice, you Christians, rejoice very much! The Lord is already near".

This is a wonderful German Advent song. They are read in the Advent season, shortly before the joyous Christmas festival. Why? Because we Christians should always return to our roots. Just as a tree is badly off if its roots are not healthy, we are not doing well if our roots are not in Jesus Christ. Jesus Christ tells us that after the end of earthly life everything will be different. Our goal should be to walk the path to Jesus Christ and God the Father. Especially in this year 2020, the year of the pandemic, in which so much bad has happened, we need this strong hope. Therefore, the end of life on earth is the beginning of a new joy, for me, for you and for all of us I hope that we will use this Advent season to walk the path that leads to a good end, namely a perfect life for all of us.

Is 2:1-5: "The vision of Isaiah son of Amoz, concerning Judah and Jerusalem. It will happen in the final days that the mountain of Yahweh's house will rise higher than the mountains and tower above the heights. Then all the nations will stream to it, many peoples will come to it and say, 'Come, let us go up to the mountain of Yahweh, to the house of the God of Jacob that he may teach us his ways so that we may walk in his paths.' For the Law will issue from Zion and the word of Yahweh from Jerusalem. Then he will judge between the nations and arbitrate between many peoples. They will hammer their swords into ploughshares and their spears into sickles. Nation will not lift sword against nation, no longer will they learn how to make war. House of Jacob, come, let us walk in Yahweh's light."

## Do you want to have Eternal Life

Do you want to live forever? That would be nice. Imagine there is a man in the forest. He calls all people to him and tells them that if they are reborn in him they will live forever. Many come to him and ask: Master, how is that supposed to be? What do we have to do?

This shows man's longing to live forever and not face death. All great cultures on earth, including the Egyptians, and all great religions of this world believe in life after death. Jesus gives us three very simple ways to have eternal life.

"Those who believe in me will not die, but will live. Even if he dies he will live". This he said to Martha, who was desperate after the death of Lazarus. He asked her: "Anyone who believes in me, even though that person dies, will live, and whoever lives and believes in me will never die. Do you believe this? 'Yes, Lord,' she said, 'I believe that you are the Christ, the Son of God, the one who was to come into this world" (Jn 11:25-27). And therefore Lazarus was raised from the dead. (Jn 11:43-44).Faith in Jesus Christ gives eternal life. He also said: "But anyone who stands firm to the end will be saved." (Mt 24:13). When Jesus said to the twelve: "Do you also want to leave?" Simon Peter answered him: "Lord, to whom shall we go? You have the message of eternal life" (Jn 6:68). That helps us too. Jesus said: "I am the living bread which has come down from heaven. Anyone who eats this bread will live for ever; and the bread that I shall give is my flesh, for the life of the world." (Jn 6:51).

When we receive the immortal God incarnate in Jesus Christ into our lives, we will live forever. He is a powerful guide to eternal life. We hear the word of God, we believe in Jesus Christ and we receive the body and blood of Christ in the

Eucharist. When we do this, we become immortal in Christ Jesus and remain in the kingdom of God forever.

## What remains forever

Everything in this world is transient; we only have it for a short time. Like that fig tree behind me. Recently its leaves were green, now they are yellow and will soon fall off. Everything we have, what we are, is subject to impermanence. What will stay the same forever?

To tell us what is really permanent, we have a beautiful story of a young man who came to Jesus because he was looking for or wanted eternal life. He says that he will keep all the commandments, that he will do everything right, that he is the best, the righteous. Jesus answered him: "If you wish to be perfect, go and sell your possessions and give the money to the poor, and you will have treasure in heaven; then come, follow me.' But when the young man heard these words he went away sad, for he was a man of great wealth" (Mt 19:21- 24). Even if people like to enter eternal life, the wealth is an obstacle for them. It cannot be overcome by human power. We become prisoners of what we ourselves have earned and owned. But if we give everything away, let go of everything and only follow Jesus with a determined heart, all our lives, with firm faith in him, then he gives us eternal life. Let us go to Jesus to inherit eternal life.

## "Black Friday" for Christians

Why is there this "Black Friday"? This trend came to us from the United States, where retailers wanted to boost the economy and sales after Thanksgiving. On this day, more than Three billion Euros in sales are made in retail and on the Internet. But now doubts about these so-called "bargain offers" are growing. I sometimes think that the prices may be raised beforehand just to make them appear lower to us, and in the end these are not bargains at all, but actually more expensive than at regular times. So it's really all about selling. We the consumers are being tricked.

What does "Black Friday" have to do with the Church? For Christians, Friday is always a black day. At 3 p.m. Jesus Christ died on the cross: "It is fulfilled"(Jn 19:30).By this he meant to say that. His mission on this earth was over. He gave his life for us. But he also said: "Come to me, all you who labour and are overburdened, and I will give you rest." (Mt 11:28- 30).That really is a hefty discount: zero percent! For everyone. Jesus does not sell us the Kingdom of Heaven, He gives it to us for free. He gives us eternal life, we have a right to it because we are His children.

Also, the word Jesus used was "It is finished" to say that his mission is over. The Greek word used for this was Tetelestai. This is the word used in the tollgates and lending houses. Jews usually borrow money for interest. You need to sign an agreement in order to receive the money. You can repay the amount in installments. When the last installment is paid, the contract paper is taken over and you have to evaluate the whole thing and write Tetelestai on it - which means that the entire loan taken out, including interest, has been paid in full. Jesus paid off all of our debts incurred as a result of our sins by giving his life on the cross as a ransom for our sins. For a borrower, the word Tetelestai should mean joy in hearing. Apart from this financial factor, Tetelestai has three different meanings.

This word was used is business which meant, the debt is fully paid.

It was also used in judgment in court system, which meant, the sentence is fully served.

It was also as a military term which meant, the battle is fully won.

So when Jesus said: "It is finished" -This is what is going to bring you rest - he meant three things. 1. Your debt of sins is fully paid. 2. The sentence / punishment for us for what we deserve as punishment, the time of being in bondage has beenfullyserved. 3.The battle against the devil and sin and all the enemies of sicknesses and diseases and viruses, the battle has been fully won.

So rest in the finished work of Cross. We are redeemed, our debts are paid in full we need not bother anymore. - Then why Black Friday? It is a glittering Friday.

## Life in Abundance

What does that mean? That I can do anything I want? That I can buy everything, experience everything, enjoy everything? That I am a free person? That goes for many of us, but neither can many. They live in poverty, in oppression, in need, there is no question of a fulfilled life for them - or can they?

There is a story. Once goats constantly complained that they wanted to get out of the stable and into the large pasture because the grass there was greener and freedom was greater. But as soon as they were outside, a wolf came and they panicked and fled back to the small stable, to safety.

Don't we do this that often? We dream of paradise, but we don't find it here. We dream of a perfect life in abundance, but despite all the work, despite all our efforts, we do not achieve it. Jesus says: I came to have abundant life. How can someone who has only lived here in this world for 33 years say something like that? He can say it because he trusted in God, accepted his life plan and fulfilled it, even though it meant a shameful death on the cross. In this way, He made it possible for all of us to receive eternal life.

# 8. FAITH

*"The upright will live through faithfulness" (Hab 2:4).*

## Hear with the Heart

When an African missionary tried to translate the Gospel of John from English to the local language where he lived, he struggled to get the job done because there weren't enough words to express many things. If he had to translate the phrase "believe" or words like belief and he couldn't find a suitable word or phrase at all. After a long struggle, he decided to enlist the help of the locals. He turned to a few educated people to help him. Most of them couldn't help him because they themselves didn't know much . Finally, someone who understood the missionary's gestures and facial expressions coined a sentence that was absolutely correct. He said "to believe" means "to listen with your heart".

## First Communion and Terror in Sri Lanka

I am very pleased that so many children will go for First Communion. First in Sandhausen and then on the following five Sundays in all five congregations in our pastoral unit. Children have been preparing for this day for a long time. They will celebrate this great day with their family, god parents, and friends, and I am glad that they will make this day a memorable one for them, with Jesus Christ coming into their hearts, for the first time.

But I am also sad about what has happened in Sri Lanka. Two hundred Christians were killed for their faith. These two aree entirely different propositions. One is a very joyous, blissful event to take place in the life of the children who are to receive the Lord in their hearts for the first time. On the contrary the other one happens to be a very bitter experience. It is like a"Good Friday experience" in Sri Lanka, in another part of the world. The joy of children to accept Jesus Christ in their lives, to receive the Son of God. Jesus is like receiving a Good Shepherd who takes every effort to protect his sheep and unceasingly run after the lost one to find them and bring them back to the fold (Lk 15:4-7).

But He also had to die on the cross for our sake for our redemption. But death was not an end for Him. His death was followed by His Resurrection. Jesus lives. He lives for us and supports us. And it is precisely this faith that God demands of us, for the good of men, for the good of the whole world. We are speechless and saddened by this massacre in Sri Lanka. Like Christ those people suffered martyrdom and were crucified. In the whole world, no religion is persecuted like Christianity. Christians in Sri Lanka who died for their faith remain a great example to us.

**How many will be saved?**

How much should one believe, how far should one live one's faith? I keep hearing these questions. Some people say: "I am a Christian and sometimes I pray, but I hesitate to attend Sunday Mass. Instead, I would rather go on a trip to a place with lots of flora and fauna". Two thirds of the population here are Christians. Why do we wonder how much we have to believe? Paul wrote to the Hebrews, who were third and fourth generation Christians after the resurrection of Jesus, even though Paul had neither seen him face to face nor had any other meeting with him. Even in this church, people thought that they could just live their lives now, that they would not have to be so strict about truly living their faith. But Paul clearly affirmed that this is wrong. According to Paul, Jesus Christ was the originator and the end of faith. Without him it is not possible (Heb 3:1-7). Without him life is nothing. If we live our faith, there should never be a fraction or a smaller percentage of it, say 20% or 50% being real Christians and the rest living according to our own whims and ideas. We have to be 100% Christians, rooted in Jesus Christ.

Paul's Letter to the Hebrews 12:1-3: says:"With so many witnesses in a great cloud all around us, we too, then, should throw off everything that weighs us down and the sin that clings so closely, and with perseverance keep running in the race which lies ahead of us. Let us keep our eyes fixed on Jesus, who leads us in our faith and brings it to perfection: for the sake of the joy which lay ahead of him, he endured the cross, disregarding the shame of it, and has taken his seat at the right of God's throne. Think of the way he persevered against such opposition from sinners and then you will not lose heart and come to grief."

## Who is poor?

Poor or rich, we are all human beings. If a person has no money, no job, no home and struggling in life to make ends meet he, is treated as poor. In some peculiar circumstances, if a person has no relationship or a family to take care and show love and concern also can be seen as poor. Some people who may be living an aristocratic life with all luxuries will be thrown out on the lurch due to natural calamities, like floods, cyclones, tsunami; losing all belongings and even livelihood, all means for survival. At that point he/she becomes poor instantaneously. This is what the world sees as definitions of being poor.

But the definition Jesus has a connotation. He said: "How blessed are the poor in spirit: the kingdom of Heaven is theirs"(Mt. 5:3).

The poor in spirit in the Old Testament means as the poor - materially poor, the Anawim, who do not have enough material possessions and whose confidence is only on God. (Is61:1;Zep2:3), Matthew adds in spirit in order either to indicate that only the devout poor are meant or to extend the beatitude to all of whatever social rank, who recognize their complete dependence on God. The same phrase poor in spirit is found in the Qumran literature (1QM 14:7). This shows that lack of material possessions, or lack of relatives and friends, or lack of a family to support, does not make a person poor. But it points to the lack of faith in God. A poor person is, one who refuses to rely only on Divine Providence.

A question repeatedly asked, especially when some renovation taking place in the church: "Is the church rich?" Yes, the Church is really rich! Who said that the church is poor? We are not poor, the Church is rich. But the Church is rich not in terms of money, but by its tradition, by its faith, by the foundation of faith. The Church is headed by a person, who lived for only 33 years on the earth. But he gained the world's largest number of followers. This record is being maintained for more than 2000 years, this man inspired people, people of all colors and languages, of all cultures and nations! They profess that this man is the Son of God - Jesus Christ. In this country too our ancestors have lived for this man and for this church. How can this fact be forgotten? The Church is rich in repentance, the Church is rich in the Knowledge of the Lord in all times - so it must be rich.

Its richness is always revealed by the faith it has in Jesus. The same faith is shared, taught, nurtured down the generations for centuries. It is the responsibility to protect, safeguard and increase this treasure, this faith and take it to future generations.

## The City Of God

The last book in the Bible is The Revelation. In Rv 21,10-14 and 22 there is a beautiful description of the City of Jerusalem - the New Jerusalem and also it says that there was no Temple in that City. Only Lord God Almighty and the Lamb were found in the Temple. I have been told that the city of Leimen was once a very famous and modern city and that the people of Baden-Württemberg have taken Leimen as an example of how to build a city and how to live there. The city of Leimen has a name.

In the Revelation of John we hear of a city. This city is a peculiar city. This city does not need sun or moon to provide light. The light comes down from heaven to this city. The glory of God shines upon it, and it is always bright, it is always wonderful. This city has four directions, and there are gates in each direction: three gates to the north, three gates to the south, three gates to the west, and three gates to the east - completely protected by God Himself. People live there without any problem. It is also interesting to hear in this reading that there is no longer a temple in this city for different denominations of Christianity or for people belonging to different faith such as Buddhism or Islam. It is a city that has only one God. That is the wonderful idea of John. Our churches have experienced again and again separation from each other and separation from God. That is why we must strive to stand on our feet somehow, we must make every effort to bring us together, because we have distanced ourselves from God.

## End of the Models

In 1978 a book was published entitled *The End of the Models* (Margarete Mitscherlich: The End of The Role Models, Pieper 1978). After a few decades, you think it was somehow right. The end of role models – Are there any role models in our society, in our Church? These days, it is not easy to find a role model. Especially in a rapidly developing media age, it becomes more and more difficult to find a great role model.

In faith we find the same situations, too.In the Old Testament, one speaks of Abraham as the father of faith, as a great example of faith. In the New Testament Mary is seen as a role model for faith. Both Abraham and Mary of both the Testaments were Jews who are quoted as models of Faith. There are also some Gentiles, other than Jews, who are shining as models of faith in Jesus. Faith is not a property of a particular race or religion. This man, a heathen, a Roman captain, a soldier, is an example of faith. This is because he had a servant, who was seriously ill. The Captain tried to help his servant by all medical means. But he remained in the same condition. The centurion asked Jesus to come and heal him. Jesus wanted to go to his house. While he was still on the way, the centurion sent a servant to Jesus to tell him, "Lord, please, you do not come. I'm not worthy that you enter my house. But just say one word, then my servant will be healed. Incredible, isn't it? Jesus was astonished by this statement and praised him. He said: "I tell you, not even in Israel have I found faith as great as this" (cf. Lk 7:9). This tells us as a church, as Christians, something important, namely that we, as ecclesial people or as religious people, must look beyond the box. We cannot expect quality only from our own people. Quality is also available somewhere else. The faith of some people of today, even if they are not Christians, even if they do not attend church regularly, sometimes seems to be stronger than the regular church going Christians.

## Faith can be found all over the World

The Second Vatican Council speaks in Gaudium et spes of the fact that there is also truth in the world, that God is also present in the world: in the humanists, in the non - Christian theories, God is also present (cf. GS 44). People live and work for God, even if they are not in the Church or are not Christians. Another point for : You may not yet be deeply rooted in faith, perhaps The Second Vatican Council speaks in Gaudium et spes of the fact that there is also truth in the world, that God is also present in the world: in the humanists, in the non-Christian theories, in the Sacred scriptures of other Religions also. God is also present in their midst (cf. GS 44).

## Do you believe strongly in God?

I have a question: do you really believe in God? For we need strong personal faith today. Like what, Martha, the sister of Lazarus had. You know the story in which Jesus raised Lazarus from the dead. Lazarus was already dead. But Martha firmly believed that Lazarus would not have died if Jesus had been there. She said, "If only the Lord was there" because she believed that Jesus would not let him die. But he was dead four days before and was buried. Jesus got the news and came to Bethany and asked Martha if she believed in him and she said, "Yes Lord, I believe". On this creed, Lazarus is raised from the dead. The impossible became possible because Martha truly believed and trusted Jesus. We often don't understand why something doesn't work in our life, why we can't make it, why things go wrong when we've tried. Martha is our role model here. When our beliefs are really strong, the impossible will happen. We can and must have strong faith.

## Nationality: Christian!

At one point it was said that Germany was not a country of immigration. But the 2011 census showed the opposite: Germany is a country of immigration. Almost every fifth inhabitant in this country comes from a country of migration. We live in a multicultural society. But what about faith? Someone wrote that Germany was a country of emigration by faith. And what about you and me? I was once Indian. But today I am a German. In other words, I have two souls in me: an Indian soul and a German soul. This goes without saying. But what ultimately defines me is the spirit in me. I would say the Spirit is the garment that I put on, which is Christ. When I was baptized, I was given a name. You are a Christian, a Christian forever, no matter how you are and where you are. You are a Christian, an image of Jesus Christ. That connects me with everyone here in this country or in the world. This is what Paul writes in the letter to the Galatians.- "For all of you are the children of God, through faith, in Christ Jesus, since every one of you that has been baptised has been clothed in Christ. There can be neither Jew nor Greek, there can be neither slave nor freeman, there can be neither male nor female - for you are all one in Christ Jesus" (cf. Gal 3:26-28).

A wonderful sentence! Yes, the sun we see today shines for all people, Christians and others alike. But especially as a Christian, I am a little closer to other Christians because I am connected to them through divinity. Whether my nationality is Indian or German has nothing to do with it. All men - black, white or "yellow" - all people could be one in God, man and woman, slaves or free, whether someone has money or not, all can be one in Christ. We are all "one" in Christ. Do we feel that? Do you feel like a Christian?

## From Limburg to Egypt

It is always exciting to be a Christian. Limburg is a story that moves us and our country very much. There was a problem with a bishop who was not properly understood for his thoughts and deeds. Quite a number of people were angry and some of them wanted to leave the Catholic Church. A small fraction of the population fought for its identity; people who make up barely 10% said "We are the old Christians. Christianity lived here for 2000 years and we want to live and survive in this country - from Limburg to Egypt."

A man's action shows what he is. Even if one causes problem, even if one threatens to destroy everything, he cannot destroy my faith. My faith in Christ cannot be seized by anyone! No one can take away my faith in Jesus Christ from me if I do not allow it. Faith and God are the most important things for me. That is why I would not leave my faith because of one person, but would continue my way because God is important to me. From Limburg to Egypt – Here are people who want to live for their faith. They want to have the joy of the Christian faith. They also want to show the whole world that they are proud Christians that they can live in this country - Egypt. We all want to tell them: We are with you! We are Christians and we are united in one God! And for all of us, Jesus Christ, God, is much more important than anything else.

## Jesus, you are the Son of God!

This would be a wonderful confession of a man who even inspired Jesus (cf. Mt. 16:13-20). A man whose academic qualification is not known; by profession he was a fisherman.

**107**

His spiritual education is also not known. This man said: "You are the Christ, the Son of the living God" (cf. Mt. 16:16). Jesus was totally excited, fascinated by that one sentence. It is interesting to note that Jesus did not ask him any more questions about this. That one man's confession was enough for his mission. The Bible says that after Peter's confession, the disciples themselves and also the way prepared for Jesus' passion. Jesus was on his way to the crucifixion.

Even a person's confessions can move God. I hear and understand that in this text. God can be moved when a person confesses to him. That is God's longing: that everyone should confess to him. It is like if parents expecting their children to love and recognize them, and the children's longing to be loved by their parents. Yesterday I was with a family with a small child. The child can almost only say "Papa". The mother is a bit sad about this, because when the dad says to the child: "Say 'Mom"'! the child immediately says again: "Dad!". In the case of Peter, this was a clear statement he said, "Yes, you are! You are the Son of God! You are the Messiah!"

The papacy today is constantly being questioned: who is Peter's successor? What does this man do? One often speaks of the power of the Pope, of the fact that he decides many things. In fact, he is infallible in pronouncing certain dogmas. The successors of Peter, the Popes, throughout their lives proclaimed and confessed Jesus as the Son of God and expressed their deep faith in him. I have seen this again and again with many popes; Pope John Paul II, a wonderful Pope, was never afraid to take on his sufferings. He always held onto his cross when he was just too weak. Or all the writings of Pope Benedict XVI, the Pope emeritus: the content of his letters was nothing other than the love of the Lord, Jesus Christ. Pope Francis constantly tries to put the service of Jesus in the foreground and shows how a Pope should pass on this love for Jesus Christ and to the people today.

Now let's put the papacy aside. It's about our confession: my confession and your confession. A few days ago I felt honored by someone who said that as a priest I would make it very clear that Jesus Christ is Lord and Savior. I was very happy to hear that. Jesus is the savior of the world, Jesus is the redeemer of the world. When we profess him, when we bear testimony of him, God goes with us. Then salvation comes close to us. We don't have to convert all people to Jesus, but when we - you and I - profess Him, it starts to work.

## You bewitched me

"You have seduced me, Yahweh, and I have let myself be seduced" (Jer 20:7). "You have overpowered me: you were the stronger. I am a laughing-stock all day long, they all make fun of me. For whenever I speak, I have to howl and proclaim, 'Violence and ruin!' For me, Yahweh's word has been the cause of insult and derision all day long. I would say to myself, 'I will not think about him, I will not speak in his name any more,' but then there seemed to be a fire burning in my heart, imprisoned in my bones."Even if it was so many years ago, even thousands of years have passed, when Jeremiah spoke the words from Jr 20:7-9, the situation is the same to this day: In Iraq people are fleeing their houses and hiding in caves and in the mountains. They don't want to become Muslims, they want to stay with their God. They want to stay Christian. They want to uphold and defend their human rights. That's why they hide. Even as people are crucified today, they remain steadfast in their faith because of this one God who loves them. You beguiled me, I let myself be seduced. You tied me up I just can't help myself, I'll stay with you.

But to confess to you and to live for you is not easy - even in the year 2021 you will only reap ridicule! If I only tell my family or friends that I am a Christian, they will laugh at me! When I say I go to church to worship, they laugh a lot. What's the point of that? Can I believe you? Can I continue to live as a Christian? The people of Iraq and Syria send a clear sign of their strong faith, even if they are persecuted and killed, they stand firm in their faith for their God in whom they believe. Where does this inner strength come from for these people? Where is ours?

An important question - why did Jeremiah still want to stay with God? Because he inwardly always belonged to God. He could not even for a moment, imagine a life without God. And what's about us? It is really worth professing as Christians that we really live for this faith, because He is the one who saved us.

## Does it have to be that way?

Today we are going to experience a bitter truth that is happening in this world. It is about the martyrdom of so many Christians who die for their faith in this world. Every 20 minutes a Christian dies in the world solely because of his belief in Christ the Lord. Is it right that these people are simply killed even though they have not committed a crime? Faith is one's own wish - and faith in Jesus and a real life on earth does not seem to harm anyone. Even so, people are always afraid of Christians and their beliefs, and they are only killed for their beliefs and not for any other fault. No! It shouldn't be like that. Our world has room for all people, regardless of which region or religion they belong to. People of different cultures, skin colors, languages have a right to live on the surface of the earth without disturbing a harmonious life. If such persecution takes place in the name of a certain god, then it makes life in their own homeland miserable for these people and it would also be even worse to suddenly have to flee to another. It doesn't have to be! When I think about it, I almost cry that people are killed for believing in Jesus, that their throats are simply cut because someone is a Christian. It doesn't have to be!

This Sunday we celebrate the Feast of the Exaltation of the Cross. Jesus says in the Gospel: "As Moses lifted up the snake in the desert, so must the Son of man be lifted up" (Jn 3:14).He had to take the cross. He was barbarically killed in Golgotha for the salvation of the mankind. Jesus already foretold His suffering and death also of His resurrection: Mt 16:21-23; 17:22 f.; 20:17-19; Mk 8,31-33; 9,30-32; 10,32-33; Lk 9,22,43; 18:31-33.If we look at the whole history of salvation through Jesus Christ, we understand: Yes, it had to be like that. It must have been that the Son of God was killed for the redemption of the world. But how can we understand that the death of Jesus can be linked to our life situation? It is faith, deeply rooted faith, which enables people to die for Christ. He gives the strength to take our crosses upon us. Those who kill people for their beliefs can only kill their bodies and not their beliefs or souls. Faith is a gift from God. People cannot take this belief away from anyone. Not even if they kill. It is a matter of pride that Christians are so deeply rooted in their Christ and even ready to die for him.

## A Royal Invitation

Is there anyone at all? The church is so empty! Why don't people come in? We invite everyone - the church is open! But the pews are empty. What's happening?

The Lord calls and waits and invites: "Come to me. I have arranged a feast for you, the best food is being offered. What do you want? You have probably never eaten and tasted better food in your entire life: only the best of the best! And there is also a fine drop!" So God invites each of us personally.

We find this beautiful invitation in the book of Isaiah. Everyone who comes is served the best dishes and the best wines. You are all invited! - I like to drink wine from Baden myself, but this reading is about the paradise wine that no winemaker can produce.

In the Gospel, Jesus tells us a parable in Mt 22:1-14. It's about the wedding feast that a king arranged and invited people to attend the banquet. The invited guests did not accept the invitation of the king and apologized for it. One was building a house, another still had to go to the field to work there, the next had no time, and another even got angry and ill treated the messengers who invited him. How would you react if you were invited by the King in person? The finest food and drinks are served, but no one comes. The invited guests just don't show up. The same goes for me as a priest and pastor when the church is empty. When I invite people to the Eucharistic Meal, the choicest thing that can be offered to a person for his spirit and soul, my invitation is ignored and slighted and the Church remains empty. There are several reasons for that. Some find Pastor Lourdu boring. Others consider the services to be old-fashioned. Or they think: who is going to church today? Maybe a great show is on TV or the swimming pool beckons. When I sometimes ask people if they want to come to church, I often get the answer: if I have time.

What's wrong with us? Why don't the invited guests come? This is a question that moves me and I would like to think about it with you. Please help me to see what has to be done so that the invited guests actually come. Actually these people really want to enjoy this great festival. Sometimes there are also people who are physically present but simply do not have an appetite for the festival. They only sit there to fulfill their Sunday worship duty, but they cannot see the fulfillment of their longing in the celebration of the Eucharist.

## Do not see and yet believe

Do I believe in him? Don't I believe in him? This is about the risen Lord coming to meet his disciples. But the disciples did not immediately recognize or believe the risen Lord. But after a while they knew who he was and started to believe him. When Jesus met his friends, the disciple Thomas was not with them. It was a terrible story for Thomas. Why does he doubt when everyone says that Jesus rose from the dead? The incredulous Thomas. It's interesting that he was looking for evidence. He said to them: "Unless I can see the holes that the nails made in his hands and can put my finger into the holes they made, and unless I can put my hand into his side, I refuse to believe" (Jn 20:24-25). Thomas is like a wonderful scientist of our modern age. One who is really looking for evidence. And I think you and I would probably say: Right. Who would just believe such a thing? Just when someone says that he has risen from the dead?

"Eight days later the disciples were in the house again and Thomas was with them. The doors were closed, but Jesus came in and stood among them. 'Peace be with you,' he said. Then he spoke to Thomas, 'Put your finger here; look, here are my hands. Give me your hand; put it into my side. Do not be unbelieving any more but believe." (Jn 20:26-27). Now Thomas began to believe that Christ had risen from the dead. He immediately understood his folly and surrendered himself to the Lord. So Thomas answered and said to Him: "My Lord and my God" (Jn 20:28).

113

At the end of this episode, Jesus gave an important piece of advice not only to His disciples including the doubting Thomas but for everybody of us as well, when He said:"You believe because you can see me. Blessed are those who have not seen and yet believe" (Jn 20:29).

We are all invited to see, and touch Jesus, who shows us his hands, shows us his side, so that the unbelieving Thomas may become a believer. We humans in the present are allowed to do the same. If we want to touch Jesus, if we want to touch God.

Of course, we can find God by seeing and touching. But we must not stop after seeing and touching. We should take the next step - to believe and to follow Jesus.

**Do You Have The Confidence?**

Faith and trust go hand in hand. A embryo in the womb has the confidence that it can live in the womb for nine months. When we go to a doctor, we trust that he will make the right diagnosis and give the right medication. When we fly by plane, we trust the pilot to take us to our desired destinations safe. This means that life always comes with trust. Nothing can be done without trust.  In the family, when the man and women get married they have confidence in each other and they express it orally and in their deeds. Life can go on only if there is mutual confidence and mutual trust. And this applies to life as Christians, as believers. We cannot live without trusting God. Even if sometimes life seems to be difficult, when dark times come to us, we still have to trust Him and have faith in God. The supposed absence of God is always a space to seek and find God. These were also the experiences of the disciples of Jesus. For this there is a beautiful narrative in the Gospel according to Mark.

Mk 4:35-31 - Jesus and His disciples were in the boat. There was a strong wind in the sea. They were very scared that the boat might go down due to the strong waves in the sea. While the disciples were awake, Jesus was asleep. "They woke him up and asked: 'Master, do you not care? We are lost!' And he woke up and rebuked the wind and said to the sea, 'Quiet now! Be calm!' And the wind dropped, and there followed a great calm. Then he said to them, 'Why are you so frightened? Have you still no faith?'"

One surprising problem emerges with this incident. The disciples - most of them were fishermen, specialists in fishing - spent their lives mainly on the water. Certainly they had always experienced the deadliest and most dangerous storms and hurricanes and rough seas. These storms were not new to them, and they were disturbed and frightened. Jesus, on the other hand, was a carpenter by trade, and he should have suddenly felt fear and excitement because of the bad weather and the rattling of the boats and the rough waves. But he went on sleeping until the disciples woke him up. This story shows us that even a person grounded in the faith can be shaken in life under certain dire circumstances.

But if we want to have eternal life, if we want to have abundant life, then it is worth believing in God.

**Faith ShinesThrough**

Easter is over and Christianity is here.Something wonderful is happening in the Book of the Acts of the Apostles. After the Ascension and after the pouring of the Holy Spirit upon them, the apostles of Jesus became famous. They cured people's diseases (Acts 2:3).They became so famous that people even tried to trust after the Apostles to reach their shadow, because even through their shadows some of them were cured. How did they do that? How could these apostles do exactly as Jesus had done? How was it possible for them?

I would say that if God can become man, if faith becomes human, then God can also shine through man. When Paul says, "I no longer live, but Christ lives in me!", - it means that I have become an image of God in which people can see God in me. The Spirit of God works in me so that I can no other than reflecting the Spirit of God in me. In the Gospel we hear that Jesus transmitted and gave the Spirit to the apostles and disciples. This means that all people who are enthusiastic about the Easter faith also live in this world as people filled with the spirit. And it also means that this Spirit works through them too (Jn 20:22). Unfortunately, sometimes you have the feeling that the church is far away. Who comes to church anyway? Even today there are people in whom we can know God. That is not easy. Neither for yourself nor for others. But my own experience shows me that God can be known in all people, small or large, young or old, sick or healthy. In their simplicity. In their mercy and compassion and in their charisma. In their faith they reflect God even in difficult situations, and none of this can happen without the Spirit working in them. Jesus rose again on Easter. That is why He is present everywhere in our midst. But He is also present in all of us. In me, in you. We have our own freedom to shape ourselves. However, if I include Jesus and the Spirit of God within me, people will eventually see or feel that I am filled with the Spirit of God. And then people will come to me, at least to reach my shadow, to be able to experience this joy of being with me. It is possible.

## True Belief

I have a question: Do you know someone who has a strong faith? I experienced something wonderful this week. Three weeks ago, a woman received the news from her doctors were that she was very ill and her days were numbered. She left the clinic after a day to die at home. Her two daughters accompanied her and I was also allowed to visit her several times. It made a big impression on me to see how she prepared herself for death. She enjoyed every day, ate her favorite dishes every day and rejoiced the time she still had. In the end, she died without fear. I think this woman had a strong faith, a belief that death cannot destroy her. For the atheists, I say: just trust life. For Christians, I say: trust in God, life will go on.

Despite all the difficulties, torments, losses, and pains that Job went through, he never lost his faith in God. The message we get from Job is that faith takes us further. And I wholeheartedly wish you all to be protected by your faith in Jesus Christ. Paul's letter to Hebrews 11:1-3 says: "Only faith can guarantee the blessings that we hope for, or prove the existence of realities that are unseen. It is for their faith that our ancestors are acknowledged. It is by faith that we understand that the ages were created by a word from God, so that from the invisible the visible world came to be."

## Just a Touch of Wind

"Vanitas vanitatum et omniavanitas" This saying is ascribed to Solomon and means: Everything is vain, everything is a mere appearance, everything is like a breath of wind and passes by, nothing remains (Ec 12:8). When we hear this, we wonder what that is supposed to mean. Shouldn't we enjoy life? What is the meaning of life when nothing is left? After all, we want to make plans, achieve goals and experience a lot. The vernacular says: the last shirt has no pockets. So it's about becoming aware of what is really important in our life. What date is really important, what planning is really important, what ownership is really important. If I want to live for eternity, what is really important in my earthly life? I think 90% of all things we do or own are not really important. Now many of us are going on vacation. Perhaps you can take a little time to think about what is really important to you. What if you died today, what do you take with you into eternity? Your possessions? Your money? Your diary?

## Faith makes you happy

The other day a woman told me that luckily she was a believer. But she lacked the joy of faith, I could observe people who have faith are happy people. Christians are special. They are the firstborn of God, the elect, the people of God. Baptism confirms that we are children of God, we are to be the light and salt of the earth (Mt 5:13-16). Being a Christian is wonderful, not boring or old-fashioned at all. Faith in God is special, and it's about sharing our faith joyfully, like a light illuminating a dark room. For this we need the community, to go with us and share our faith. I hope for you that you will find people who exude joy in the faith. And if someone is having no joy, ask him or her where the joy of Jesus' love has gone.

Heb 12:18-19, 22-24 says: "What you have come to is nothing known to the senses: not a blazing fire, or gloom or total darkness, or a storm; or trumpet-blast or the sound of a voice speaking which made everyone that heard it beg that no more should be said to them."

"But what you have come to is Mount Zion and the city of the living God, the heavenly Jerusalem where the millions of angels have gathered for the festival, with the whole Church of first-born sons, enrolled as citizens of heaven. You have come to God himself, the supreme Judge, and to the spirits of the upright who have been made perfect; and to Jesus, the mediator of a new covenant, and to purifying blood which pleads more insistently than Abel's."

## Moses' Hands up

Harry Potter in the Old Testament? A story about magic? In the Old Testament we have a story that speaks of the battle of the Israelites against the Amalekites. As long as Moses raised his hands, Israel was successful in the battle. But when he let his hands rest Amalek was successful. However, Moses' hands got tired soon, so they brought him a large stone to sit on. Meanwhile, Aaron and Hur supported his hands, one on one and one on the other, so that his hands would stay stealy until sunset.

Today we often ask: Why do we need God? He does not ask us whether the trees should grow, whether the sun should shine, God works in this world without ifs or buts. Nevertheless, we humans must do our part to gain eternal life. And for this we have role models, like the saints and mediators between us and God, who support us and make our way easier. - A woman recently came to confession with me with heavy burdens in her soul. After that, she cried with relief and said she felt so free afterwards. Indeed, God forgives us all of our sins and transgressions, but the priest pronounces absolution as the mediator between God and man. Yet everyone can help others to find God, feel Him, and gain salvation. Our society needs God's power and actions. You too can be such a mediator when you talk about God with your children, grandchildren or friends.

Ex17:13-16: "And Joshua defeated Amalek, putting their people to the sword. Yahweh then said to Moses, 'Write this

119

down in a book to commemorate it, and repeat it over to Joshua, for I shall blot out all memory of Amalek under heaven.' Moses then built an altar and named it Yahweh-Nissi meaning, 'Lay hold of Yahweh's banner! Yahweh will be at war with Amalek generation after generation".

## Belief and Superstition. Friday the 13th

Friday the 13th, you left that day behind you. How was that? Did you have bad experiences of accidents? Did you fight or have to live without food or water? Friday the 13th. A bad day. We dreaded this day long in advance. Some executives, including some employees, who cling to such superstitions in their private lives, bring these negative expectations with them into the office. You avoid organicing the meeting on Friday the 13th. None of the letters would be signed by the executive on the 13th, and the subordinates would be strictly instructed not to mention the date as the 13th in the letter. Superstition is the opposite of belief. Many think that superstition is better than belief. What is belief It is the confidence that someone else will take care of me who says: I am with you, don't worry, no matter where you are and who you are. And that someone is the one who created you, me and the universe; He is the one who guides, guides and protects us. No matter what date you write or start doing things, nothing adverse can happen to you.

In the Gospel of Matthew there is a parable in which a king wanted to invite all his friends, but no one came. Then he went out into the street and invited everyone he met to a party in the palace. So is God. He invites all peoples to a great festival. He says: You don't need to shed tears, you don't have to be afraid anymore, I am with you. Everyone is important to God. We never have to be lost.

Of course I have free will to decide. But superstition can break me if I identify myself with it, consider myself important, think that it's all about me. Faith says it's not about me, it's about someone who takes care of me, who protects me.

There is also a lot of superstition in my own culture. But no superstition can ever win against belief or science. We could try to get rid of whatever paralyzes us and thereby become free for the greater glory of God.

## Too late

In our life there is often a "too late" syndrome. The train had left. I should have arrived in time, but now I'm too late. I wanted to visit a friend, but I was late. I wanted to do certain things, but it was too late for that. I wanted to be reconciled, to ask for forgiveness, but this man may already have died. So we often experience a "too late" syndrome in our life.

And we suffer because our soul somehow had this longing for it. It is also about faith, the longing to believe in Go and to be with him in order to experience God. That is the longing and the task of every human being. And when? Now and here!

Although God is always and everywhere, I can only experience him here and now. At this moment. If I postpone it may be too late for me. If I want to believe, I believe now. If I want to pray, I have to pray now. I only have this moment to make a decision and act. We shouldn't wait too long, especially not for our belief in God.

## The 68-man Program

Let us especially remember those who saw 1968. Upheavals, rebellions, criticism. Even today it seems to me that many people who were born in the 1960s and are still alive today are undeveloped. They live in the past with all its bitter misery. People who only complain, who see nothing good and think that nothing can be done right. They think everything is bad. It's like a cardiac arrhythmia in our society. Why do you always have to complain about everything, whether in your club, at the party, at work, in your relationship? You find something bad everywhere. These people did not understand that life is positive. Many good changes, enormous developments have taken place in all areas and areas of life, but they do not accept them. They are just people with memories of times gone by. Such people lack one thing above all else. It's belief in God. Faith in Jesus. If they could only believe in Jesus, who through his words and deeds turned away old superstitions and rituals, they would understand new things. New insights are very possible.

## Become a child of Christ by Faith

I can send you a happy message. This weekend, three adults are preparing for their baptism. The starting point of your trip is St. Ilgen. And on this weekend a big festival will be celebrated in the Evangelical Church in St. Ilgen, where it celebrates its 100th anniversary. What does this mean? Evangelical theology is based on people's beliefs. And that is the theme this weekend when Paul writes to the Galatians. Through faith we become sons and daughters of Jesus Christ (Gal 2:16). What role does faith play when people like these three adults are baptized today? It's about a relationship. Paul writes very nicely: At baptism they are given a robe. And that garment is Jesus Christ. When someone wears this garment, there is no longer any difference between people. No slaves, no free people, no Jews, no Greeks or in our sense no Russians, no Germans, no Indians etc. The other day someone told me that a reporter had gone to a kindergarten and interviewed a child there. He asked her: Well, how was kindergarten? The child said: Good. There are a lot of refugees here. The reporter asked: Are they foreigners? The child replied: No, only children. That is exactly the point. When we are together in the name of God, by our faith we are all children of the same God. And although there are many refugee children in our country, the children do not see them as foreigners, but simply as children. This gives foreign children the dignity of simply being children. And so it should be with us as Christians too. Our faith should move us to see everyone as children of God, regardless of differences such as region, religion, nation, language, etc. All Christians are equal if they believe in Jesus Christ as their goal and their way. And these three adults will receive this wonderful dignity in a few weeks when they are baptized in St. Ilgen.

## Do the Work of God

Today we're just sticking to the subject of bread. Our God also takes care of physical needs. The Gospel says that Jesus fed 5,000 hungry people with five loaves of bread and two fish. The disciples of Jesus have one concern: They want to accomplish the work of God.

They wanted to act just like Jesus. They have seen many miracles from Jesus. They wanted to live like him. So they asked him, "How can we do the work of God?" Jesus said to them, "You cannot do that. But there is one thing you can do. You can believe in the one God who sent him." That was the answer of Jesus. To be honest, bread is extremely important to us. We have done everything for a breaf of bread. Bread is the most important thing in life. But bread has gotten cheap these days. Then we ask: What is important to me? Can I even do the works of God? If I have everything in my life, if the food I have is filling me up, what else could I use? Maybe I can give the answer that Jesus gave: "Believe in Jesus". We just don't have that. We humans have different needs. We can satisfy our hunger with bread, but can we fill our souls with it? Our society needs faith. Faith helps us move forward. If we believe in Jesus Christ that he is the bread of life, that he is the nourishment for people and that he gives himself to us, then our souls will be strong and healthy. We possibly can buy a pound of bread for € 1.40. But the question is, do I believe in Jesus Christ? Here we have a long Christian tradition of faith in which people still find Jesus and are strengthened through him in which He is still the bread of life. For you and for me?.

## Suffering belongs to Man

Suffering belongs to everyone. Someone once said that there are only two groups of people who do not suffer: those who are not born yet and those who have already died. All people experience sufferings at some point in their lives, disappointments and struggles. Nobody is spared from this. So how can we move forward in our life?

In the Bible we have an impeccable and sincere personality named Job. He was a great man. He had everything, family, wealth, possessions. He feared God and avoided evil (Jb 1:1-4). Satan became restless when he saw Job's faith in and love for God. So he said to God that just because Job had everything in life, everything was well organized, and he was satisfied, he would praise God, but if he were to withhold all these comforts, he would surely blaspheme God. God allowed Satan to test Job on the condition that he should not touch him. (Jb 1:6-12). In Satan's first trial, Job lost his wealth, his children.

Despite these dangers, he did not lose his faith (Jb 1:22). In the second text, he developed a terrible ulcer all over his body.

Even then his answer was: "'If we take happiness from God's hand, must we not take sorrow too?' And in all this misfortune Job uttered no sinful word" (Jb 2:10). But in the midst of all our sufferings, God is one who weeps for us and would never forget or leave us. We don't have to go through all of this alone. Since He is with us, we endure everything. We can even suffer again and again as a result. God takes care of us not to get lost. He is with us. It is precisely in suffering that we can reverse our faith and trust it. We can become firmly rooted in our faith and say from the bottom of our hearts that God is with us always and at all times, in pain and danger.

# 9. FEAR

*Moses said to the people, "Do not be afraid! Stand firm, and you will see what Yahweh will do to rescue you today"*
*(Ex 14:13).*

## Do not be afraid

It is wonderful that we can continue to be connected through these video sermons. Even if you have to be at home due to this pandemic and lockdowns, you can still hear and share the words of the Holy spirit. This time is difficult, it is getting tighter and the lockdown is inevitable. My ministry as a priest is to encourage all of you during this time of panic. Even if we cannot be together physically, we can be connected through the media - a million thanks to God for giving people the wisdom to invent such a wonderful device. This is how we stay in contact with each other. When we are alone, young, old, sick, or healthy, no matter what condition we live in, it is natural that we should become anxious about this new, emerging situation. Our nature is community life. I had an interesting brochure about the work of professional ministry, of which my professional colleague is the leader.

The title of today' s sermon is: Don't be afraid. This is a period of trial for all of us. The question before us is how to deal with fear. Our God is the God who has a personal relationship with every human being. He's not far away, he comes towards us and says: Don't be afraid. An overview of the word Fear Not, or words with related meanings appear 365 times in the Bible. That is, God reassures us every day and whispers in our ears incessantly whole year. There is an excellent narrative in the New Testament, in the Gospel of

Matthew, in which Peter was seized by fear and Jesus breaks this unwanted fear (Mt 1:22-32).

We see in the narrative that Peter wanted to walk on water in rough seas like Jesus did, and Peter wanted to reach Jesus. He was on a boat in the middle of the lake. Jesus agreed and wanted Peter to come to him on the water. But Peter had no confidence, after a few steps he went down, he was about to sink and screamed in fear. Then Jesus came to him and took him in his hand to save him and asked: "Why are you afraid, I am with you!" Then they both boarded the boat safely. And: "Do not be afraid", because He is always with us.

Especially nowadays I can say: the more we let our trust in God grow, the faster our fear disappears. That is the wonderful thing. When we trust God, he is always by our side. We are mortals; we are busy with viruses and diseases right now. But we don't have to be at the mercy of fear. Therefore, I invite you to overcome your fear when you hear the words of Jesus and believe: "I am with you always; yes, to the end of time"(Mt 28:20). That is Jesus' promise to us. With this great encouragement, we can move on no matter what lies ahead.

## Fear of God knows no fear

Many people ask me whether we really need the fear of God. Do we have to fear God? But that is not the exact meaning of the word. Rather, it means: Reverence for God, the right attitude towards God and his will. It should induce people not to break God's commandments. A good example of a godly man is Job. We can find some more instances, where the reverence for God as fear is portrayed in the Bible: 1) The other criminal, who was hanging on the cross near Jesus spoke up and rebuked him. 'Have you no fear of God at all?'

(Lk 23,40); 2) Joseph's answer to the wife of Potiphar: "How could I do anything so wicked, and sin against God?" (Gen 39:9). In his first letter Peter writes: "If you are a stranger you should fear God. Here the word stranger does not mean to separate people based on their nationality or religion or race, language, but here it refers to those who have forsaken God and go astray, who refuse to love and believe in God. So we should be a bit afraid of God here in this world, but in the sense that we align ourselves to trust God so that He can be in our lives. Because with it we align our thoughts and our way of life to God. It's not that extraordinary. There is also often awe of important people who have great influence or accomplish great deeds or had revolutionary thoughts that raised humanity to a higher level, like Mother Theresa, Nelson Mandela, Mahatma Gandhi - these people have an influence in society and all over the world. So fear of God means living so that I can come face to face with God. It pays to be afraid of God, because that will make a difference in me today, namely that I can live as God is: merciful, loving, understanding. This is very different from fear."The fear of Yahweh is the beginning of knowledge" (Prov 1:7).

## Overcome Fear

In our midst, many people live with the fear in politics and business or in society that they will lose their position at any time. There are also people who are afraid of others in office, especially their bosses and senior executives. You are afraid of making mistakes. They are afraid of being paralyzed or blocked - internally. "People are terrible sometimes!" said someone. There are people who enjoy seeing the sufferings and tears of others. No animal and no other living being feels the longing to see another living being suffer and cry. Only the peak of creation, man, has this sadistic desire - to enjoy the sadness of others. In the gospel we have a story in contracts to this evil desire of men.

There is a wonderful story in the Gospel of Mark about a paralyzed man from Capernaum who was bedridden. Jesus was in a house. The house was full of people who came to see Jesus, and Jesus started preaching to them. Four men, who wanted Jesus to heal the paralyzed man and believed that only Jesus could heal him, carried the man on the stretcher on which he was lying. Since they were unable to enter through the door because of the crowd, they broke the roof of the house and helped him by taking him to the roof of the house. They opened the roof, lowered the stretcher, and held it in front of Jesus. When Jesus saw their faith, he said to the sick person: "Child, your sins are forgiven". This was viewed critically by the scribes and they thought that Jesus was blasphemous.

He knew their thoughts and gave a straight answer. Then he said to the paralyzed man, "Rise, get your mat and go home". With that, the patient was cured. The healing was holistic. Not only was he physically healed, but his soul was cleansed of all his sins (cf. Mk 2:1-12). In the miracle there was no direct request from the paralyzed person for his healing through Jesus. He did not know what was happening to him until he was healed and stood up at the command of Jesus. The four good-hearted men prayed for the helpless man. To heal the man, they did not hesitate or were afraid of damaging some-one else's home. Even when they saw the crowd in the house, they did not turn back. They really wanted the man to be healed by Jesus. Their heartfelt desire gave them the courage to act. Her determination and firm belief in Jesus gave new life to a sick person who had lost hope of healing. We also do not need to be afraid or hesitate to do good to others. We should try by all means to help those who suffer in a simple way and to enable them to lead a decent life in society. There are many people who live in a paralyzed state without anyone speaking for them. They are voiceless people, they are the marginalized and deprived of their right to a decent life in society. So let us step forward to shake off our fears and hesitations and become the voice of the voiceless. This is what God wants from all of us. We humans are not all bad. We don't just think badly of others. We think well of them too. That is why this world lives. A great philosopher poet of my native Tamil, Thiruvalluvar, said: "The world lives on goodness." Because you and I are good people, this world lives on. Perhaps, like these four men, we can check our daily lives to see if anyone around us needs our help. Maybe I can show another Jesus, show God, so God can do what is best for this man.

## The end and the Fear

The church year is slowly coming to an end, we are ap proaching Advent and the end of the church year. There are many texts in the Bible that are introduced on this subject.

I accompanied a seriously ill person whose days were numbered. He was in bed for months. He had partial memory loss. Sometimes he wasn't clear in his words and actions, but sometimes he had clear moments. When I asked "How are you?" he always said "good" even though he knew he would not live long on earth. But he was afraid of approaching death - the end of his life. There are many people who do not die from disease, drugs, or any other circumstance. But purely out of fear of death. When I also think about my death, I am no exception, sometimes fear seizes me. And I ask myself: How do I deal with my life, how do I live, what will be my end?

Do I have to be afraid? No. The Church Year shows me that there will be a flourishing future. The season of autumn gives us hope that everything will grow again, that new things will come. It is not the end of my joy, but it is the beginning of a new life. We often have problems with fear of death; we are afraid of other people, afraid of God. We do not have to fear him in the sense that our God is a cruel God and would punish and judge according to our deeds. But this sentence "The root of wisdom is fear of Yahweh; those who attain it are wise" (Ps 111,10) has another meaning. Here it means the awe and respect that we must show God. When we start to worship God, it means that we are on the way to gaining wisdom. This type of fear of God is always welcome, and it is exactly what we should all have. When we're scared, we don't unfold, we hide and make ourselves small. When we fear God, we give room to evil within us. Fear is a condition we humans shouldn't have. We can live without fear if we believe in God.

That's in everyday life, with colleagues, friends, relationships, too. We can always strengthen our trust, just don't worry. God is the one who wants us to live without fear because He loves us. Even if we sometimes get angry and weak, it would not lead to a separation from God because of our faith and our love for him. As soon as we become aware of the shortcomings, we can immediately return to Him. He would never shut the door on us. HE would never turn his face away from us. He is full of mercy (Lk 6:36) and ready to forgive us for all the sins we commit and he is happy to hug us again as his own beloved sons / daughters.

# 10. GIFTS OF GOD

*"You have in you a spiritual gift which was given to you when the prophets spoke and the body of elders laid their hands on you; do not neglect it" (1 Tm 4:14).*

## Satisfaction - a Gift from God

It is very rare for people to be satisfied. Whatever they own, whatever higher position they hold, they never seem to be satisfied with what they have. They compare themselves to others; they want to go up higher and higher. They forget to count the abundant blessings that are showered on them without they asking for them. God has sent everyone to this earth with different talents, blessings, and graces. Nobody is sent empty by Him. So it is up to the respective human person to recognize the treasures hidden in them, dig them up and put them in the limelight, and use them for the best benefit for themselves and for the benefit of all of humanity. It is time to learn to be happier and to be able to say that there is enough of everything. I have everything I need. If we don't achieve this satisfaction in life, we will waste our lives making a list of what we lack, what we don't have, and what other people have. With these constellations, we lose the true joy that would have come from all of the gifts and blessings God has already given us. This type of dissatisfaction will lead most of us to seek further ways and means to get what we believe we lack, to achieve by all possible means, perhaps even at the expense of others' lives. This would plunge our lives into misery, be problematic, and result in the loss of our dignity and respect. Our peace of mind would be lost, our entire body, mind and soul would be disturbed. This can be explained in the following short story.

A man lived in poverty. He struggled to make ends meet. But he wanted to own lots of gold coins and keep counting in his life. He always asked God for it during his prayer. He used to pray to God to say, "God, give me one hundred gold coins and I will count them again and again and be happy." God, who one day answered his prayers, decided to grant his wish, so one night he sent an angel with a beautiful basket, and asked him to put it at the poor man's doorstep. The angel did the job. When the man came out of the house the next morning, he saw a beautiful basket that he had never seen before. He looked left and right to see if anyone was watching. When he realized that there was no one watching him, he hurried into the house, closed the door, sat down in his room and opened the basket, took off the lid and discovered lots of glittering gold coins.

Overwhelmed with joy, he began to count them. He was glad that God had finally answered his prayers. He counted 99 coins. He had doubts. He thought that God surely would not have made any mistakes. He would have sent 100 coins. To be sure, he counted again. The total remained 99. He counted again, twice, three times. The result was the same 99 coins. He began to doubt his neighbour, who had known what he prayed for and had laughed at him. Then he began to doubt his wife and son, thinking that one of them had stolen "the missing gold coin". Through guesswork and false suspicions, he now racked his brain over the "non- existent coin". So he was not satisfied with the 99 coins that were already available. His mind became corrupt and full of doubt, but at the same time he was unwilling to ask openly for fear of losing everything he had; if he asked his wife and son, they would find out about those gold coins that he had now owned, and they could buy various things that they could desperately need for their simple life. However, he believed that God had sent him 100 coins and that one of them was stolen by someone. So he just wondered where and with whom the missing coin was and no longer even counted the 99 coins that were originally his heart's desire. He failed to count the blessings in the form of 99 coins and was concerned about the "not yet born" coin.

This story teaches us to be content with all that we are and have and to enjoy life with a heart full of gratitude to God for His tremendous blessings and graces. If we do not live with such a sense of fulness, we will try to make up the missing things with crooked deals and thereby pile up sins and wicked vices. Therefore, John the Baptist warned and advised the people, saying: "There were tax collectors too, who came for baptism, and these said to him "Master what must we do? He said to them "Exact no more than the appointed rate". Some soldiers asked him in their turn "What about us? What must we do?" He said to them: "No intimidation! No extortion! Be content with your pay!" (Lk 3:12-14).

## More beautiful, richer, better, more graceful

Being nicer, richer, better. Who does not want that? A flower blooms, a person grows, and people always long for perfection. Perfection is desirable. But what do we do when we are not who we want to be? There are some people who say, "I'm not pretty. I'm not rich. I'm not that good." A flower is pretty and beautiful because it doesn't ask itself that question. She knows when the sun is too strong that her head is drooping. Still, I think the flower is pretty because it knows that it is what it is. Paul speaks in the letter to the Corinthians: "God's folly is wiser than human wisdom, and God's weakness is stronger than human strength" (1 Cor 1:25). In my weakness I find new strength. There I learn the Spirit of God. Then I experience the grace of God. That means that I respect my weaknesses, my blockages and my mistakes, and that makes me better. Life as a whole is a test for all who strive for the better, the more beautiful. In the end, it is not what I have achieved, whether I have become more beautiful, whether I have become better, whether I have become richer, but the joy with which I experienced my existence." My grace is enough for you: for power is at full stretch in weakness" (2 Cor 12:9). God said. Yes, his grace is enough for us. And that's why I want to tell you: stay the way you are, and that's wonderful. If you are asked to be a rose, stay a rose and spread your scent. That is the grace that is bestowed on you. If you are a rose, don't imitate a lily and stick with it. If you are trying to imitate a lily and would rather become a lily, you will lose both the rose and the lily. So be happy with what you have.

## Be full of Joy

Joy - I've had some experiences related to joy lately. I want to meditate with you a little bit about them. A child was waiting for the father. After a while the doorbell rang -. The child ran in and called, "Papa!" - an expression of joy. At home the woman was doing something funny. The man watched and then laughed: "Ha ha!" - there was joy there too. The other day a nurse told me that her internship had been extended. Then I spoke to her superiors. When I got the answer that she didn't have to do the internship for six months, but that three months would be sufficient, she was really happy. And one more experience: a lady suspected she had breast cancer. We discussed a lot when she told me she had this disease. Then we had to wait for the results of the investigation. The time came. I was worried. Then she called me and said, "No breast cancer!" It was a real joy to feel. We humans need joy because we constantly experience different stressful situations. We have to suffer again and again. So we always need good news. This is what Jesus expects from us because he is the root of happiness in our lives. He wants us to enjoy our source. We hear a wonderful example in the Gospel of Matthew, in which we see how John the Baptist slowly doubts whether Jesus is the right Messiah or whether he should perhaps wait for someone else (Mt 11:2-11).Then Jesus said, "Go back and tell John what you hear and see; the blind see again, and the lame walk, those suffering from virulent skin-diseases are cleansed, and the deaf hear, the dead are raised to life and the good news is proclaimed to the poor" (cf. Mt 11:4 f.). This is good news that the blind can see again, the lame can walk again, that the lepers are healed and can live normal life in society. This is good news from Christianity. If the sun is shining on me right now, then it is perfectly fitting that I reflect on this joyful news with you today. We don't need to think at all, we just need to enjoy the creation around us, the good news we hear and see, good experiences in our own lives. So be happy about all things - big or small.

## What's Work

The world celebrates Labor Day on May 1st. In this reflection we want to look together at what "work" is. We have many religions in our world, many cultures, many languages, but one thing that unites and brings all people together is work. People work independently of cultures, languages, religions, nations. We work every day. In different areas. Some people work in the office, some outside, some work with their heads, some with their hands. And so there are different types of work. It is interesting that not only humans work, but also animals and birds also do. It goes without saying that all living things work. There are wonderful passages in the Bible where people have to work. And sometimes there are also examples of the behavior of the ants which are busy gathering food for the winter

(Pr 6:6-8, 30:24-28). Paul says you should work, because without work there is no bread. So work is not only a gift from God, but also a task that we have to do. We can't just put our hands on our laps and sit around at home. Sometimes when I think about it, one week adds up to sixty hours of work. But I am glad that I am needed, I can work. And why are we doing our job? I would say: God is the best worker. According to the Bible, he created the world in six days. That is, if we are in the image of God, we too are called to be. We cannot refuse to work. We have to work until we die. And so the work becomes holy and divine. If God is the Creator, a worker, then we should also become workers in order to create, to produce. At the same time, we should tear down what is out of date and build something new. All of this is part of the job. And today, when we take this video recording on May 1st, it is also the Catholic holiday for Saint Joseph. He is venerated as a worker, as the patron saint of workers. Yes, Saint Joseph was a laborer, a carpenter. He worked and nourished the incarnate God Jesus and the mother of God, Mary from his income. And if we take Saint Joseph as an example today, one thought tells me: I should not only make my work dependent on the reward or what I get for it, but I should do my work with all my heart. If we only worked for money - of course we have to be paid - the work would not be fulfilling. We should work with all of our mind and heart, energy and time. That would be a great satisfaction for everyone.

## Save Time or waste Time

Do you have time? No, I don't have that much time. We hear these words often.Do we have time - or not. And especially at a time when people live much longer, 70, 80, 90 or 100 or even up to 110 years yet we don't have time. In the gospel we see Jesus speaking about time. His disciples were constantly busy with work and did not even have time to eat or rest. Therefore he asks them to go to a lonely place to rest (Mk 3:21). Time is a gift, something that I can have. I can't save time. But I can plan the time well. How can I plan my everyday life? I can plan in the sense that I have some of this time myself. It is clear that our time is determined by strangers. When I go to work, I need a lot of time. But even during the day there is always time that I can use for myself. I decide how much time I plan for myself, for example, for a good night's sleep, for a delicious meal, for a wonderful drink or for a good conversation with a friend and my spouse, so that I can use my time to do it for me and those around me are doing well. And especially I take time for my prayers. So that I meet my Creator, who strengthens me so that I can make my everyday life easier and more qualitative. Time is a precious gift from God and we should always use it for the best of ourselves and others. But I can waste my time too! By just doing nothing, or by wasting my time doing strange things that are not useful to me, anyone else, or God. We have to be careful with it. Don't waste it, use it well - for yourself, for your God and for your environment.

## 18 years: Ordained Priest in the Parish Garden in Leimen

Today I am sending you a personal message: On May 18, 2003, I was welcomed by the then Auxiliary Bishop of the Archdiocese of Freiburg, Rev. Dr. Paul Wehrle, ordained a priest in Freiburg Minster. To be a priest means to be a friend of Jesus, to live in and with him, to proclaim the Word of God, to bless people, to forgive sins. It's not just a job, it's a calling and a wonderful experience. I have been on the road with this assignment for 18 years.

First I was in Karlsruhe, where I did my internship in St. Peter and Paul. I did a lot with young people, acted in theater, and started various activities. There I celebrated my "Primiz", my first service that I held alone. Then I was in India in my hometown, where I also celebrated that day with 4000 people in a church service, and then returned to Freiburg, where I belong to this day. The Bishop of Freiburg is, so to speak, my spiritual father, "my boss". Later I went to Markdorf, where I had my first job as a pastor. It was a wonderful and intense time and I still have contact with many people there. I worked a lot with young people, founded the baptismal group and in three years learned a lot from the congregation and the pastor at the time. Then I moved to Wiesloch, where I was a chaplain for two years. My particular concern was pastoral care for young people, and I also regularly visited the prisoners in the Wiesloch juvenile detention center. In the second year I did my parish exam there. These two years have fulfilled and strengthened me. In 2008, I finally handed in my Indian passport and received German citizenship. It was a movements decision for me. Then I should go to Leimen. I promised immediately because obedience is important and because I vowed to be obedient when I was ordained a priest. At first I was responsible as a pastor for Leimen-Nußloch- Gauangelloch and initially only had one chaplain by my side. From 2008, I was alone. I had to learn a lot, I had no training as a manager or a leader and I was often "on my nose". But I had people by my side which helped me and were by my side.

In 2011, I was asked to take over the second pastoral care unit in Sandhausen and St. Ilgen, because today there is simply a lack of priests. It was not easy, but I approached this task with great courage, in the service of Christ, because people need a priest. Since then I have been heading the large pastoral care unit Leimen - Nussloch-Sandhausen for seven years, with all ups and downs. But in the meantime I've arrived here, I have many trusted people by my side, who are on the road with me, who have gone through a lot with me, who have always encouraged me and discovered the kingdom of God with me.

After eighteen years in priesthood, I am grateful for this calling. I see my priesthood as a gift from God. It is wonderful and I am delighted to be able to live in God's grace and blessings. And I'm looking forward to many more years of video messages and a fruitful life in and with this community.

## Today and now is important

Too many people are stuck in the past. They just think about what happened earlier, what the negative effects they had been, what wrong decisions they had made. Should I have studied something else? If I had taken another job, would I be better off today? If I hadn't done so much evil, would I have suffered less? Or we're just looking what could happen: If I go to the doctor tomorrow, what will he tell me? When I get a message should I call my boss? Do I think about the worst possiblity? Will I get the job I'm applying for? I'm already worried about what hasn't happened yet. But life takes place in the here and now. If we speak to someone now because something is important to us, if we call someone now to ask how they are doing, it is worth it.

If we could go shopping now, we could cook dinner. Exactly now. I wonder if this is not a sign of the "plagues of mankind": dwelling on the mistakes, failures and misfortunes of the past or worrying too much about what will happen in the future. This attitude of people leads to the fact that they do not see the happy and worthy moments of today and cannot fully live them and enjoy them. That is why Jesus also taught us (Mt 6:34): "So do not worry about tomorrow: tomorrow will take care of itself. Each day has enough trouble of its own". Feel the love now and today that is shown to you by your fellow human beings, and the love comes from God.

## Subjugate the Earth?

When the weather is nice, many are out and about during the holiday season to enjoy nature, experience the beauty of creation, find peace and relaxation and recharge their batteries. The earth was given to us as a precious gift, and in a sense we are partners in the rulership of God because we were created in His image and likeness. That is why we participate in the work of God. We act on behalf of God. And that's exactly why we have an immense responsibility for this world. More than 150 plant and animal species die out every day; 150 tons of food are thrown away every year; the rainforests are being cut down for profit, although we know the fatal effects on the climate; man pollutes the earth, air and water with his waste products; the seas are drowning in plastic. Are we like God when we do this? Pope Francis expressly says that we have no right to do so! When this earth suffers, God suffers. We have the right to live here, but we have no right to abuse that right. When some exploit the earth just for their own interests, they are acting against God himself. Everything is interdependent, everything works together. We should be grateful for creation that nourishes us and gives us everything we need for life and makes us happy. There are many atheists who deny God or materialists who only accept the visible world. But if they only allow matter to come into their own, they have to respect this matter, this earth, guard it and not watch everything collapse. We have such environmental awareness here in Germany, there are so many laws on climate protection here. But do we also think of the countries from which the raw materials come, in which we produce for us? Everyone knows the conditions of the workers and the environment there. Even so, little is being done to change that, and we are destroying these countries and the people there.

I wholeheartedly wish you a lot of joy in this wonderful creation, enjoy your vacation. But never forget that each individual has a great responsibility for the earth, precisely because we are in the image of God!

## Peace - the Gift of God

On this feast of Pentecost we hear that Jesus always said: "Peace be with you!", when He came to men. Each language has a word for peace - pax (Latin), peace (English), Shalom (Hebrew), Pace (Italian) etc. But what does peace mean? Is it just the absence of strife or war? No, peace is a heartfelt attitude that begins with everyone. Someone once said, "I am my greatest enemy." What it means is that I must first be at peace with myself, forgive myself, comfort myself - and then my peace comes to others. In my relationships, in friendships, at work, in the community, in my country, around the world. Peace is like a hug for myself, for people, for creation. Peace be with you! This is a wonderful gift from the Risen One. God is invisible, but when he dwells in my heart, he alone can give me peace, peace and harmony. But I have to start working on it myself. Let us ask ourselves: Am I peaceful with myself, with other people and their different worldviews, with nature, am I peaceful with God?

# 11. GOOD NEWS

*"But you must always behave in a way that is worthy of the gospel of Christ" (Phil 1:27).*

## The Gospel, the Good News

Gospel - This word comes from the Greek and means "The good news". The gospel brings the good news so that we can hear and read about Jesus Christ. The gospel has great power. After Jesus' death and resurrection, the disciples went around the world and the gospel inspired people in different places that many became Christians. It first spread to Jerusalem, Rome, Constantinople (Today: Istanbul, Turkey), Antioquia (in Turkey) and Alexandria (Today: Egypt), later to Armenia, the first country to become a Christian country, then the whole of Europe after the third century, Asia, Africa and in the 15th-16th centuries. America knew Christ in the 19th century. Today Christianity is the big religion in the world.

The good news! Who wouldn't want to hear good news in our world where we are surrounded by so many terrible things? And what's the good news?

You are not alone. You are not just a number, but important in the eyes of God, a child of God. Wonderful that a mortal can say that he is worth something. In his life and actions, Jesus Christ showed again and again how every single person can find his or her worth. Namely in the great love that comes from the Creator, from the Father. In this love man should shape his life fraternally so that the whole world becomes one community.

And that's why missionaries went all over the world,

145

especially the Benedictines and Divine Word Missionaries from. They traveled all over the world preaching the gospel to adults, children, young and old, healthy and sick, happy and grieving. Because in the words of Jesus Christ there is something wonderful for everyone: the gospel.

## The Good News

At the moment the weather is gray. Today I heard on the radio that it might not get any lighter after all, it will stay dark. As I think about it, I remember many examples from Job's life found in the Book of Job in the Old Testament. I visited someone at home yesterday. This person said to me: "Pastor, we have to be careful and prepared now, because this year the world could end!" It's a mood that isn't necessarily very happy. It's a dark mood. The Mayan calendar moved many people. Many have created their own interpretations, and many others have used them to scare people. There are even people who built houses in which supposedly nothing could happen to them. Such people who believe in the day of doom are now waiting for the "day" when the world will end and they alone will be saved. So there are very interesting people in this world. Is the world going to end?

The Gospel also says something similar. In Mark's Gospel 1:15, Jesus says: "The time is fulfilled, and the kingdom of God is close at hand. Repent, and believe the gospel".

So He announces the fulfillment of the time and that people should prepare for it. What for? "For the kingdom of God is at hand:" Repent and believe in the gospel! For Jesus, the time has come for everyone to believe in the gospel. If he wants to have his existence fulfilled, it is important that man believes in the gospel. What is the "gospel"? The "Gospel" for the evangelist Mark is nothing else than Jesus Christ himself - and this also applies to the Gospels of Matthew, Luke and John. Jesus Christ, the Son of God, is himself the "Gospel". The word "Gospel" comes from the Greek and means "good news". The good news for every person "in this world there is nothing but Jesus Christ." Believe in the Gospel! That means: Believe in Jesus Christ himself! For every person, if he wants to have a fulfilled existence, there is ultimately only one thing: to believe in Jesus Christ. Jesus Christ, the Savior of the world, the Son of God who is still alive today, in the 21st century. But before we believe in Jesus Christ, we need to take one more s tep - repentance. We should really ask ourselves what visions and desires we have, whether we can relate all of this to Jesus.

I wish you a good search in yourself, and also the joy of finding everything in Jesus Christ! The time is fulfilled. Repent and Believe in the Gospel!

## The new Teaching

Today let us reflect on Mk 1:24-27: In Capernaum, Jesus went to the synagogue on the Sabbath and taught. And the people were very troubled by his teaching; for he taught them as one of divine authority, not as the scribes. In their synagogue was a man possessed by an unclean spirit. He started screaming: "What do you want with us, Jesus of Nazareth? Have you come to destroy us? I know who you are: the Holy One of God.' But Jesus rebuked it saying, 'Be quiet! Come out of him!' And the unclean spirit threw the man into convulsions and with a loud cry went out of him. The people were so astonished that they started asking one another what it all meant, saying, 'Here is a teaching that is new, and with authority behind it: he gives orders even to unclean spirits and they obey him."

What does this mean? Here, a whole new doctrine is proclaimed with authority. Even the unclean spirits obey his

147

command. And his reputation quickly spreads throughout the Galilee area.

A very moving story. Did you also feel that it moved you? In any case, the people in Capernaum were very affected at the time. They felt moved by this event.

People were confused. For the first time in their lives they had seen a man exuding divine authority and preaching a new doctrine. The Gospel of Mark says: This new teaching was different from that of the scribes. What does that mean? The new teaching of Jesus Christ is more than the law. The new teaching of Jesus Christ is very simple and new and is different from the people who moved from their homes to abandoned places like the Qumran and appeared before people to speak about strict laws. The new teaching of Jesus Christ touched people's everyday lives. Wherever there are people, there is Jesus. The new teaching of Jesus Christ moved everyone in everyday life. He had authority over evil spirits and this was encouraging news to people. The authority and the new teaching of Jesus Christ are still relevant today after 2000 years. I invite each of you to feel this new teaching of Jesus Christ, which is just as relevant for the individual as it is for the Church and society and for every country. Perhaps it is important for us Christians to reflect on whether or not we are affected by this new teaching about Jesus Christ today. The church, too, should consider again and again whether to do so or to keep to the old law like the scribes. Jesus wants to free us all from all possible clutches. Jesus wants to free us from everything that binds us, from everything that humbles us. We can wait eagerly for Jesus: when we are bound, when we are depressed, when we can no longer get up, when we cannot fully live our lives. Believe in Jesus and that belief will help you and me and all of us.

In the days to come, let's try to have a little experience of whether or not the authoritative message of Jesus of Nazareth touched you, like as it did to the people of Capernaum 2000 years ago.

# 12. GRATITUDE

*"To you, God of my fathers, I give thanks and praise for having given me wisdom and strength" (Dan 2:23).*

## Thanksgiving

I am looking forward to reflecting on the subject of "Thanksgiving" with you today. Thanksgiving - it's nice in the parish garden. We had a lot of sun this summer and it's raining right now. We have fresh air and we have life here on earth. When we live in this beautiful world, we feel that we should be grateful for what we get from nature, for the sunlight, the rain, the fruits, vegetables and flowers, all so fresh and so beautiful. I haven't paid anything for the rain, I haven't paid anything for the fresh air I breathe, I haven't paid anything for the water that comes out of the earth. So I never paid for the bare minimum. Everything is a gift, a gift from the One who created this world, a gift from the One who loves you and me. The Bible says: "For he causes his sun to rise on the bad as well as the good"(cf. Mt 5:45). He gives us everything, no matter how we are, because God loves us beyond measure. In the Gospel of Matthew, Jesus says:"Look at the birds in the sky. They do not sow or reap or gather into barns; yet your heavenly Father feeds them. Are you not worth much more than they are?"(cf. Mt 6:26).

We don't need to worry! But everyone is worried. You and I are worried. The birds in the sky, the lilies, the grass in the field have no worries. Why do we worry? When we worry, there is also doubt and fear. How many people suffer from fear today! Thanksgiving helps everyone personally to have a certain trust that God who created us will take care of us. I can work and earn money, but in my heart I should remember that the Lord who created and protected this plant, grass, sun, will protect me too.

## Look what you are

The "Bräunling" farm shop is located in Nussloch. This is a business that sells the products of creation on earth. Men and women work very hard here so that we can get potatoes, apples, other fruits and much more. I was amazed to see what creation unfolds from such a small plant. A great gift from creation, a great gift from nature.

These days we celebrate Thanksgiving day in all churches, especially in Catholic Church. We bring everything that the earth has given us to the altar and say to God: "Thank you! Thank you for everything you have given us!" We are very happy that nature and creation give us so much. We even get a lot of what we have for free: the sun, the air and the water. So many things that we need most are given to us for free. That is why we humans thank our God for everything we have. At this point I would like to lead you to a different thought - especially at a time when performance is required. We are in a performance society. We have to produce a lot, we have to give a lot. The great philosopher Immanuel Kant wrote "Look what you are! What you are is more important than what you have; and what you have is more important than what I have is much more than what I give. Man cannot be judged by what he gives, but by what he has and ultimately what he is. If we think about the dignity of every human being, every animal, every plant, then we will all realize how great our God is, who gives us everything, thank you Lord!"

## I haven't paid yet

This happened in Italy. An old man of 93 was admitted to hospital in Italy for treatment for the corona virus. By the grace of God he was healed and released from the hospital. The hospital authorities gave him the bill for the treatment. When the man saw the bill, he began to cry aloud. The doctors and everyone in the hospital thought he was crying because he did not have money to pay the bill. When asked the reason for crying, he gave an answer that made the entire hospital cry. The 93-year-old said: "I received the bill. I am not short of money. But I have reason to cry because you billed me a large for ventilation, that is, to give me air to breathe. For 93 years I have breathed the air for free. God never asked me to pay for the air He gave me to breathe and to stay alive. For a few days here I have to pay a lot of money for the air you deliver. It shows me how much I owe God. He has always given me enough air to breathe and stay healthy and alive. It never occurred to me, to be grateful to God for all these free gifts that he gave us without our asking. We just take it for granted and never bother to thank him. From now on I will consciously thank the Lord for the air, for the water and for nature, that he gave me for my survival until I mine last breath."

Are we aware of these things? Have we ever thought of thanking the Lord for giving us the air to inhale and exhale? For the water he gave to drink and for other uses? Why don't we become sensitive and gratefully fold our hands in front of his presence and say: Thank you, Lord!

## Correctly say Thank You

Thanks very much! Thanks very much! For two years we have been or are on the road with the "Spiritual Word" of the video sermons. You supported me with your watching, with your thoughts and with your comments. Thanks a lot for this. Today, after two years, we have the harvest festival again. I was visiting a family the other day and the mother prepared dinner for the child and put it on the plate. The child didn't say anything about it. Then the father intervened immediately: "Yes, and what do you say?" Unfortunately, the child did not answer. The father repeated his question in a loud voice: "Yes, and what do you say?" Then the child said: "Thank you!" "Thank you". The woman has been in hospital for seven days. Her illness has not yet been diagnosed. The doctor comes after seven days and brings her good news. How grateful will she be? Two weeks ago we heard the bad news from Italy. Some refugees were dying because they were standed at sea. If these people had been saved, if these people had been given their lives, what kind of "thank you" would they have said? "Thank you" is not just a word. Thank you is an expression of my own need. When I say thank you, I feel relieved of the hardships I had and therefore say thank you. Thanking simply means: It was good for me, it made me feel alive and gave me new strength. That is actually the meaning of thank you.

Today I am in the Gauangelloch Church - a beautiful church. The parishioners have put a lot of effort in designing the Thanksgiving Altar. This is also an expression of the heart. It's not just about buying something for a few hundred euros and then putting it down again, but really thinking about how important and necessary these individual gifts are for myself. And therefore say a word of thanks to God. I bring my need to God and say: "Every day I live with you and in you, I draw energy from the sun, from the rain, from the earth, from the various fruits of the earth that you have created, and above all from your love and mercy and also through my faith in you ". Do you feel this "need"? When we feel that need - that we need faith, love, and the fruits of the earth - we will truly thank Him with all our hearts.

## Thanks to all Volunteers

I would like to thank all volunteers, regardless of their afffliation to any church or political group. I think it's great that you are here. Volunteering is a term that I had to learn when I came to this country. I see with great gratitude that there are so many people who love to work for others. Which state could live without the selfless commitment of the volunteers, which church can survive without the contribution of certain men and women? Volunteering is really an office to be honored. Because this service comes from the depths of the souls of people who say: "It doesn't work like that, I have to do something." This can be for other people, the needy, the disadvantaged, the environment or animals. We live in a world that is not perfect. But precisely because the world is not perfect, it needs all of us in order to become perfect. I mean, God's plan is that everyone can volunteer to help, not for merit and fame, but for a sense of sharing and doing good from the heart. This can still lead to suffering and pain. But even with volunteering you need a little willingness to make sacrifices. This year we remember a bishop who lived in Brazil: Bishop Oscar Romero. He was there for the poor and needy and was shot dead during a mass. Many mourners and the poor will always remember him because they had the good feeling that there was a man who could be relied on to help them in their time of need.

When you do something good, remember that you are blessed by God and that your heart is very close to God. If you take God's place on earth with people in critical moments and give them a helping hand, you are truly a part of God.

## Seven years of Video Sermons

It is good that you have been accompanying me in my video sermon for the Internet magazine "Leimen-Lokal" for seven years now. I would like to thank those who make this possible every week and who have not missed a week for the video recording. Thank you, too, for your loyalty. Thank you very much for your comments, for your reflection, and for talking to you about the subjects from the Spiritual Word.

I would like to tell you something: As a young man, I had a major language problem. By the time I was 27, I stuttered so much that I couldn't even pronounce my own name fluently. And such a person has been talking to people and even in front of a camera for seven years! How can that be? Jesus healed me. Through spiritual practice, through my belief and through my trust in him, I have been healed so that I can now speak freely. And not only in my mother tongue, but also in German.

I am so grateful to have received this gift from God. My strength comes from him, that I can speak freely about my faith to others and convince them. Seven is a perfect number, it appears a lot in the Bible. It is not for nothing that the 7th day of the week is Sunday, the day of rest for us, just as God rested after his creation. Seven is also a healing and sacred number for me, and I am grateful and happy that I have been able to communicate with you here for seven years, because I remain true to God's word and gladly share my joy and experiences with you.

## No time to thank the Lord

A beautiful miracle of Jesus is recorded at Lk 17:11-19. He cleanses ten lepers. While traveling through Samaria and Galilee on his journey to Jerusalem, he met 10 lepers. They kept their distance - according to Jewish custom and law, which forbids lepers to live freely in society and to dwell separately in a deserted place, they were treated as outcasts by both civil society and the religious community (Lev13). All ten shouted in one voice: "Jesus! Master! Take pity on us.' When he saw them he said, 'Go and show yourselves to the priests." As per Leviticus Laws, the Jewish lepers when they were cured were to show themselves to the priests, who would examine and attest the cure. They had to make the offerings prescribe das per law and then they could join the society (Lev 14). When they left, they found that they were cleansed. Only one man returned to Jesus, fell at Jesus' feet and thanked him profusely. He was not a Jew, but a Samaritan, an outcast, separated from the Jewish community. When Jesus saw the gratitude of the Samaritan, he cherished him for seeing the grace of God working in and through the person of Jesus who healed his illness. The Samaritan recognized Jesus as divine. Jesus expressed disappointment when he saw the 9 Jews who belonged to the house of Israel who had not recognized the healing power of Jesus in their bodies. Only the stranger had the time and the heart to come back to thank Jesus. The sight, the faith and the salvation of the Samaritan were connected with each other. The Samaritan "saw" and believed and was saved.

One thing here, one more note. The nine Jews had religious duties and rituals to perform. They were in a hurry to join mainstream society. While they were sick, they didn't mind join- ing the Samaritan, and all ten voices asked for a cure. The moment they were healed, they did not see the power of God through Jesus, but they "saw" that they were standing next to a Samaritan who was an outcast. So they had to leave him behind and go to the priests and show themselves.

But their feeling of ingratitude was noticed by Jesus and he praised and praised the Samaritan, who had the heart to thank for the benefit received. No matter the urgency of our affairs, we should never fail to express our gratitude to those who have helped us and to God. We should be grateful to God and to people who come on our way in times of need and help us. Gratitude is a very great virtue.

# 13. KNOWING ONE SELF

*"Such amazing knowledge is beyond me; a height to which
I cannot attain" (Ps 139:6).*

## Accepting one's own Self

We have to accept ourselves as we are. We are all not one
hundred percent perfect. Each of us has our own strengths
and weaknesses. But most of us live with masks. Not the
corona mask. Corona mask will disappear sometime after
Corona leaves the country. But in order to hide our own
inadequacies, our own transgressions, our own inabilities, we
cover ourselves with masks of various kinds. It will always be
better to accept our strengths and weaknesses clearly and
openly. That would always be safer for our lives. I would first
check whether I even know myself. The moment I know myself,
my strengths and weaknesses, my advantages and
disadvantages and also my limitations, I will probably act
differently. I often exaggerate or understate my doubts as to
whether I can really create something on my own, with my own
intelligence and with my own personality. The moment I am
convinced that I can do something and then commit myself to
its implementation - or not because I honestly admit my own
limits, because I know myself - my credibility begins. When
people reproach me and tell me, for example, that I am a bad
person, or say "you are exaggerating" or "you are
underestimating me", then I should first ask myself: Am I
credible to myself? Did I act correctly? Have I been faithful in
this matter? Am I being honest with myself? "And then I make
a decision or find an answer whether or not I am believable.
The moment I don't know myself, don't see my strengths and

weaknesses, people see me as implausible and also tell me that because they saw that I cannot keep what I promised.

## When did you think of Yourself?

When was the last time you thought of yourself? Someone once said: Everyone thinks of themselves, only I think of myself. - Even in kindergarten, our children learn to say: I want this, I want to be the best. And it goes on in school. Only the best get on. Of course we always try to move forward, everyone wants to exercise their rights. Actually, there is nothing negative about people wanting to develop, achieve something, show what they can do. But it can also quickly turn into something negative if, for example, in business or politics only one's own profit or reputation is seen as the most important thing, often to the detriment of others. If I think too much and forget my surroundings, if I forget that I live in a community and thus depend on others, then I am no longer open to God's grace because I only look at myself and no longer at God or my fellow human beings.

Two men came to church to pray. One was very confident of himself and put himself above all others. The other, on the other hand, knew that he was a person with flaws, but believed that only God's grace could save him. It's about being too proud of your own achievement, putting yourself above everyone else and looking down on others - and losing sight of God. Lk 18:9-14. Jesus told the parable to those who consider themselves pious and despise other people.

## Socrates: I know I don't know anything

"I know I don't know anything" This sentence is attributed to Socrates. He was a great philosopher who always questioned everything. Why is something the way it is? Why is something happening while it is happening? Why do people act the way they do? He didn't have an explanation for everything, but he never stopped asking questions. And the conclusion of his thoughts was: Know yourself. The soul is more important than anything else, more important than the body, property or money. Because the soul really makes a person. We are so much influenced by our environment that we behave as everyone else is expected to do. In doing so, we lose ourselves, lose sight of our own soul, and with it what really defines us. As soon as I realize who I really am, I will act differently. In the Holy Scriptures we meet the Pharisees and the scribes who complained deeply to Jesus about his disciples. "Why are they doing this or not that? Why don't they obey the rules of our religion", they asked him. Jesus tried to explain to them that what is important is not what is outside, like observing many rules and laws, but what is inside a person, his mind, his soul. For the body is perishable, but the soul can live forever (Mk 7:1-23). Socrates lived 500 years before Christ, but his knowledge was the same: only when I get to know myself do I know at least a little. But a person can never know everything, even if he is educated and learned. But we will know everything when we are with God because He is omniscient.

## I see Black

There are not a few who see in everything black. Everything in the world is bad, people are bad, and their lives are bad. You are dissatisfied with everything. Democritus, a Greek philosopher, also known as the "laughing philosopher", lived about 400 years before Christ. With irony and satire, he showed people how to behave. He said: People want to own the whole world, even if they cannot take any of it with them to the grave. People are so afraid of death that they want to live as old as possible. But when they are old they whine that they are old.

People are always looking for something new, but when the new is there they are not happy. They want the best in the world, gold, precious stones, but for that they devastate the whole earth. Ironically, Jesus held up a mirror to the people. He was a man who could laugh. Laughter is a grace. And even if everything looks black, there is always a salvation. The sun is still shining behind every dark thundercloud, it's not gone, even if you can't see it at the moment.

Somebody in Leimen once told me that there was a solution for every problem. Our problem is that we are not looking for a solution, we are trying to create a problem for a solution. While healing a deaf person, Jesus said when he touched his face: "Open yourself." And the blockage dissolved. This also applies to us: if we block ourselves by only seeing the negative, the bad, we are like deaf people who no longer know anything about the world. We can laugh, we can be happy because God is there for us so that we can give hope to other people and find a solution to any problem if we want.

**Dream - Dream Big**

Everyone on earth has dreams. From children to teenagers, the adults to the elderly, all have dreams in their own way. So everyone with certain talents and intelligence is sent to this earth. Nobody, neither man nor woman, is sent "empty". Everyone has a special gift and that makes them unique. Some people might realize their talents or intelligence and they plan a goal and dream of achieving that goal, sometimes they make their dreams come true. The ex- President of India, A.P.J. Abdul Kalam, invited the youth to "dream". He wanted the youth, the future leaders and sculptors of the nation, to dream for the building of the nation. In front of him there as an English saying that calls everyone to "Dream - Dream big". While we are dreaming, we should never never be a curmudgeon. Only when we dream big can we achieve at least a significant part of it. But all of our dreams should never be based on selfishness, nothing should be self-centered, but rather serve for the benefit of other people or for a common cause. "One who aims to shoot at sky alone would be able to shoot at the top of the tree".

In the Bible there are two prominent personalities associated with dreams who had the ability to dream and also to interpret or understand their dreams and act accordingly. Through them the world has seen many wonders and benefits. Both were called Joseph. Old Testament Joseph, son of Jacob, who is introduced in the very first book of the Bible (also of the Old Testament) of Genesis. We find the other Joseph in the first book of the New Testament, namely in the Gospel according to St. Matthew. Old Testament Joseph was given the gift of having dreams and of interpreting them as well. Because of this gift, Joseph suffered much. His own brothers became jealous of him. Jacob, his father, had developed a special love for Joseph because he was born despite the old age of his parents and was adorned with a long tunic (Gn 37:3). Additionally, Joseph also had a dream about being led by the Lord. This sparked the anger of the brothers and they wanted to get rid of him. But due to the intervention of Ruben, the older brother, Joseph was thrown into an empty and dry cistern. Then he was sold to Potiphar, a courtier of the Pharaoh of Egypt. During his stay in Egypt, Joseph experienced many struggles, temptations, and even imprisonment. This in turn resulted in his whole family, father and all brothers and their families coming to Egypt. All of this is reflected in chapters 37, 39-47 of the Book of Genesis. So Israel became a great nation in the land of Egypt. They had prosperous lives for a long time before they were made slaves by the new pharaoh who knew nothing about Joseph. Joseph of the New Testament came from the house of David. He was a carpenter by trade and the husband of Mary through whom Jesus, the Savior Jesus, was born. The announcement of the birth of Jesus was communicated to Joseph only through a dream. Joseph was betrothed to Mary of Nazareth. But before their marriage was consummated, Joseph learned that Mary was pregnant. Since Joseph was a righteous man who did not want to publicly expose and shame Mary, he decided to secretly part with her. But an angel of the Lord appeared to him in his dream and informed him that Mary had received the power of the Holy Spirit and that she would give birth to a son. Joseph was asked to name this child Jesus. Joseph immediately understood the will of God. He had a crucial role to play in the plan of God the Father's salvation. He immediately obeyed God's will and accepted Mary as his wife and became the foster father of Jesus, the Massias and savior of the world. He protected Jesus from the cruel hands of Herod, who planned to kill the baby Jesus. When the angel instructed him in a dream to flee to Egypt, he exalted him to take Mary and the baby Jesus with him and to live there until he was asked through a dream to leave Egypt again and to settle again in Nazareth. (Mt 1:18, 2:23). So Joseph became the head of the Holy Family, who is venerated as the patron saint of families, the church and also the workers. He had the honour of feeding the Creator of the world through his own profession of carpenter and he was also the one who taught this profession to Jesus, the Creator (the Logos) (Jn 1: 1-3).

Now it is our turn to identify our goals and dreams. Dreams - dreams big and achieve great things - for our own benefit, for the benefit of our families, our workplace, our church, our society and for the benefit of the whole world. Let's become dreamers from now on!

## All just Water

Our world is surrounded by water. Two thirds of the planet are covered with water. Our body is mainly made up of water. Our body should consist of 80% water and other liquids. The unborn child grows in the mother's amniotic fluid. All life is based on water. Thales of Miletus, a philosopher who lived in the 7th century BC. Lived at the grave of his teacher and recognized: "Everything flows, nothing remains as it is. Everything must pass away so that the creative, the new can arise. Just as a fallen tree is decomposed, its nutrients are released back to the ground so that new trees can grow there". -"So he called a little child to him whom he set among them. Then he said, 'In truth I tell you, unless you change and become like little children you will never enter the kingdom of Heaven. And so, the one who makes himself as little as this little child is the greatest in the kingdom of Heaven" (Mt 18:2-4). What does that mean? This life is not a stagnant, but is always in progress. Everything is transient, everything flows. Old becomes new, death becomes new life. We must not stop at old ideologies, we have to give space to the new. In our western world in particular, many people no longer want to have children. But we need children, we shouldn't encourage abortions, weshould try to stop them. Only then will there be a future for us, for humanity. If I reject children, I destroy myself. If I don't give life a chance, my life is not fulfilled either.

## Become who you are

Many great philosophers, such as Socrates, Aristotle, Kant and Schopenhauer, have repeatedly thought about this sentence: "Become who you are".

We spend a lot of time doing activities outside of our apartments or houses. We go on vacation, go to the cinema, to the restaurant and meet up with friends. But these philosophers say that we should find ourselves first, recognize who we are before we deal with the world.

When I ask someone: Who he or she is, I don't have to know what religion they belong to, what job they have, how much they earn. What I want to know is what wishes he has, what worries, what longings he has, what strengths or weaknesses he has. I want to know what kind of person he / she is. When we recognize ourselves when we are at home with ourselves, then we can get along better with ourselves. There are many struggles in the world, not only outside but also within oneself.

It's a big challenge, a big step, to deal with myself and see who I really am. Become, who you are. Who are you? You are a child of God. The most important thing is not to have more prestige, to be more powerful than others, richer or more popular. The important thing is that I realize that I am comfortable with myself. Am I already doing this or should I still find out who I am?

## Is your Reality Real?

There was once a man in a hospital for the mentally challenged who was very afraid of cats. The doctor tried to explain to him that he was not a mouse, but a person and therefore did not need to be afraid. The man replied: "Yes, yes, I know that I am human, but I am worried that the cat should also know that I am not a mouse, but a human being." This man had lost touch with the real world.

We live in a world in which we often cannot determine the authenticity of things and reality. If we can check something directly, it seems simple: is this snow real? I can tell when I touch it. Is it really cold I notice that when I take off my jacket and then freeze. But what about the things that I can't check? Are you real?

We have a fine example of the revelation of reality of Jesus at the time of his baptism. This shows who Jesus was; the Messiah, the Son of God, filled with the Spirit of God, who took up his cross and suffered for the redemption of all people. At his baptism a voice came from heaven saying:"You are my Son; today have I fathered you"(Lk 3:22).

This shows who Jesus really was. We should ask ourselves: what makes me real? Do I show who I really am, not only my strengths but also my weaknesses, or do I play something else for myself and others? Is my life worthy of Heavenly Father's praise for saying, "You are my beloved son / daughter that I rejoice in?"

## How do I Live?

It is rainy season. When it gets dark early, when it rains a lot, it will be a good time to ask myself: How do I actually live my life? We actually live as we learned from parents, from grandparents who taught us their values, from the society that shaped our worldview and goals. But it's a very important question that we should ask ourselves before it's too late.

Do we only live for others? For what they think of us, how they judge us? What car we drive, what clothes we wear and in what kind of house we live in? decided by what others think of the Do we just do anything just to please others? Jesus said, "I have come so that they may have life and have it to the full" (Jn 10:10).

Jesus lived very well for others, but in a positive way. His goal was to enable others to live as fulfilling lives as his own. In the Old Testament, the prophet Amos vehemently opposes the rich who have dishonestly acquired their wealth and live at the expense of others, especially at the expense of the poor who have nothing to eat.

In the New Testament, Lazarus is said to have lived in great poverty and disease. Until his death he ate the leftovers of the rich man (Lk 16:19-23).

How do I live my life a human life can only succeed if one lives for others, not just to please other people. Jesus lived his own life authentically, he knew what life means: living in abundance means to live himself and for others.

No matter where we are and how we live, we hope and expect others to think and talk about us well. We constantly meet people who have something to say about us, directly or indirectly behind our backs, which happens much more often than you think. But when we learn about other people's thoughts and words, it does something to us. When the remarks please our ears and mind, we feel happy. But if they taste sour, we would like to do without them, they don't want to swallow so easily. We raise so many questions: "So are you talking about me like that? Why? Who are you to talk about me? What right do you have?" - Well, if the remarks are, he / she is a wonderful person, he / she has many talents, or he / she is pretty, always well dressed and smart, always happy, that's okay. But derogatory remarks like: he / she is boring, stupid, ugly, cheeky, arrogant, proud etc., then we don't want to hear them or we take them to heart. Only by absorbing the derogatory remarks and analyzing them can we find the truth in these statements. But we shouldn't just ignore it when we hear unwanted comments and be self- critical enough to admit our real mistakes and shortcomings.

## Live for the Others

It is a wonderful idea that we can be there for others, so that we can care for others with devotion. I attended a funeral for a woman who was very popular in the area. Until recently she was working in the St. Joseph Kindergarten and last year she knitted 170 socks for adults and children. People only say good things about her.

If we lived alone, just worried about ourselves, no one would be interested in saying good things about us. It would just be noticed that we have been selfish people all our lives.

However, if we can do a little, if we can do whatever we can for others, these little things will also be seen and praised as great for the good of others. Jesus said: "If anyone gives so much as a cup of cold water to one of these little ones because he is a disciple, then in truth I tell you, he will most certainly not go without his reward" (Mt 10:42).Maybe we can think about our attitude towards life, towards society, towards the world? Do we only live for ourselves? Every action leads to a resonance with the others, has an impact on our direct or indirect environment. Of course there will always be someone who speaks badly of us. We can't please everyone, they don't understand our motives, even if we have done good. But we know in our hearts that we have done good, and sooner or later, over time, they will realize and understand it.

## You are the temple of God

"Do you not realise that your body is the temple of the Holy Spirit, who is in you and whom you received from God?" (1 Cor 6:19). We humans have many things in our bodies - blood, water, bones. But are we also aware that we have God within us? That's a brilliant thought from Paul, isn't it? We humans are sacred vessels for God.

3000 years ago the Israelites were nomads. In order to always have God with them, they carried the most holy ark of the covenant with them. When they settled down, they built a tent and placed the ark there. Later a temple was built and the ark of the covenant was placed there. If people wanted to be close to God, they had to go to the temple. Often they came from far away.

Paul told us something wonderful. He said "every person is a temple of God". Everyone has God in them. We don't necessarily have to go to a church, temple, or mosque to be close to God. We are special because we have the love and goodness of God within us. It doesn't matter whether we are Hindu, Jewish, Muslim or Christian. This applies to everyone. We have to take good care of each other because God lives in everyone.

## Obsession / possession

People who are possessed by demons and evil spirits are called possessed. In our society here you hardly ever see something like that, but in my old homeland there are still many who go to churches, temples, mosques to be liberated. They have tangled hair and make strange noises, they make strange movements. Being obsessed is not easy. I would use another word to describe obsession, namely the word conflict. Being obsessed is really like being a shell for something else. For another mind. A spirit that is evil. He comes to me, he takes all my strength from me, he sucks my strength out so that I can no longer be me, but he or she has to be a person if I am a ghost. I feel so many spirits inside me, so many voices. We read about such experiences in the Bible too.

In the Gospels we see that Jesus had encounters with evil spirits or with possessed persons. A concrete example can be found in the Gospel of Mark. Jesus performed a miracle and cast the demons out of a person who lived in the tombs. His condition went so far that not even chains could hold him back. He cried loudly and injured himself with stones. His condition was pathetic. This man met Jesus who was nearby. But when he saw Jesus in the distance, he ran to Jesus and prostrated himself before him. The man shouted in a loud voice (these were the words of the demons who were in this man and even identified them who Jesus was):"What do you want with me, Jesus, son of the Most High God? In God's name do not torture me!"(Mk 5:7). Jesus knew that it was the evil spirit who spoke to him. He commanded it to come out of the man. On the command of Jesus, the evil spirit left the person and he became free and he even wanted to follow Jesus, but Jesus gave him a higher responsibility - the man was sent as Jesus' ambassador to preach what he saw, heard and experienced. In reality, we are also obsessed with many bad vices that cause us to be occupied by these things and to act awkward and unacceptable in the homes, offices, and society. But if we surrender to Jesus and prostrate ourselves to him and ask him to dissolve all these bad vices in us, his one word would be enough to make us clean and set free.

There are many things in society too. Many types of demons stand in the way of people, societies and nations, bringing wars and chaos into the world. If we cast out such demons by standing together in unity and showing our mutual solidarity, we can break away from such obsessions and undesirable traits.

We are obsessed with different things, with different people, but also with different ideologies. We should get rid of all of this. Otherwise we'll run around like madmen in this world. Jesus can definitely help us with that. "Quiet! Get away from him, from her!" Yes, Jesus is ready to set us free. Are we ready?

## Eagle and Chicken

You may know this story: A man once found a young eagle in the woods that had fallen out of its nest. The man who found it didn't know it was an eagle. He thought it was some kind of bird that had fallen out of the nest. He took the bird home with him, and the eagle grew up among his chickens and soon behaved like a chicken too. It didn't fly, but stayed on the ground, picking up grain like chickens. One day a friend came to his house. When he saw an eagle among the chickens, he was surprised. He told his host, "This is not a chicken, this is an eagle. He can't stay on the ground, he has to fly." The man just said, "No, no, this bird doesn't think it's an eagle. It grows up like a chicken and may not like to fly away." But his friend didn't like the idea. He thought the eagle should fly high in the sky. He shouldn't be on the ground with the chickens. So he decided to teach the eagle to fly. He put the eagle on his arm and lifted it into the air. "Fly high, you are an eagle!" The eagle did not fly, but fell back on the ground with the chickens. Then the man led him up a high mountain and showed him the vastness of the sky, the horizon and said to the eagle: "This is your kingdom, you do not belong on earth and you belong to heaven. So fly! To heaven!" At first the eagle hesitated, but when it saw the sun rise and the glorious expanse of the sky, it spread its wings and flew out into the sky. This is Paul's message. "We are not made for earth but for heaven" (Col 2: 20-3: 2). We are eagles.

# 14. LOVE OF NEIGHBOUR

*"You must love your neighbour as yourself" (Mk 12:31).*

## Serve instead of Wanting to be First

It is good that you are the best, that you are the first. It comes from instinct: every living being tries to be the first, the best. When a lioness finds a meal, she goes and drives away everyone else and she is the first to be allowed to eat. This is in the instinct of the living being. Man is endowed with spirit and reason. He's trying to find a ranking. When he realizes he's too slow, he always tries to be the best, the first. Sometimes you give in to others - and sometimes you don't. That's always the tension in people.

Divinity is different. In the Gospel according to Mark (Mk 9:33- 37), we hear the words of Jesus: "If anyone wants to be first, he must make himself last of all and servant of all" (cf. Mk 9:35). Jesus himself has shown this in his life by saying to his disciples The Son of Man must suffer. He must die. He is to be killed (cf. Mk 8:31; Mk 9:31; Lk 9:22). Glory comes after this "becoming small", after this "being dead". Divinity means to be small and to have been killed and suffered even before. After that , glory and success will come.

That may not fit in the eyes of the world, but God is different. He turns everything upside down and demands that we give in. By humbling oneself and becoming a servant of all, one can become the greatest in the kingdom of heaven. For God loves those who humble themselves, who love their neighbours as themselves and with a loving heart to serve.

## I love Her

When I read from the letter of Paul to Romans (Rm 13:8) I have nothing else to say other than: "I love you! I love you and I love you!" Only love owes you to one another. If you love others, you fulfill all the laws. That's how Paul writes. It's wonderful if I love you, isn't it? Very often it is the case that I have problems with some people. I keep realizing: Too bad, I can't really love this or that person. – Love is not just sexuality; love doesn't just mean I get something from someone else. Love is not just a feeling, but much more. In the book of Prophet Ezekiel, God says to the Prophet, "Son of man I have appointed you as watchman for the House of Israel."(Ez 33:7).

A lover is someone who cares about others. We also notice this with the small children when we say at home: You, take care of your sister! I will come back! But we will never tell a child to take care of another if we are reasonably sure and are aware of the fact that that child has no love and affection for that other child at all. "Watching" actually begins with love. Or by warning others. In the Gospel Jesus says: "If your brother does something wrong, go and have it out with him alone, between your twoselves" (cf. Mt 18:15). Love also means warning. When I say I care about someone, I have to love them. If I don't have love for others, then I can't take care of them or warn them.

To show love to another person therefore means to pay attention to the loved one for the good of the person, to care for his life, to provide help and last but not least to point out his shortcomings and mistakes and to warn him not to take a dangerous path. Love doesn't just end with chatting, laughing, eating together and lingering in some places of entertainment. It is much more than any of that.

# Suicidal

"I'm tired of life. I don't want to live any more. I don't see any sense in life anymore. Nobody likes me. I have a lot of problems. I have so much debt. I'm so sick - incurably sick. The world is really crap." Today a lot of people are grumbling and murmuring like this, and they are living with lots of frustrations and inferiority complexes, and somehow they want to end their earthly life. Have you ever thought of committing suicide because you are totally disappointed and powerless, because you feel that no one likes you? You haven't seen any sense in your life anymore? Have you ever had such an experience of being life-weary? Or in spite of leading an honest and righteous life, you feel you have been exploited and that has caused you utter disappointed and made you to think committing suicide?

In the letter of Paul to the Philippians, we hear "I am caught in this dilemma: I want to be gone and to be with Christ" (Phil 1:23). Why did he say that? At that moment his situation became very bad for him. Everything seemed in vain to him. Life was no longer interesting to note He had founded various churches. And in the end it was nothing - pure disappointment. So he said, I actually long to enter into glory with Christ. But at the same time Paul also said: "And yet for your sake to stay alive in this body is a more urgent need" (Phil 1:24). It is very interesting to note that Paul wants to live for others. That's why you can say to yourself when life gets difficult: Yes, I will continue to live - simply because of you or for you! - You don't always have to say that out loud, but you can think so, because the world lives only on goodness, only on people who radiate goodness, only on people who really give security. This world lives through them. In this sense Paul said very clearly: "I will go on living for you. "If at some point you have the feeling".

"I am really tired of life. I just want to go. If I go, everything will be better." Then say to yourself or teach your mind to speak to yourself: No, there is always a little hope for us to go on living! If you feel useless, look left or right, or look at someone, a child or something you like and tell you, yes, that's why I stay - I am not alone in life. My life is not just mine. My life is actually there for the others. If I give my life for others, it will be wonderfully blessed by God. I meet Christ expressed in the language of Paul.

## I wish you Love

The most abused word in the world is "Love". This is often very inflationary. There are many ways to love. From childhood to death, people love. As a child we all love our parents. In the teenage, another branch grows, it is friendship, and in the next stage, it is a love between the lovers, the love between opposite sexes, which will culminate in marriage. Then it is a love between the couple - the husband and the wife. Then the parents would have children and they would pour all their love on their children. And at ripened age the love turns to be a deeper one, as grandparents. Thus the cycle goes on down the generations. So there are different kinds of love, but what is interesting is that love still smells like a rose. It love still exists. All life is there to learn how to really love. There are various attempts. There are different experiences and expressions we have in our lives. Even when I live alone, I love. I can't live without love either. So what could real love look like? And Paul explains the value of love in his first letter to the Corinthians in chapters 13:1-13. The conclusion of the chapter tells of the greatness of love.

*"As it is, these remain: faith, hope and love, the three of them; and the greatest of them is love" (1 Cor 13:13).*

Love is a fine thing. Love doesn't ripen, it doesn't brag, it doesn't bloat. Love does not seek its own gain. It enjoys truth. If we love so much it will be heaven. But often we abuse this sacred aspect of life, for our own personal gain. Loving with the motive to get something back is reprehensive. If this does not happen, we will not be merciful. We don't forgive. We even punish people by withdrawing our love.

True love accepts everything as it is, see everything as positive. If we lived the love of our religion, we would have fulfilled what our religious leader Jesus showed us. He was a man of love. That's what he was born for, that's what he lived for, and that's what he gave his life for on the cross.

## Give more than you take

This year brought us many good experiences, but there were also difficult times. I look back on the year with a smile, but there were also some tears. "Giving is more blessed than taking," Jesus said. Was it so for me, for you? We humans always consume something, we consume, even when we breathe, we take something from the world. There is always something we want. But if everyone just takes, how does that affect creation? Giving is more blessed than receiving. If I take a lot, I should give a lot. It is better for those around me and for all of creation. Perhaps during this time, so near the end of the year, you can reflect on what you have taken from yourself and given in return to the people around you, nature and the world. Perhaps you are pondering the ways you have helped others, even if it was in your own family, on your own street, in your own community. Whether in the family, at work, in church, in the government or in nature. If you have given too little proportionally, now is the time to make up your mind to cultivate the habit of giving more than you take from others and the world. If we all just had the attitude that we were taking something and not giving anything back, the world would soon be poorer in terms of resources and virtues. So maybe you are thinking of choosing the motto for the coming year: "Give more than what you have got" - either from people or from nature, just as Jesus gave us the most precious, namely: His life. Are we ready to give our lives for the benefit of other people?

# 15. MISSION

*"Go out to the whole world; proclaim the gospel to
all creation" (Mk16:15).*

## How are You?

Mission: The word generally means an operational task that is
usually carried out by higher authorities. Usually this is a group
of people or a committee of people who are sent to another
location or country to negotiate, establish relationships, or the
like. In the Christian context, it is a body of people who are
sent by a church to carry out religious work, especially
evangelization, also to establish schools and hospitals to serve
humanity. Jesus commissioned twelve of his apostles for his
mission. He wanted them to go to all corners of the world to
preach the good news. In the book of Acts 14:21-27 there is
an account of the mission of Paul and Barnabas. Paul and
Barnabas preached the good news and gathered a
considerable number of disciples to continue their work, and
they returned to Lystra and Iconum and then to Antioch. Then
they traveled through Pisidia and reached Pamphylia. After
proclaiming God's words in Perge, they went down to Attalia.
From there they sailed to Antioch, a city in what is now Turkey
with 18000 inhabitants, where the believers were called to be
Christians for the first time (cf. Acts 11:26). Upon their arrival,
they called all the people of the Church and informed them of
the missionary work they were doing among the Gentiles and
opened doors for them to believe in Jesus. This "Jesus
Movement" began in different cities, from Jerusalem to all over
the world. Paul and Barnabas therefore came to their old
churches to talk to the people there and to inquire about their
welfare. As a priest, as a pastor, I would like to ask the

question: How are you? How is your belief today? Do you still believe in god? Do you even need a god?

For 2000 years your ancestors, believed in this God who bore life in the midst of various strokes of fate with all political and social problems. Can you still believe or are you waiting for faith to take hold of you at some point later when a stroke of fate strikes you? Or should we get even more problems in society? Or if we should get poor? Are you waiting - Why do we have to wait so long? If we have already learned beforehand to walk with God, to live with God, then an extreme situation in our life will not be so dramatic, then we can act well. But we can only do that if we start now. So why wait any longer? We can already believe in Jesus today and proclaim his message.

## Mission Sunday

This Sunday the Catholic Church celebrates World Mission Sunday. The word "mission" has several meanings. In the Christian context, the Church sends a group of men and women to do religious work, spread the faith and evangelize in different parts of the world. It was Jesus who sent his disciples to preach the good news. He had trained his disciples for three full years so that the preaching could continue uninterrupted after his death, and it continues to this day. World Mission Sunday - Today is our mission to bring the whole world together. In the 19th century missionary work began very intensively, especially from Germany. Many missionaries traveled around the world to fulfill Jesus' mission. I well remember the great stories of the SVD missionaries who travelled around the world; whether it was hot or cold there, whether dry or wet, no matter what language the people spoke there, they went around the whole world. It was already the beginning of globalization. These missionaries wrote down everything that happend in every place, in every village they came to, in every continent they settled, from which modern ethnology and anthropology, which is studied in many places today, has gained a lot of inputs. World Mission Sunday is a festival of dialogue: Jesus brought and showed the dialogue between God and the world. Missionaries especially ensure the dialogue between nations and cultures, but also between religions. We help Christians and people of other faiths to live in peace and reconciliation. That really is the goal of all of us. World Mission Sunday gives us dialogue and peace.

## Exit from the Church

Many people have left the church with us. I have been writing letters to people who have left the Church, especially in recent years. 99% of them didn't answer. I know it's not against me, but it means something refered to our country. Four professions were very important in the past - the mayor, the doctor, the teacher and the pastor. But today they are becoming less important.

In the book of Prophet Malachi (cf. 2:7-14), which dates back to around 500 BC., God speaks against the priests. He says: "The priest's lips ought to safeguard knowledge; his mouth is where the law should be sought, since he is Yahweh Sabaoth's messenger. But you yourselves have turned aside from the way; you have caused many to lapse by your teaching. Since you have destroyed the covenant of Levi, says Yahweh Sabaoth, so I in my turn have made you contemptible and vile to the whole people, for not having kept my ways and for being partial in applying the law."

The above indicates the attitude and behavior of the priests during this period, which is still perpetrated by most of them. You dictate what others should do, but you don't do anything yourself. You collect money and make yourself comfortable. In short, they set a bad example to the people, very inadequate for a priest to come forward to serve the people and guide them on the right path, without showing any bias and making no distinction. But in reality, all of this only happens in today's society. Similarly, Jesus makes it clear in the Gospel when he says: "The scribes and the Pharisees occupy the chair of Moses. You must therefore do and observe what they tell you; but do not be guided by what they do, since they do not practice what they preach."(Mt 23:2-3). At the end of the instructions Jesus also teaches them not to call anyone as a father, since they only have one Father who is in heaven (Mt 23, 9) He also instructs the priests to humble themselves. He wants the greatest among them to be servants of the people. He who exalts himself is humbled and whoever humbles himself is exalted, was the last word of this passage (Mt 23:11-12).

A priest should have empathy with the people and thereby bring and proclaim the love of God to them. Then he would really do justice to his profession as a priest.

The priest is now called to live by these ideals. We are all co- workers of God, as the Bible writes about people (cf. 1 Cor 3: 9). There is no one higher or lower, everyone is the same. But the office of priest should be an updated translation of love today, as Bishop Klaus Hemmerle wrote. If we do that - we as priests, then we are role models in this society; then maybe many people will come to us again to feel the secret of love through us, in us and from us. In the coming days, you will likely visit the graves of your loved ones as well. These were the people who really experienced this love, radiated it and showed it to you and us. This love is also the decisive factor for the priest and for all Christians.

## You are sent

This special greeting is sung by the priest at the end of the Mass. It comes from Latin: "Itemissaest" and means "You are sent". Jesus gathered his 12 disciples around him "Thesetwelve Jesus sent out, instructing them as follows: 'Do not make your way to gentile territory, and do not enter any Samaritan town; go instead to the lost sheep of the House of Israel. And as you go, proclaim that the kingdom of Heaven is close at hand. Cure the sick, raise the dead, cleanse those suffering from virulent skin-diseases, drive out devils. You received without charge, give without charge. Provide yourselves with no gold or silver, not even with coppers for your purses, with no haversack for the journey or spare tunic or footwear or a staff, for the labourer deserves his keep" (Mt 10:6-9).

Jesus insisted that the disciples should only rely on Divine Providence. You should never waste time gathering up any things or thinking about their needs. The focus should only be on the mission for which they were sent. He assured them that if they entered a house, the residents of that house would take care of them. Food and accommodation would be provided. Jesus wanted the disciples to have a free mind to focus on God and proclaim his kingdom. The people who received them should also take care of them. In the Second Vatican Council 50 years ago it was said that the congregation is the family for a priest. Therefore he can live alone.

## Spread the Word

I was in my old homeland in India some time ago. There I had the pleasure of many things, objects and cars from Germany. Even in the advertising it was said again and again: "Made in Germany". "Made in Germany" "Made in Germany" - that's what it says always and everywhere. "Made in Germany" -

Germany stands for quality. The products are wonderful. Even if the products are sometimes not that great and may not be of high quality, the motto is: "Made in Germany". Parroting! Our country is one of the largest exporters in the world. We export a lot. All of this is happening not just because of the quality that we eventually achieved, but also because of the storytelling, the sharing, and the promotion. Is it the same with faith? Is it the same with God? Why are we afraid to share our faith? Why do we hesitate to say that God loves you and me? How come? Will a president or chancellor openly say "I believe in God" when they vote? If he or she did something like that, defeat would likely be inevitable. But, on the other hand, will a president in the United States be elected if he does not say these words? Why do we hesitate? Why don't we say something like that? The people around Jesus spoke of it after Easter, especially the Emmaus disciples who had seen Jesus going with him from Emmaus to Jerusalem (cf. Lk 24:35-48). They continued to tell what they had experienced. They almost couldn't stand it because they were so moved by Jesus who rose from the dead. Peter, who said loudly and openly that he was touched by Jesus Christ, lived for his faith (cf. Ac 3:12-15-17). Maybe we have this Easter experience too. With our great wealth of faith, our good ecclesiastical past and our spiritual history, we do not necessarily have to stay at home anywhere. We can come out and say to anyone, "Faith is a little more, maybe even better than knowledge, better than reflection."

## Investiture

This Sunday is a very special festival for the communities of Sandhausen and St. Ilgen, because an investiture service is celebrated here. Investiture is a very old word that is used very rarely in our society. Investiture - what does it mean? I nvestiture - I was "invested" as a pastor for the parishes of Sandhausen and St. Ilgen. I was first called by God to become a priest. And now it's my job to be pastor for Sandhausen and St. Ilgen.

In our Church there are different ministers, religious, deacons, priests and bishops, cardinals and the Pope. I was used as a priest for these congregations. There are many hospital and military chaplains and I am now called and appointed pastor.

Today the picture of the pastor is out of date. I am not a shepherd and people are not sheep. My job is comparable to a soccer team; I'm like a captain. The captain has a team consisting of employees, pastors and many volunteers. With them I do something good for people. It's about taking care of the people who are entrusted to me. There are many thousands of people in consisting communities who can and should feel comfortable with me. That's my job. My own coach is God himself. He sends me into this office and I want to carry it out with his help, with his strength and with his grace.

## Traveling without Luggage

Are you preparing for a trip on this vacation? You will need to pack everything you will need during the trip. And you have to take enough clothes, upholstery with you, but then you have to be careful that the suitcase doesn't weigh too much! We have a problem with obesity, not just with our bodies, but with our suitcase as well.

Jesus tells how his disciples should pack their things. What should they take with them to get to the people? You shouldn't take anything with you. Yes, even with just foot waer! No storage bag, no money! (cf. Mt 10:9; Lk 10:4). Just go ahead. But what's the point of it? There is one thing they should take with them: the Good News. The Good News should be received by all disciples. What kind of good news is that? "Whatever house you enter, let your first words be, "Peace to this house!" (Lk 10:5). You should have peace in your luggage, you should go into the houses as peaceful people. And if someone does not accept this peace, you are to shake off the dust from your feet (cf. Mt 10:14; Lk 10:10 f.). Maybe that could be discussed. But I would say that if I can't get any further with the peace I have from God, then I have to remain credible and say: I'm unfortunately not welcome here. All churchmen, all people, who work in the church, must have this peace with them. Very often, or for a very long time, the Church has not done this. We haven't made peace. Perhaps today we have reason to really think about it: When I go out into the world as a pastor, as a religious, I ask myself: Do I have peace?

## Peace in my luggage?

What about me if I have no peace? As a world or as people who really expect something from the church, they have the right to demand peace from their church, from their people who come to them in the name of God.

## The Salt of the Earth

There are different religions, ideologies and denominations in the world. There are representatives who say: "You can come to us. You feel better with us. You can do what you want. Be free!" But there are certain religions, like Judaism or Christianity, that demand something from the people, that is, I can't just be what I want. I have to become and be something. Jesus says in the Gospel: "You are salt for the earth, you are light for the world"(Mt 5:13-14). The two objects or two symbols. We know what light stands for! Salt is a very precious thing. There was a time in Europe when people even wanted to pay are everything to get salt. Salt is the most important spice we have. Without salt we cannot eat anything, without salt we cannot enjoy anything. Salt even cleanses the wounds. Salt is the best preservative.

In a book by Benedict XVI, the Pope Emeritus, I read a sentence to the question: What does it mean, "Being Catholic"? Is it anything better? He writes: "Being Catholic is good because there is a certain continuity in the life of the Church with ups and downs over 2000 years. And that's actually the salt. Salt gives this continuity." Christians are like salt. Jesus continues: You are also the light of the world. We know this very well: when there is darkness around us, then we need the light. Especially at a time when everything is bright, when night turns into day, we sometimes do not feel the importance and necessity of a candle. But I know one thing: when I was little, there was no electricity in our house. We always needed a little light. Jesus says: You are the light of the world. He would like to say: You are the divine light that makes people's lives bright. You are the salt of the earth and you are the light of the world. Not only will we or have to become, but we already are. Jesus says: You "are" - you and I "are" the salt of the earth and the light of the world. As adults we ask ourselves: is that true? Is it really true?

## Who is in the Church?

Are you a Roman Catholic? Protestant? Orthodox? Or a person of an evangelical church? Which church do you belong to? I will be very interested to find that. I'm standing here in front of a Catholic church. To be more precise, in front of a Roman Catholic Church. Our pastoral care unit, in which we were previously called: Roman Catholic Parish Leimen-Nussloch- Sandhausen, now has this name from January 1st, 2015.

I take you into history. In the beginning, when the church was built, this happened in very different places. Especially in Jerusalem, Rome, Constantinople, Antioch and Alexandria. So the Church was born in different cultures in different places and slowly spread. The Catholic Church, based in (Vatican) Rome with the Pope as the supreme pontiff, today has around 1.254 billion people. In the Orthodox churches like the Greek Orthodox, Russian Orthodox, Serbian Orthodox and Romanian Orthodox churches. There are now over twenty five in the world. All of this had a beginning, like everything else. In the book of Acts we hear of the conversion of a centurion named Cornelius. In the beginning, Jews followed Jesus and referred to themselves as his disciples. After that, the pagans also slowly developed their faith in Jesus. That was a big deal. It was impossible for Jews or Jewish Christians that Gentiles could become Christians at all. The full story is in Acts chapter 10. This was the first baptism given to the Gentiles. The conversion of Cornelius is of great significance. Its significance for the church as a whole results from the narrative itself and from the emphasis on the two correlative visions of Peter and Cornelius from the way in which the author of the book Luke consciously links this incident with the decision of the Council of Jerusalem (Acts 15:7-11, 14). We get two lessons from this. First, God himself made it clear that the Gentiles should be accepted into the church without being forced to follow the Law (10:34-35, 44-48). Second, God Himself showed Peter that he must accept the hospitality of the uncircumcised. The problem of the social relationship is found between Christians who were converted from Judaism and Christians who were converted from Paganism in the narrative (10:10- 16, 28-29). We can see many other interesting things in this episode.

"Fear God" and "Worship God" are terms used for the Jewish religious people who prevent people from entering into the Christian faith before circumcision. Peter is advised to put aside his scruples about legal purity. God has purified the hearts of the Gentiles, and although their bodies are uncircumcised, they remain pure. The immediate practical conclusion is that Peter need not fear contact with the uncircumcised. There is just as much division today as there was before. Today there is the same outrage as before. Let's just look at what's going on in the Catholic Church. Even today there are different classifications in we hear: 'You do not belong to us'. I hear remarks like that the Russian Church would not accept all other churches as Christians. And so there are churches in every country that say: You do not belong to us. And when the Protestant churches emerged after the Reformation, there were further divisions. Today there are more than 35,000 churches, small and large that do not accept one another. In the Gospel Jesus says: "Love one another, as I have loved you" (Jn 15:12). A great word that we Christians have not yet understood.

People are still marginalized because "the others" do not belong to us. It is a great reminder from Christ that after 2000 years we should finally understand that we cannot exclude anyone because God himself does not exclude us. God allows all people to be equal. And that is why Peter says that God does not look at people, from which origin, from which nation, from which culture this person comes, but he looks into the heart. And when the heart is there, who am I who could afford to marginalize someone? It is high time we accepted people regardless of their origin and did not exclude them. We can take different theological directions, but that does not mean that the other cannot come to us.

## Restore Hope

There are more and more "sleeping villages", i.e. places where people only live and sleep, but not much else happens. Hardly any shopping opportunities, no opportunities for joint activities, for leisure time or coexistence. You can also see that in Gauangelloch: almost all shops have been given up in recent years, one bank is closed, there is only one small grocery store with the essentials. Everything you need or want to do should be bought or done elsewhere, because there are no more options in this place of residence. But there is a movement to change that, and not just in Gauangelloch. The people are committed to making villages more livable again. People want to have a community again, to share common activities in sport, culture and religion.

It is not for nothing that the church is in the middle of the village. But not many people go to church these days. As a result, a village or a city loses its center, its core. The philosophical, social, cultural and religious life, which can always be the linchpin for people, is to be revived. As a priest, I say that the glossing over of our lives should be given to God. If we only take care of our earthly and human concerns, we are lost to our core. I want us to shape our lives together, help one another, be there for one another and create a community worth living with God as the linchpin of our life

## Sow even if not every grain germinates

The Catholic Church lost almost 400,000 members in Germany alone in 2019 when they left the Church. This is terrifying in a church that has been around for 2000 years. This is also daunting for me as a pastor. We wonder what we Bishops, priests, volunteers can do to create new models, to find new ways, but somehow the church fails. That is a sobering truth. Yet the mission of the church is to be missionary, to follow Jesus, and to bring the good news to the people. You can't just wait and hope that maybe more people will return to the Church. There is a beautiful parable in the Bible: A farmer wants to cultivate his field and throws out seeds. Many seeds fall between thorns, on rocks, by the roadside, but there are enough seeds that can fall on good soil and germinate there. I think it's great that this farmer is not thrifty for he throws a lot of seeds. The church must also be like that; she must not stop sowing the good news (Mt 13:4- 7). Perhaps the mistake lies in the fact that the church does not speak the language of today and therefore the content of the message and the offer of the church do not fall on fertile ground. But it has to get the message across to people, whether they want to listen or not. The message may fall on rocks, but it will also fall into the hearts of good listeners. I've always been pleased that I've come across a lot of good floors in my work. We are all responsible for sowing the Good News because it is THE message that brings salvation and blessings. I invite you to sow with me because I believe the Church has the potential for new growth.

## Diaconate

The inauguration of the new old people's home in Nussloch is taking place today. There are three such houses in my pastoral unit. Would we be here without the contribution of the Church? The Church is involved in social services and support / care facilities around the world serves in Africa, India, and many other locations. I also have 130 employees and around 100 of them work in the social sector. There are also many private groups and clubs. Can't the state take care of it? Why does the church do it? Because the church has the mandate of the early church to be active in diakonia. At that time, seven men were appointed who were sent into the world by the apostles to help the poor, the mourning, the hungry, the weak and the sick. The office of deacon is derived from this. But not only the state, not only the church, not only the deacons have to help the people, but each individual should come forward to help the needy. Jesus says, the moment we help someone, the glory of God is revealed. When we act like Jesus, the apostles and the deacons, the presence of God manifests itself here in this world. This applies to all people who are loved by God and who pass on his love.

## I'm ready

"I am ready", as you often hear. These words of assurance are given when the pilot takes off or a construction worker when he gives a sign to sart work. When I was ordained, the bishop asked me, "Are you ready?" When you say this, it means fulfilling someone else's expectations and doing what is necessary. Peter calls all Christians in the world to be ready to take responsibility for instilling hope. All Christians should be ready to give an answer of hope. Our world suffers from hopelessness in relationships. I'm looking for someone to give them hope. I heard many friends and parishioners in the past few days telling me that that they have hope. And I'm especially grateful for the people who gave me hope in crisis situations. Hope is not a utopia, it is very real. Christian hope is not limited to the present or the near future, but exists forever. God who loves us, He never will ignore us, He will always protect us and always go with us. That gives me hope for my life and the whole world.

## Sheep among Wolves

Jesus, while sending his disciples on His mission said "Look, I am sending you out like sheep among wolves" (Mt 10:16).

Should we go to people who "eat" us like a wolf, as sheep? It also means being a Christian. Going out into the world as Christ's messengers can encounter difficulties and opposition that can even lead to death. We can encounter rejection, even hatred. The road is not always wide and comfortable. We may have to fight our way through rubble and thorns. But our mission is to proclaim the kingdom of God! That is what it says in the Gospel of Mark. Jesus said:"The time is fulfilled, and the kingdom of God is close at hand. Repent, and believe the gospel" (Mk 1:14-15).Christians are on their way to proclaim just that: God is close to you. Look at your life. What changes can you make in your perspective, your actions, your attitude? We don't do anything new. We are only following in the footsteps of Christ's disciples, who carried out the mission of Jesus even after his death and gave their lives for this mission.

## Mission is on the doorstep

An honest question should be answered honestly: Do you know the man Jesus? Do you really know him? What a provocative question! You can easily say that we have been in a Christian country for generations and follow the faith and how can we say that we do not know Jesus. It is realistic, however, that we have lost a whole generation: Many younger parents allow their child to be brought up in the Christian faith because of the compulsion of the elders in the family. Church membership is tolerated and church tax is paid. But four in ten people want to leave the church. Many have no idea whether God really exists or they just don't care. So what will happen in 50 years? Will these children who were baptized today know who this Nazareth man was? Will you know Jesus? Jesus Christ has shaped us positively for 2000 years, he cannot and must not simply disappear from our lives. This Jesus is God's best message to us, he can save everyone, give everyone eternal life. It doesn't make us small, it makes us big. We are children of God and can live full lives. And we have the mission to go out into the world and tell everyone: Jesus lives.

We don't need the people who just pay their church tax. We need disciples of Jesus who have been touched by Jesus. Only then can they, like the apostles, go to the people with conviction. There is still a lot to be done because the harvest is great!

Feel touched by Jesus. A wonderful life will await you and it takes you with Jesus to other people. Knowledge means more than just knowing the name, knowledge also means friendship. Mission is necessary not only in Africa or Asia, but on your doorstep, in your surroundings and in your life.

# 16. NEW MEANINGS

*"You will be called a new name which Yahweh's mouth will reveal" (Is 62:2).*

## Simon Peter's Mother In Law

Being a Christian is very simple: you don't think so much about how you can live it. Jesus visited his friends. He learned that Simon Peter's mother-in-law was ill (Mk 1:29-39). The Gospel of Mark tells us that he grabbed her by the hand, and the fever went away. The mother-in-law got up and served Jesus (cf. Mk 1:31).

What does this text tell us today? This is very ordinary story of Jesus visiting a sick person. The fever went away and this person served Jesus. I would interpret it this way: Jesus visited people in everyday life. We can also do that, we don't need a lot of experience. We do not have to start Lent to experience God because God Himself comes to us in our daily life. God comes in when I live my everyday life. When I work, when I eat, when I play, Jesus comes into my life. There comes Jesus, touches me and says, "I am with you." Even if I don't have great faith, even if it looks very dry in my life, even if I think that I have no more joy, the finger of God is still present in my life. Jesus touches me every time I live my daily life. It often happens that there is some change in me. Many do not realize that. Sometimes I feel bad for days. But at some point I have the feeling that I am feeling better again. I don't know why, but I feel it's better. Maybe it's the same in your life. I see this as a presence or touch of God in my life. Jesus touches me, God touches me to make me feel better.

Simon Peter's mother-in-law did only one thing: she served Jesus. This is how the gospel reports. Serving has different meanings. I would like to emphasize one meaning: faith. A servant is usually entrusted to his lord. He lives with this and so there is no reason to be afraid, nothing to worry. He rejoices to be with his Lord. When I serve, I feel good. This is nothing but to believe. If we want to serve God, I need faith in Jesus - I rejoice that He is there, that God is there.

## DoTell

I recently met a young person from my parish. I asked him, "How do you tell at school that you're a ministrant?" He replied: "Oh, that's very embarrassing. I don't want to tell my school that I'm a ministrant or any other person working in the Church. My comrades laugh at me when I just say I'm a ministrant. - So I don't tell anyone about it!"

There is a story from the life of Jesus (cf. Mk 1:40-45): a leper ran towards Jesus and asked him for healing. Jesus healed the leper and told him: "Mind you tell no one anything, but go and show yourself to the priest, and make the offering for your cleansing prescribed by Moses as evidence to them". Don't tell anyone about it! This is somehow a strange command for the man healed . But the man walked away and told everyone about it. This is the so-called "silence commandment", which we discover again and again in the Gospel of Mark: Jesus commands especially the evil spirits: Silence, be silent! (cf. Mk 4:39) or silence and leave him! (cf. Mk 1:25). There is a motive for this. At the end of the Gospel of Mark we hear an angel say after the resurrection of Jesus:" But you must go and tell his disciples and Peter" (cf. Mk 16:7). So it's about telling, but only after a good result, after a real life experience. I can't really tell you about something if I'm not excited about. If I am a football fan or a fan of a singer, I will tell you about this person or this club based on my personal experience with it. And why cannot I, express it also from the experiences of my faith? We can tell everyone about it, but first of all we should have good experiences with Jesus. Jesus works miracles in me every day. I should report on it. But first I should gain experience, experiences that inspire me, that just get under your skin. "When the heart is full, the mouth overflows" a proverb says. If my heart is full of joy because Jesus heals me, because Jesus helps me, because Jesus is present in my daily life, then I can tell you about it too. Do not tell anyone about it until you have had a deeper experience! Even today, even in church, even in my own world, I learn that Jesus heals me and protects me with his blessings.

# 17. OPPRESSION

*"You on the other hand have eyes and heart for nothing but
your own interests, for shedding innocent blood and
perpetrating violence and oppression" (Jer 22:17).*

## Oppression

Any person in authority be it in office, or at home, or in
society, or in politics or even in the Church administration, could
exercise his/her authority or power on a weaker or less- fortunate ones, or minorities, in harsh, cruel or unjust manner. In
some cases the oppressed people are forced to take extreme
steps to end their lives. Oppression of any kind must be
abharred in any society.

## Oppression in the Bible

There are a number of passages in the Bible that condemn
oppression. Our God Yahweh never liked people oppressed
by the authoritarian people, kings, religious leaders. Let us
read a few words of God from the prophets and learn not to
exploit, not to manipulate, not to oppress people, especially
the marginalized, widows, less fortunate and strangers in our
places, but to treat all people equally. For people, no matter
where they come from, whatever religion they may profess,
whatever language they speak or whatever  religion they
belong.  For they are created by  God in his image (Gen 1:26).

The commandments given by Yahweh through Moses to the
Israelites read as fokons.

You shall not oppress an alien, you well know how it feels to be
an alien since you were once aliens yourselves in the land of

Egypt. (Ex 23:9). The Israelites already had suffered oppression when they were slaves in Egypt. Yahweh God wants Israelites that, after they have suffered themselves and as they know the hardships and torments, they should not treat others infliting similar pains and torments. This means that God does not want them to take revenge in any way for what they once suffered as slaves in Egypt. "You will not exploit or rob your fellow. You will not keep back the labourer's wage until next morning. You will not curse the dumb or put an obstacle in the way of the blind, but will fear your God" (Lev 19:13). Lev 19:11-17- These commandments regulates. They are social behavior summed up in the commandment asking people to love one's neighbour. Similar injunctions are found in all the legislative passages of the Pentateuch.

"If you do not exploit the stranger, the orphan and the widow, if you do not shed innocent blood in this place and if you do not follow other gods, to your own ruin, then I shall let you stay in this place, in the country I gave for ever to your ancestors of old"(Jer 7:6-8). - The Lord spoke through the Prophet Jeremiah who preached the message from the Temple of the Lord to the people who were entering the Temple for worshipping Him.

"Do not oppress the widow and the orphan, the foreigner and the poor, and do not secretly plan evil against one another" (Zc 7:10). - The Lord spoke against oppression of widows and orphans through Prophet Zechariah.

Almost all the prophets In the Books of Prophets condemned oppressions like defrauding, hate, robbing, exploitation which were rampant among the people of Israel. Hence Yahweh God had to speak again and again on these things in order to make a change in the minds of the Israelites, turn them towards Him and make them live righteously.

Oppression in any form is not good for a good society, for a good family, for a good organization institution and in Church, too. We should learn to respect human persons as they are, irrespective of differences which most often were thrust upon society by people.

## Violence Starting from Home

By violence we mean a swift and intense force, rough or injurious physical force or treatment (causing death or injury in humans (also in animals, birds etc.). Unjust and unwarranted exertion of force or power as against rights and laws. Violence can be caused by words, thoughts, actions of subtle things, but strong enough to cause deep wounds in people's hearts. Some countries have laws to protect small birds and animals. But in some cultures violence is built in. In countries like India there is gender inequality that still exists even among the educated. In some conservative families, women are not allowed to accept work even if they are educationally qualified to get a decent job. Even their movements are restricted. They have no say in important family decisions. Only men have all authority. Since such practices have been in vogue for centuries, built into the culture, the hidden violence is not felt so much, it is seen as routine, habit and right way of life.

Children are also subjected to a kind of slavery at home. The ambitions and desires of the parents are imposed on the children regardless of the child's own preferences and desires. In the long run, this makes a very strong adverse effect on children. Children experience a lot of psychological stress and tension. As they grow up, they grow up with violent mentalities and inflict violence on others in their families and societies.

Elders in the family are neglected. This too borders on violence. The elders are seen as a burden and as crap to throw away once they are physically and financially disabled. Relationships with them are seen as irritating and unbearable. But the people who treat their elders like this forget one fact. One day they too will grow old and depend on someone. The treatment that they gave to their own parents or in-laws will be given to them because their children will grow up with it and see what they do to the elders in the family.

The Bible fittingly says for such people: "A full measure, pressed down, shaken together, and overflowing, will be poured into your lap; because the standard you use will be the standard used for you"(Lk 6:38).

# 18. PARABOLIC LANGUAGE OF JESUS

*"I will speak to you in poetry (Parables), unfold the
mysteries of the past" (Ps 78:2).*

## What is a Parable?

Parables are educational and memorable stories that teach
people important lessons in daily life. They convey deep
messages and are the central teachings of Jesus. Parables
make up one third of the teachings of Jesus. A parable always
stands for one lesson. We shouldn't just skip this and bring in
various other lessons at our will and desire. Parables teach
only one truth. In order to understand the parables, one should
become very familiar with the socio-political-economic-
religious-cultural-geographical situations and circumstances
at the time of the narration of the parables. Parables are found
only in the three synoptic gospels - Matthew, Mark, and Luke.

Matthew contains 23 parables

Mark contains 8 parables

Luke contains 24 parables

## Why did Jesus speak in Parables?

Jesus spoke to the people and his disciples in parables. All
three synoptic gospels contain parables of Jesus. Once the
disciples came up to Jesus and asked why he was speaking
in parables. He answered them with the words: "Because to
you is granted to understand the mysteries of the kingdom of
Heaven, but to them it is not granted"(Mt 13:10-11).

A parable is a figurative speech. Understanding this language requires reflection. Only those who are willing to explore their meaning can get to know them. Understanding is a gift from God given to the disciples but not to the rest of the people (masses). In Semitic fashion, both the disciples' understanding and the dullness of the crowd towards God are ascribed. The question of human responsibility for dullness is not dealt with, although one can read about it in Mt 13:13. The word mysteries, as in Lk 8:10, Mk 4:11, is used to denote a divine plan or resolution that affects the course of history that can only be known when it is revealed. Knowledge of the Mysteries of the Kingdom of Heaven (Mt 13:11) means, to know the kingdom of God presently in the service of Jesus.

## Which seeds Bear Fruit?

In the Gospel according to Matthew, Jesus talks about different kinds of fruits or the fertility of the seeds (Mt 13:3-8): "Listen, a sower went out to sow. As he sowed, some seeds fell on the edge of the path, and the birds came and ate them up. Others fell on patches of rock where they found little soil and sprang up at once, because there was no depth of earth; but as soon as the sun came up they were scorched and, not having any roots, they withered away. Others fell among thorns, and the thorns grew up and choked them. Others fell on rich soil and produced their crop, some a hundredfold, some sixty, some thirty". That shows us that they are differenct people. We can never create equality in this world: in terms of quality, skills and intelligence. We don't know why this is the case. This remains a mystery. But we can ask ourselves how we ourselves can grow and bear fruit with these given situations. Sometimes people are like the seeds that fall on the way. We say: I do not understand why, that is the case.

A good thing just goes by me! Or that at some point I say: I never got it. That's why I never became what I wanted to be! There are also experiences such as seeds falling on rocks. We are so fascinated by something and would like to do something and start. But over the time we don't longer desire it, or other things become more important than faith in God. Then the initial euphoria will quickly sprout but also quickly wither. These are then the experiences of people like the seeds that fall under the thorns. They want to move on somehow, but there are so many worries, other people, problems or new situations that are so distressing to these people that they can no longer grow. Finally, as the Bible says, there are seeds that fall on good fields. That is you! That's me! Even though we sometimes experience falling on rocks or thorns, we are still good seeds. We are allowed to bear fruit. It doesn't have to be a hundredfold – maybe thirtyfold is enough? Sixtyfold? We will succeed in this.

**Be the Leaven**

Leaven - that is the subject of our reflection today. (Mt 13: 33-34). Jesus told us that the kingdom of heaven should be like leaven. He said a woman took some leaven and mixed it with three measures of wheat flour. The leaven was in the flour the whole night. Then, behold, the next day all three measures of wheat flour were leavened and ready for baking. The kingdom of heaven is like leaven. What is that supposed to mean? The leaven is only a small part. And that little part turns all of the flour into leaven. It has a wonderful result that all of the flour is acidified. Jesus compares us all to leaven. Even if there is nowhere life, no peace and no community; if you and I work for it, then we are like leaven. The leaven adds flavor to the food.

Otherwise everything will be boring and tasteless. The leaven gives the whole flour and bread the desired taste.

What can we do to make our society like leaven? Many people have worked for the kingdom of God before us, and there will be some after us who are leaven for our society. A church doesn't always have to show what it is. It just has to be there, just with this belief in God - with a deep belief! If you have this belief, that's enough. My ancestors or your ancestors lived this belief. You were the leaven. Little by little it went on, step by step. So we can ask ourselves: Am I like leaven like my ancestors? And what kind of sourdough am I? Can I offer "taste"? Or am I "tasteless" myself? Can I offer life or am I "lifeless" in myself? What am I?

# 19. PRAYER

*"(Yahweh) May my prayer be like incense in your
presence, my uplifted hands like the evening sacrifice"
(Ps 141:2).*

## What is Prayer?

Gn 4:26: "This man was the first to invoke the name Yahweh".
- People began to call God by his personal name, Yahweh,
which is given in the Bible as the Lord. This is part of the Yahwist
tradition. The Elohistic and priestly traditions later place the
revelation of the divine name in the Mosaic period
(Ex 3:13-14, 6:2). This seems to be the origin of the prayer.

Prayer, simply defined, is a dialogue between man and God.
Invocation of the heart and soul to almighty God. A spiritual
communication with God of worship in supplications,
adoration, thanksgiving, confession, petitions, etc. Prayer is
performed by individuals, in groups and communities,
institutions, places of worship and in families, etc. The best
prayer for Christians is what Jesus He taught us himself: "The
Our Father" (Mt 6:9-15). Prayer helps us to go nearer to God,
and prayer is the greatest force in the world.

## When / how do you Pray?

This can be a good interpretation of prayer. What is a prayer?
Or when and under what circumstances do we really pray?
Prayer is not something that just happens when we kneel down,
fold our hands, close our eyes and focus and expect things
from God that meet our expectations and desires. But
thinking positively and wishing well to others is a real prayer.
When you sincerely pray for a friend or relative for their good,

that is a real prayer. When you hug a friend. Shake hands, pat on the shoulder as a gesture of consolation and comfort in times of pain and sadness - it's a prayer. When you cook something tasty and healthy for your family, friends or a sick person to nourish and heal - there is a prayer in these dishes. When we send away our neighbours and loved ones and tell them, "Have a good trip," "Take care of yourself," "Be safe," etc., that is a prayer. As you help someone in need by giving your time and energy, pray. When you forgive someone with all your heart, that is a great prayer.

Prayer is a vibration, a feeling, a thought. Prayer is the voice of love, friendship, genuine relationship. Prayer is an expression of your silent being. So keep praying always, in every deed and moment of your life. By this, your whole life becomes a life of prayer. Life is prayer and prayer is life. "In all your prayer and entreaty keep praying in the Spirit on every possible occasion" (Eph 6:18).

## "The message of Pope Francis on prayer - February 2021

In essence, everything becomes part of that dialogue with God (prayer). Every joy becomes a reason for praise. Every process is an opportunity to seek help.

According to the Pope, prayer "is always alive in life like the embers of the fire. Even when the mouth does not speak, the heart speaks."

The Pope also said: "Do not look for the perfect moment to pray. We can pray anytime. We can pray with words or in silence. Don't pray for tomorrow, pray for today. Already today Jesus will really come to us.

## "Ask, Seek, Knock"

"Ask, and it will be given to you; search, and you will find; knock, and the door will be opened to you" (Mt 7:7). He did not stop with that. To affirm his statement He also cites certain examples "Is there anyone among you who would hand his son a stone when he asked for bread? Or would hand him a snake when he asked for a fish? If you, then, evil as you are know how to give your children what is good, how much more will your Father in heaven give good things to those who ask him." What a definite assurance! It is not enough that we deepen our faith in God and turn to God for all our good and bad desires and needs, not only to ask him but also to thank him for his tremendous compassion and unconditional love.

Prayer and Christianity are inseparable. From waking up in the morning to the time we retire to bed, there is a prayer for every activity of ours. Through prayer we receive strength to meet the challenges of the world, to conquer in times of tests and trials, we get healing from diseases, pains, get solution for our problems and struggles of life.

The assurance of Jesus for prayer is found in all the four Gospels.

"I tell you, therefore, everything you ask and pray for, believe that you have it already, and it will be yours" (Mk 11:24)

"Then he told them a parable about the need to pray continually and never lose heart" (Lk 18:1).

Jesus told us that prayers should be a continuous process. If an intention, which is genuine, is asked for repeatedly would never go unanswered. He spoke about a persistent widow who won the heart of a judge, who neither had fear of God nor had any respect to human beings. Yet he rendered justice to the widow because of her persistent prayer.

"Until now you have not asked anything in my name; ask and you will receive, and so your joy may be complete" (Jn 16:24).

## According to His Will

Once, three trees in a forest prayed to the Lord expressing their wish for what they should become in life. The first wanted to become a king's throne in the palace. The second wanted to become a ship and go around the world in the sea. The third wanted to be made into a beautiful piece of jewelry or an idol that should be adored and cherished by people. Time passed. The first tree was bought by a shepherd from Bethlehem, who built a nativity scene out of it and kept it in his sheepfold. After a few years a man from Galilee took the second tree and gave it to the carpenter to build a boat to float in the Sea of Galilee. After a few more years, the Roman soldiers came and took the third tree to make a cross to crucify the criminals. All three trees wept for their misery day in and day out. Their dreams were shattered. They wanted to occupy high positions in their lives, but now they were a manger in a sheepfold, a boat on the Sea of Galilee, a cross in the House of Commons that was used to store the tools used to punish the criminals.

But one day a couple came to the sheepfold. The woman was pregnant. She gave birth in the sheepfold and the woman put the child in the manger. Angels from heaven perished at the manger. Chants of glory and praise were sung; heavenly music and heavenly light adorned the manger. From the an-gels' messages to their masters, the shepherds, the manger learned that the child lying in it was the expected Messiah and the Lord. There was no limit to his joy. The inns that closed their doors to the couple had now disappeared. But the sheepfold and the crib that housed it are still preserved and people all over the world come and love this place. Yes, they were Mary and Joseph who happened to be staying in the Bethlehem sheepfold. Jesus was born there and placed in the manger. The crib has understood its worth.

The boat in Galilee was usually out at sea and the fisher men used it to catch the fish. Once a man with a glowing face came and got into the boat. Lots of people were running around the place. He spoke beautiful things that made the boat very happy and comforted. Many miracles happened in this place. The boat was amazed to see and it began to think that this person sitting in the boat was no ordinary person. Storms and high waves were not known to this boat. Sometimes it was badly damaged and sometimes minor damage was done. Once the same person traveled along the Sea of Galilee with his disciples in this boat. Suddenly there was a storm and the sea turned rough. The disciples screamed in fear. But the man who was sleeping in the boat got up and said something. The sea became calm immediately. Such a miracle had never happened before in the life of this boat. Soon the boat realized that he was the Messiah, the Son of Man.

One day the cross that was in the basement was taken out. It wept bitterly. It wanted to be worshiped and adorned and held in high places, but now some criminal would die on it. What a misfortune. It thought its prayers were in vain. The cross was placed in the hands of a man named Jesus. The moment he touched the cross felt great. It assumed that the person who carried the cross was neither an ordinary person nor a criminal who deserved such punishment. The moment of Jesus' death made the cross tremble. The earth shook. Rocks were split. Tombs were opened and the dead came to life. The centurion shouted, "Verily this was the Son of God." The cross now clearly understood that the person who carried it was the true God.

Overall, we can see that the prayers of all three trees, just not to their expectations were answered in God's way. If the wish of the first tree for his prayer had been granted, the throne would have been thrown away or burned if the king who sat on it had been defeated or died. If the wish of the second tree had been granted, the ship would have been destroyed or disappeared over time. But the boat that Jesus traveled in was recorded in the Bible and people will read about the boat until the end of time. If the wish of the third tree, which it prayed for, had been granted, it would have been kept in a display case or room for some time. If a new art of ornament or a new form of idol had come on the market, the old would have been abandoned and displaced. But the cross - it has been venerated ever since. And it's a permanent symbol of Christianity. The cross and Christianity cannot be separated.

Therefore, our prayers should be "Your will be done". God's ways are not our ways. We are limited in time and space. We are limited. But God's view is limitless, endless.

**Whose father is He?**

Once a rich man invited a poor man to have dinner in his house. He wanted the poor man to come in through the back door. He made him sit on the floor. Then he brought food on a plate and held it up to the poor man. When the poor man wanted to eat, the rich man said: "Wait first, we pray, then you can eat". The poor man also folded his hands and was ready to pray with him. The rich man started "Our Heavenly Father". The poor man repeated "Your Heavenly Father". The rich man corrected him and corrected him: "Our Father". The poor man repeated the same mistake again and said "Your father". The rich man was upset. He said to him: "Why do you keep making the same mistake? Why do you say your father instead of our father?" The poor man said, "Lord, I pray right. If I also say Our Father, then we will both be children of the same father. If we are children of the same father, you would not have asked me to come in through the back door. You would have asked me through kicking in the front door and sitting the other at the dining table and we would both have taken our meal plates, we would have sat down next to each other and eaten. But you didn't do any of that. You did the opposite. Then how can I do it Call our father?" The rich man was shocked to hear the poor man's explanation, which seemed absolutely right to him.

We pray the same prayer every day. When we pray in church, we call everyone with one voice and say "Our Father". But when we come out of the church, do we still feel that oneness - as children of the same father? We should think about it. There should never be a gap between what we pray and what we live.

## Whose prayer would the Lord answer?

Once a missionary walked through a thick forest. A lion came by. The missionary was frightened. Immediately he knelt on the floor. He closed his eyes and began to pray to Jesus to help him in this critical situation. A few minutes passed. The missionary felt as if nothing had happened to him. So he slowly opened his eyes to see if the lion was gone or not. But to his surprise, the lion also knelt with closed eyes and lifted both of his legs and prayed. The missionary was so happy because he had evangelized the lion by example and praised the lion for his piety. Out of curiosity, he asked the lion what he was praying for. The lion asked him to be silent because he had not finished his prayer. A few minutes later the lion opened its mouth and said, "I thanked God profusely for giving me a very nice dinner. For God was sending me my food in the form of a strong human person like you." The missionary was on the verge of passing out and falling over.

Now is it up to us to ponder and see whose prayer the Lord would answer?

Is it the missionary's prayer? Is it the lion's prayer?

## Praying for Common Causes

Praying for others, especially in their hour of need, is one of the best practices. When wars and natural disasters affect the harmonious life of people around the world or in any part of the world, prayers can be addressed to God to intervene in the lives of suffering humanity and help restore normalcy. For the sick, the abandoned, the orphans and the oppressed, prayers for their well-being can be said with generous hearts. For all countries, for all people who are confronted with extraordinary things, crisis prayers can be addressed to God in order to free them from their present calamity. Today, by the time of the pandemic, the whole world is faced with the coronavirus and prayers can be offered not only for the sick but also for those who care for them - the doctors, the nurses, the volunteers and everyone who cares Help the sick at home and in the neighbourhood directly. Not only do such prayers produce great results, but they shower abundant graces on those generous, selfless people who waste their precious time and energy praying for others rather than putting their own requests and wishes in the presence of the Lord.

## Prayer of the Two

This Sunday we celebrate World Mission Sunday. A small fraction of the population fights for its identity, people who make up barely 10%, say, "We are the old Christianity! Christianity has lived here for 2000 years, and we want to live and survive in this country."

This Sunday the Gospel text is about two men standing in the temple to pray. They were a Pharisee and a Tax Collector. "The Pharisee stood there and said this prayer to himself, "I thank you, God, that I am not grasping, unjust, adulterous like everyone else, and particularly that I am not like this tax collector here. I fast twice a week; I pay tithes on all I get." The tax collector stood some distance away, not daring even to raise his eyes to heaven; but he beat his breast and said, "God, be merciful to me, a sinner." This man, I tell you, went home again justified; the other did not. For everyone who raises himself up will be humbled, but anyone who humbles himself will be raised up" (Lk 18:9-14).

Of the two prayers, the Pharisee's prayer was self- boasting, critical of others especially of the tax collector. The danger of spiritual pride is very real in the life of those who stand out from ordinary people. In prayer the self- righteous Pharisee spoke about himself. He cataloged his meritorious deeds, initially negative, that he did not have the vices that are common to other people. His boasting peaked when he compared himself to "that tax collector". Then he boasted positively by writing out his merits in the form of works of supererogation, by doing more than the law requires. Although the law did not require two fasts a week, he kept it. Although the law required the tithe to produce agricultural products (Deuteronomy 14: 22-23), he paid tithe of all his forms of income. This is how the Pharisee justified himself before God. It is not God but himself who has "justified" himself. He relied on himself and not on God's righteousness. The tax collector, on the other hand, was in contrast to the Pharisee. He recognized his own sinfulness. With contrite heart he spoke about his unworthiness to stand before the presence of God at all. He relied on God's mercy and forgiveness. His prayer was pleasing to God and he returned a person who was filled with God's grace, freed from God's forgiven sins. Nor should we justify ourselves in prayer. That is God's work. We must always stand before him humbly and contrite. There is no point in boasting in the presence of God, who sees every moment and every movement of our whole life.

## Praying is not just Asking

The church in Leimen, like all churches in the world, stands here as a place for prayers. I have just entered the church to pray. A woman is already here and I ask her, "What is your prayer to God now?" She replied " For me, prayer means being close to Jesus. And the presence of Jesus is fully felt by me in the Church. His closeness is given to us by the Holy Eucharist, but also in silent adoration". Saint Theresia of Gerhardingen said: "Prayer is for man like water for a fish. You can't stop praying, you pray fervently and always. And such a man is always close to Christ".

Praying is not old-fashioned, but it is existential. People come to pray, be it in a church, a mosque, or a synagogue, to be close to God. Prayer should come from the heart. It should connect our whole existence with God. It is not like a request to always ask God about one thing or the other. He is like the Father in knowing our needs and fulfilling us as if we were essentially needed. He fills us with all graces and leads according to His will. Prayer is a dialogue with God. You come into contact with your Creator, with your whole life and with all your strength. Prayer also means thanking the Lord for the life we have received and which we can enjoy. We could thank the Lord for everything that happens in our lives. And we praise

God's wonderful creation. Our churches are open to everyone. Eucharist means to be close to the Lord. Come to church and spend time in prayer. Or sit still and look at Jesus in the tabernacle and hear what He says in your heart. This type of meditative and silent prayer experience would definitely give the soul a freshness, peace and bliss that words cannot describe. It is beyond description and imagination.

# 20. QUIET / SILENCE

*"There was silence in heaven for about half an hour"*
*(Rev 8:1).*

## Theophany in Silence

Theophany means manifestation of God or appearance of God to man. We learn from Scripture that various biblical person-alities have experienced theophany. On many an occasion they experienced theophany or in silence. In the lines below we can see some biblical personalities who experienced how God quietly revealed to them in silence.

• Hagar, Sarai's pregnant slave, had to leave home because of the mistreatment of Sarai. She was wandering around in a desert in spring. The desert is a place known for its silence. There the angel of Yahweh appeared and asked them to return home. The angel also revealed the name of the child who was to be born to her as Ishmael (which means God hear or God hears) with the assurance that her descendants will be too numerous to count (Ishmael's descendants are Arabs the desert). Hagar gave a name to Yahweh, who spoke to her: "You are el Roi (El Roi means God of vision)" (Gn 16:7-13).

• When Moses was tending his father-in-law Jethro's flock, he came to Mount Horeb, the mountain of God. There he had the Theophany experience in the midst of a burning bush. Of course a mountain top is always silent. There was a deep silence there. When God appeared to Moses, it was in a silent atmosphere He revealed to him (Ex 3).

Elijah's experience – Elijah fled to save his life and reached Mount Horeb, the mountain of God. There he was told: "Go out and stand on the mountain before Yahweh". Elijah was there as he was told, waiting for God to visit him. At that time a mighty hurricane split the mountain. But the Lord was not there. There was an earthquake after the hurricane. God wasn't there when the earthquake occurred. There was a great fire, but the Lord was not in the middle of the fire. After the fire there was a low murmur and Yahweh was there. Elijah covered his face and went and stood at the entrance to the cave in the mountain. Then a voice spoke to the prophet. (1 K 19:9-14).

Even now God speaks to us in silence; He lives in us and with a soft voice he guides us and reveals himself to us. If we only believe in him and listen to him, we can recognize him and always live in his presence and be protected and blessed by him. Instead of always being surrounded by noises and unwanted thoughts, we should create a space of silence for Him to talk to. That would make our life on earth worth living.

## More beautiful through Silence

Do you want to be beautiful? I have a suggestion for you; just look at the lilies or the flowers in the fields. In spring you can see that the flowers are blooming everywhere. It's wonderful to just look at them. Why are they so beautiful? A philosopher and theologian of the Catholic Church once said: "Because they can be silent. Nature is always silent; therefore there is also day and night: at night nature is silent. And during the day the sun comes out and the birds start to sing. But they are silent. And that's why they're beautiful. We are amazed. "(From: Sören Kierkegaard: The Lilies in the Field - Three Confessions). But for us humans the opposite applies: We have to make cosmetics. We use many things to make ourselves beautiful. There are different ways of making ourselves more beautiful. We don't really need any of this if we can be silent.

In the Gospel of John we read that Jesus visited his friends Lazarus, Martha and Mary. Martha was very keen to offer the guest Jesus the best food. She was very busy. But her sister Mary just sat at the feet of Jesus. She just listened to what Jesus said. Martha was very angry about that. She couldn't understand why Maria was acting like this, but wonderd why her own sister was not helping her. Then she came to Jesus and said: "Lord, do you not care that my sister is leaving me to do the serving all by myself? Please tell her to help me" (cf. Lk 10:40). I think she was right, wasn't she? As a host, you have to do everything. You would do that too. But here something paradoxical comes to light" Martha, Martha,' he said, 'you worry and fret about so many things, and yet few are needed, indeed only one. It is Mary who has chosen the better part, and it is not to be taken from her" (cf. Lk 10:41 f.). How can we understand that? Quiet, going in, strengthening is very important - especially at a time when night turns into day, work at night, partying at night and sleeping during the day. It would be good to pause, to be silent and to listen to the word of God, or to other people who are close to our hearts; so that we can feel what God wants to tell us or what others want to tell us. We only have one mouth and two ears, which is a sign that we should hear more and speak less. Maybe we'll try it together in the next few days. Let's try it in this week.

## Feel God in Silence

I don't always have a good feeling about it. Sometimes I'm scared, sometimes I mourn. Sometimes I get desperate about why life is the way it is. One woman said that her husband left her when a wonderful event happened in her life. One man told me that he was very good at his studies. He then started a company. Then at some point everything broke. He wanted to rebuild everything and took out a lot of loans, but in the end he couldn't save the company. He almost became homeless. Even today he is not fit because his wife left him. A child told me that it was terrified of going to high school for some reason.

These experiences do not only apply to a few people in our time and in our world. Lots of people have problems. People long for change, rest, time out and so on. I also want to enjoy something in my life. But how do we find that? This requires wisdom and life experience. On the one hand, we experience the strain and tension of life; on the other hand, we hope for something better and more pleasant. But how do we find the way there to achieve this and also to find our inner peace? In Scripture we see how Elijah found his God (cf. 1 K 19:9,11-13). Interestingly, a storm passed Elijah, but God was not in it; after that there was an earthquake, but God was not perceptible in it, then there was still a fire, but God was not in it either, but in the quiet murmuring that followed he recognized God.

This Elijah story gives me new insights: I can't find my peace even on vacation if I don't get involved with God, if I don't find my God, who wants to give me peace. I have to concentrate consciously so that I can really rest. Not everyone who lies somewhere on the beach will find peace, but those who really look inside and listen to God what he wants to say to them - these people experience much more inner peace. We don't need to complain about anything, we just hear what God wants to tell us individually. - I look for an undisturbed place that is comfortable for me. I sit there for half an hour and rest - not alone, but with God. This is how I get double the peace, double vision and double the strength for my life.

**Take a little Rest**

Now is the time when many of you want to go on vacation and have a good rest and relax. Rest is an important part of our life. One calculation says that a person who is 80 years old spends 25-30 years sleeping. Almost one third of life is spent sleeping and resting. Rest is very important to us humans. Jesus also said: "Those who are afflicted and have to bear heavy burdens come to me, I will give you peace". And he also always took time to rest, also together with his disciples. Does that mean only sleep? It's much more than just what we see in Jesus, it means being alone with me, with myself. Not to get bogged down in thoughts and programs, in obligations, but to come to yourself. We spend our whole lives doing other things, being there for others, achieving goals. Rest means to come to God, to be thankful, to feel the goodness of God and also to experience and enjoy the goodness of people. I as a person need love. I am loved and when I am loved I feel better. Rest is a time when I discover the goodness of God and the people in my life so that I can receive strength and joy. God wants us to have peace, recharge our batteries, be happy and feel new strength. For we all are loved by God.

## Bear in Silence

The journey to Holy Week begins on Palm Sunday. We will learn from the Gospels in all worship services what this path meant for Jesus. He knew his life would end in a few days. I am particularly touched by the pain in his soul. The fact that people celebrating him and shouting Hosanna later shouted, "Crucify him!". I think it was a lot worse. I compare that to the situation today. People are afraid, especially the infected, the patients in the intensive care unit or the lonely people in quarantine. That is exactly what Jesus experienced. He too was afraid, felt abandoned and lonely, but he knew that his father was with him. Although Jesus asked for a moment of fear that this goblet should pass up to him, he put his life into the care of his father: not my will, but your will happen. And as

Jesus surrounded his pain is unique: he was silent. When people left him, he remained silent. When he was beaten, he was silent (Is 50:5-6, 53:7). Even before Pilatus he was silent, although he could have liberated himself with a word from death on the cross. Also at the height of his work and his life silence was the power source for him. Silence in the assurance that his father is there. This silence can reach God, in the silence we can connect with God, feel salvation.

So I do not talk about the silence of the graveyard, but about active silence in the knowledge that my body and my soul belong to God.

# 21. TRANSFIGURATION

*"I was gazing into the visions of the night, when I saw,
coming on the clouds of heaven, as it were a son of man.
He came to the One most venerable and was led into his
presence" (Dan 7:13).*

## The Specialty of the Feast of Transfiguration

Jesus revealed His divinity to three of His apostles namely
Peter, John and James on the top of a Hill, which is
traditionally known the Mount Tabor. This day is celebrated as
a Feast in the Catholic Church on 6th August of every year.
St. Thomas Aquinas refers this as "the greatest miracle
performed by our Lord Jesus Christ". This is one of the five
instances which were the turning points in the Gospels. The
rest of the four are Baptism of Jesus, Death of Jesus on the
Cross, Resurrection of Jesus and the Ascension of Christ. The
Church has attached great importance to the Transfiguration
of our Lord for 2-3 centuries AD. St. Jerome promoted this
with considerable efforts. In the 4th century AD, the Saints
Evagirius, Pontinus and Gregory of Nissa brought "Theology
of Lights" out of the transfiguration of our Lord. From the 9th
century AD, this festival is celebrated in the western church.
Pope Calistus announced in 1456 that the festival should be
celebrated in the Catholic Church on August 6th every year.

## Jesus on Mount Tabor

Today the Catholic Church celebrates the feast of the
"Transfiguration of the Lord". What does the transfiguration of
Jesus mean? Jesus took three of his disciples, Peter, James
and John, with him to Mount Tabor and transfigured himself in

their presence. This was an incredible event for the disciples. They were completely enveloped in the presence of God and His light. They would rather have stayed there to capture this wonderful experience. But at the same time, Jesus had to endure suffering, even to the point of death on the cross. Jesus experienced both: his confirmation as the Son of God, through which he shared in the glory of God, although he was human, but also what was to come. And later he also said: "Father, it is not my will be but yours may be done". We are dependent on other people, family, friends and our partner. If they would all leave us, it would be fatal. We need a sense of belonging. But beyond belonging to people, Jesus learns to belong to his Father and proclime that he is the Son of Almighty God. Even as a person in this world, he kept saying that he was the Son of God. We too can have this experience as children of God, because God also confirms to us again and again that we are his children. However, being children of God does not mean that we are only lucky; it can also be painful and bitter experiences. Jesus, as the Son of God, also suffered the painful death on the cross for our salvation. Before he suffered, he revealed his divinity to his disciples. But he accepted the Father's plan to suffer, to die, and to obtain eternal life through death. Suffering and pain have been transformed into the glory of the resurrection in which we can partake as children of God.

## Mountain Experience

The transfiguration of our Lord in a mountain is given in all three synoptic gospels. The disciples Jesus took with him were very close to him, Peter, John and James. We find it in Mt 16:1-9, with Mk in 9:2-13 and with Lk in 9:28-36. All three are talking about the same thing, but with a few small differences here and there. In all three Gospels the transfiguration takes place after Jesus proclaimed his suffering and death on the cross and his resurrection. The disciples could not break the idea that Jesus was going to die on the cross. Their expectations were in something else. He took these three close disciples and revealed his divinity on a mountain top. According to Mark, the Transfiguration is not only concerned with the teaching of Jesus about suffering and resurrection, it is also an anticipation of the resurrection and glory of Jesus as Messiah, Son of God (Mk 8:29, 9:27). He gives a special reference to the time "after six days" in Mk 9:2, which connects the Transfiguration with Peter's confession (Mk 8:27-30). Mark did not identify the location of the event (as a mountain). Matthew and Luke state that it took place on a mountain. For Mark who was the first evangelist to write the gospel, the event itself was important, not the location.

Jesus has transfigured himself before the eyes of his disciples, which means that Jesus' appearance has visibly changed. In the Gospel of Luke, the event occurs while praying to God. All three Gospels speak of the presence of Elijah and Moses talking to Jesus. Elijah stands for the prophets and Moses stands as the representative of the law. In Jesus both the prophets and the law symbolized the fulfillment in their presence. (Lk 24:27,44). In the Gospel of Matthew, when Jesus announced the suffering and death, Peter was angry and said that such things would never happen to him (Mt 16:22). Jesus got angry and scolded Peter by saying: "Get behind me, Satan" (Mt 16:23). During the transfiguration Peter desired that Jesus should remain in that divine glory forever. That was why he suggested making of three tents one for Jesus one for Elijah and one for Moses. He did not want to go down from the present state. It was comfortable and pleasant. But Jesus had to take up the Cross. That was why he came down to earth; that was the Will of his Father who sent Him. The transfiguration event affected all disciples, especially Peter, therefore Peter was able to keep it in his memory long after this event and convey it in 2 Pet 1:16-19 in his letter. As we reflect on this wonderful event in the lives of Jesus and three of his disciples, we should also share the wonderful experiences that the disciples had. Jesus is the Lord and God who is always present in our midst and if we just go to Tabor (we don't have to travel all the way to another country to climb Tabor, it is in our minds and in our hearts), we too can have the great experience these three students had there, here and now in our lives.

## Get to the Top

Right now I'm standing here in a field and looking at the blue sky. Do you also long for the top? Somehow it is anchored in us humans, this desire to get to the very top. You can see it in the mountaineers. It is acheiving the seemingly impossible, exceeding your own limits. On May 29th, 1943 Sir Hilary and his Nepalese Scherpas succeeded in conquering the 8848 m high Mount Everest and standing on the roof of the world, where there is hardly any oxygen left, where it is freezing cold, where many have already failed or lost their lives. And despite all the dangers, people want to get to the very top, they have the vision even higher, even higher.

The Bible reports that Jesus climbed Mount Tabor with three friends, to the top. And there these three men saw Jesus be-ing transfigured. A voice came out of a cloud and said: "This is my beloved Son, you shall listen to him". They experienced the presence of God and divinity in Jesus, who shone from within. This experience was so extraordinary, so special, so empowering. But they too had to descend from the mountain, like every climber, back to the ground, into everyday life. However, they have never forgotten this experience of pure joy. If we manage to listen to Jesus, he will take us all the way to the top. Whether in everyday life, at work, in our relationships, in the community or in the state. Together with Jesus we can do it.

## Experience of the three Men

Three men who had known him for three years went up a mountain with Jesus. And something fascinating happened: Jesus suddenly became very different from what they had known him to be. He was transfigured. They were so fascinated by it that they stayed with him. God does not sit far from us in heaven. He is here with us. He invites us to discover something fascinating in him every day: in his creation, with other people, every day.

If we do not lose this fascination, our life is fulfilled, in any situation. Let us only think of what fascinates us every day. In all this fascination we always can recognize the beauty, the divinity and the power of our God.

# 22. TRUE / TRUTH

*"Purchase truth — never sell it" (Prov 23:23).*

## The Message Pope Francis on Truth: (Lenten message 2021)

The Pope also spoke of the truth at the message of Lent: "Accepting and living the truth revealed in Christ means, first of all, opening our hearts to God's words."

## The Price of Telling the Truth

On this day we celebrate the feast of the beheading of John the Baptist. John the Baptist was accepted as a prophet in his days and was held in high regard by the people. He was a courageous person, he spoke the truth without fear. He was beheaded for speaking the truth and pointing out his sin in the face of the king.

Herod the king arrested John and put him in prison because of Herodias, his brother Philip's wife. For John told him: "It is not lawful for you to have her". Although Herod wanted to kill him, he was afraid of the people because they worshiped him as a prophet. But at a birthday party for Herod, the daughter of Herodias performed a dance in front of the guests and delighted Herod so much that he swore to give her everything she wanted. When asked by her mother, she said: "Give me John the Baptist's head, here, on a dish…" and had John beheaded in the prison" (Mt 14:6-11).

The above incident in the Bible shows us that people who lived after Jesus were killed because of their truthfulness to Jesus not only that but people who were contemporaries of Jesus were also put to death for telling the truth. Confessing the truth for God's sake has always been risky, even today. But that doesn't mean that one should avoid telling the truth and living it. That will definitely be rewarded in this world as well as in the next world. So holding on to the truth is always good.

## Loving in Fact and Truth

*"Our love must be not just words or mere talk, but some thing active and genuine" ( 1 Jn 3:18)*

A wonderful sentence from John's letter. It fits well with the development of North and South Korea. I was in Seoul, South Korea in 1989, and there were demonstrations and a great longing to reunite these two countries. But how many years had passed? And how far have they come?

Loving is a matter of the heart, It is not enough you find beautiful words for it. You must really to put it into practice. Every day, every second, our hearts work. When it stops working, we don't live anymore. So our love must be that it is in fact and truth. If I love someone, it must not just be lip service, but must be visible in the deeds.

We say often 'I love you' . But do we do it from the heart? Are we telling the truth? Love has its price. We have to cross our own limits. We cross them, as these two countries did for the first time.

Our world suffers from the fact that we are not always truthful in word and deed. Jesus set an example for us and is therefore an example for all people. John says in his letter that all people who see the Son of God in Jesus Christ will feel the Spirit and love because Jesus was born not only for a certain group, but for all of us, including Northern and Eastern Europeans South Korea.

## Testimony to the Truth

At present, the media is full of reports about rulers and people who have seized power after a revolution or the removal of rulers. The craze for more power is everywhere and clearly noticeable.

Jesus came into this world as the Messiah, the Redeemer of mankind. But the people did not recognize him as their savior.

In John's Gospel, Jesus stands before Pilate like a criminal and is called King of the Jews (cf. Jn 18:33-38; 19:12-16; 19- 22). Jesus had a motive, namely, to bear witness to the truth (cf. Jn 18:37). But the people did not recognize him (cf. Jn 1:10 f.). People expected something different from him. This led to the crucifixion and death of Jesus. Jesus was firm in his motto of bearing witness to the truth. That is why the church founded by Jesus still has this task today: to bear witness to the truth, to fulfill what Jesus taught through his disciples. The church should be the one who can testify to the truth. Only then we will be the Church of God.

# 23. UNCLEANNESS

*"It is the same with this people,' he said, 'the same with this nation, in my view - Yahweh declares - the same with everything they turn their hands to; and whatever they offer here is unclean" (Hag 2:14).*

## Clean and unclean: Old and New Testament Views

In the Old Testament there were are divisions as clean and unclean in many aspects of life - eating, other habits, ways of life and so on. The things that the Old Testament calls unclean (Hebrew word tame) are the opposite of things who were called clean, pure and holy. Impurity disqualified a person from worshiping in the temple. The emphasis was not on filth, but on God's definition of what is clean. Since the words clean and unclean also referred to animals, God used these categories to show which animals He intended to be sacrificed and eaten.

"Animals and foods were also divided into clean and unclean classes.The clean might be eaten the unclean were forbidden. Only clean animals might be offered to God as sacrifices" (Zondervan Expository Dictionary of Bible words 1991 p.169).

Aside from the rules and regulations prescribed to them, the Israelites also had "traditions of their elders," which included the regulations and practices added to the Law of Moses by the rabbis. All of these had to do with the ceremonial ablution (Halakha - Jewish law), which required that the water for the ritual washing of hands and feet and for bathing should of course be pure and unused. The

Israelites were not allowed to eat before bathing. They should also wash or bathe their hands and feet when they return from the market. They shouldn't eat what they brought back from the market right away. They should wash it first and only then were they allowed to use it for cooking or eating. There was also the ritual of washing of utensils. In Jer 2:22 the use of soap is mentioned in connection with the washing ritual.

Unclean in Scripture means "to be defiled, polluted, unhealthy, defilement of religious character, and moral or spiritual impurity". The word defilement describes a sinful and unfit condition (Is 6:5).The Old Testament distinguishes between what is clean and helpful or acceptable and lists unclean and unacceptable (Lev 10:10).

But the New Testament deals more with the spiritual application and lists uncleanness or moral defilement along with fornication and other sins as works of flesh (Gal 5:19-21).In the Gospels, "Unclean" describes those who were possessed with unclean spirits (devilish).Uncleanness in Gospels also mean sin and it says sin separates man from God. Because of Sins we are all like unclean things (Is 64:6) and believers are not called to uncleanness but to live in holiness (1 Th 4:7).We are not to yield our members to uncleanness but to righteousness and holiness (Rom 6:19). In the Book Acts of the Apostles Peter - who was hesitant to eat the unclean things that were shown to him in his vision - was advised to eat them (Act10:9-16). The Bible relates following this law to being holy and being like God. "You have been sanctified and have become holy because I am holy" (Lev 11:44)."To keep the commandments and laws of Yahweh, which I am laying down for you today for your own good" (Dt 10:13).

Jesus also spoke in this way (Mt 7:9-11).Through Prophet Isaiah, God declares that His thoughts and ways are different from our thoughts and ways (Is 55:8-9). The Leviticus priesthood was given the responsibility to teach the Israelites the difference between the holy and the unholy and to help them discern between the unclean and the clean (Ezk 44:23).

God declares, He that is holy and He wants us to be holy (Lev 20:7) as his sons and daughters (2 Cor 6:17-18). John 1:12 and 20:17 and many other scriptures confirm this concept. Our Father wants us all to be like Him - holy and pure.

The teaching about uncleanness arises from the concept of the holiness of God (Lv 11:44-45). It is in itself a miracle that freedom from uncleanness and guilt is possible through God's grace. Inner holiness and purity of heart are possible through the exercise of faith in God and in Christ's work of redemption and obedience to his truth.

**How Jesus saw Uncleanness**

It was not so important for Jesus and his disciples to pay attention to the external cleaning of their hands and to bathing before eating. This was viewed critically by the Pharisees and scribes. To this, Jesus gave an appropriate response, quoting that on the one hand they were breaking the Lord's commandment at will, but insisting on other commandments that were not so necessary. He also says that whatever people eat would never defile people but what comes out from the mind and mouth alone would defile a person - like envy, adultery, theft, false witnessing and blasphemy (Mt15:1-19; Mk 7:1-23).

# 24. VIRTUES

*"With this in view, do your utmost to support your faith with goodness, goodness with understanding" (2 Pet 1:5).*

## 500 Years of Reformation

500 years have passed since the establishment of the Evangelical Church. In Germany, Martin Luther was commemorated with a public holiday. What did we do? On this day we had a nice joint action under the motto "We are pulling together". Catholic and Protestant Christians jointly set a sign of unity. In 1517, 500 years ago, Luther published his 95 theses to reform the Roman Catholic Church. He wasn't the first to try this. Before him, attempts were made now and then, for political reasons, to separate from the Catholic Church. Unfortunately, for political reasons, people then suffered a lot and were killed because of these differences. I would be happy if we could escape a breakup. Luther and many other reformers were not concerned with dividing the church, but with correcting something else. I think they wanted to correct the church's mistakes. After 500 years of Reformation there is only one message: to look to Jesus Christ. Whether Orthodox, Catholic, Protestant or Free Church, there is only one message: to find unity in Jesus Christ. He wanted all to be united (Jn 17:21). In our western world especially, we cannot afford to neglect or forget Christ. For in Christ we are all one. And that's the message; that after 500 years of separation, we don't look at how different we are, but what unites us. Every person has his own house, his own apartment, but that does not mean that we are not brothers and sisters. This is our task for the next 500 years: to travel together, to show our

profile as Christians and to live. Today, it is more important than ever to show the society that we are one and contribute together to the well-being of all people, and thus to live Christ's legacy in our country.

## Do we have to be One?

Do we have to be one? Many countries in Europe no longer want to be member states of the European Union. If not all nations but at least many people from different countries. Do we have to be one? It is also difficult for the Catholics, Evangelical and Orthodox Churches to come together and to agree on a common ecumenism. Do we have to be one? Man, woman, family – to be together for such a long time, 30, 40 or 50 years? Do we really need to be one?

That is the theme in gospel ecumenism: that we should all be one. This was the high priestly prayer of Jesus. If we look at our past in Europe, it was a longing of the people during the terrible world war. They wanted to get back together. The longing for unity arose after the war, especially in the 1960s. And it was precisely at this time that the Catholic Church came with the Second Vatican Council, where on November 21, . . . . . . . . . . . . . . . . . . . . . *Unitatis Redintegratio,* the Church expressed the declaration that we should carry the soul of unity within us. Sometimes we even have to justify ourselves for wanting to be a unit. But there are also many politicians who are fighting to hold Europe together. And especially today, when we see Pope Francis accepting the Charlemagne Prize. Simply to show, that Europe should remain a common continent. There are always new and sometimes tense attempts to stick together.

In my opinion, this longing for unity should actually be present in every person. And if we want to relate all of this to the high priestly prayer of Jesus (Jn 17:21) namely that all should be one, we see that He begins the oneness with His Father. "As you, Father, and I are one, so shall all be one." Unity begins with God himself. He forms a unity with his Son, and this mystery of unity is to be conveyed to us. We should all be one too. Somehow we humans cannot do that. But I have a tip for you: unity in diversity. Only if all people, all cultures, languages and skin colors maintain their independence and still maintain unity with others, only then will we be successful. A narrow mix of denominations, nations, and peoples will never work. So we want to try to respect each other's differences and at the same time form a unity.

## Be Unusual

Be unusual - what does that mean to us? This is the teaching of Jesus Christ. He taught us this way of life, which should bring a comfortable life for God and others. In what way are we supposed to be unusual? In his famous Sermon on the Mount, Jesus made it clear how one could behave in unusual ways. In Mt 5:21-48 six examples of the behavior required of the Christian disciple are given. Each deals with a commandment of the law, preceded by: "You have heard that it was said to your ancestors or an equivalent formula, followed by Jesus' teaching in respect to that commandment "But I say to you" thus their designation as "an antithesis" Three of them accept the Mosaic law but extend or deepen it (21- 22, 27-28, 43-44) three reject it as a standard of conduct for the disciples (31-32, 33-37, 38-39).

**We can have a few examples explained to us.**

Mt 5:21-22 Teaching about Anger: "For I tell you, if your uprightness does not surpass that of the scribes and Pharisees, you will never get into the kingdom of Heaven. 'You have heard how it was said to our ancestors, You shall not kill; and if anyone does kill he must answer for it before the court. But I say this to you, anyone who is angry with a brother will answer for it before the court; anyone who calls a brother "Fool" will answer for it before the Sanhedrin; and anyone who calls him "Traitor" will answer for it in hell fire."

Anger is the motive behind murder, as the insulting epithets are steps that may lead to it. They as well as the deeds are all forbidden. (Raqa is an Aramaic word meaning "imbecile" or blockhead a term of abuse); So Jesus wants us not even to show our anger in words, not to speak of the deeds, which would end up in murder.

The following verses 23-24 also show another way. Usually repentance comes from the one who offended the other. But here the offended is asked to drop the sacrifice in front of the altar and go to whoever offended him to be reconciled before making a sacrifice to God. Mt 5:43-44. It is customary to love our neighbours and loved ones and also those who do us good. But Jesus shows us another way and He wants us to adopt unusual behavior. Loving an enemy is a tough exercise. But Jesus goes a few steps further and asks us to pray for our enemies. The Old Testament (Ps 139:19- 22) assumes that hating evil people is right and there is a nothing bad in hating a person who causes evil. That was probably the usual way of life back then. But Jesus changed this and He wants us to be unusual - He wants us to show mercy and compassion to the evildoer, that we love and pray for such people. For this he brings the example of his Holy Father, who makes the sun rise on the wicked and the good and lets the rain fall on the just and the unjust.

So, in order to become children of our Heavenly Father, we should all behave in unusual ways. Let us all "BE UNUSUAL" in our thoughts and actions.

## Pride versus Humility

Humility is one of the greatest virtues to take us closer to God. In order to accept one's own weaknesses and sinful ness, one needs humility. Only when a man can be humble can he accept his own weaknesses and sins. The Lord also says:"Anyone who raises himself up will be humbled, and anyone who humbles himself will be raised up." Humility is an often misunderstood word. Humility is an essential characteristic of Christian life, without which eternal life is impossible. Why is humility so important? It defeats the pride that is the root of all great sins committed. The Lord also wants us to learn humility from him in the gospel of Matthew (Mt 11:28-30). In the book of Proverbs we find many verses that teach this virtue (see 11:2, 15:33, 22:4).

Our first parents Adam and Eve succumbed to the pride of wanting to live without God. The sin of pride preceded disobedience. They wanted to be equal to God. If we made an honest effort to examine ourselves, we would surely find that we have often allowed pride to rule our lives in order to gain priority and get first place in everything. It only leads to egoism to always think only of ourselves and always and everywhere to look for a place of honour. St. Louis said: "A proud man is looking down on all things and people". Pride blinds our eyes to see the things or people in front of us. It only lets us see ourselves. That is the reality for most of us. But the reality is always difficult to accept. But if we accepted pride and turned it into humility, it would be to our advantage. Pride keeps us away from the truth about ourselves from realizing that we are

243

the creatures and that God is our Creator. Pride, the bad vice has a counter-virtue, which is humility. Every Christian should cultivate humility. Humility is truth. Knowing the truth is always good, and the truth always helps us.

Humility is the virtue that Mother Mary practised. She was full of humility when she said: "You see before you the Lord's servant, let it happen to me as you have said" (Lk 1:38) and surrendered herself to the Will of God.

John the Baptist humbly said:" "I baptise you with water, but someone is coming, who is more powerful than me, and I am not fit to undo the strap of his (Jesus') sandals" (Lk 3:16).

Jesus humbled himself and obeyed the will of the Father and took up the cross to meet a shameful death.

## A just world? 200 years after the birth of Karl Marx

Everyone has a bank account with more or less money in it, Nobody wants to lose it. Karl Marx celebrates his 200th birthday on May 5th. He was born on May 5, 1818. He was a great revolutionary who taught that all should have the right to wealth. He advocated that would be no more social differences. But this idea didn't last. So far, neither the socialist nor the capitalist form of government has succeeded in achieving a classless society. Originally this concept of equality comes from the Acts of the Apostles. It can be found in Acts 2:42-47. There we read about the life of the early Christian community, the believers in Jesus Christ.

"These remained faithful to the teaching of the apostles, to the brotherhood, to the breaking of bread and to the prayers. And everyone was filled with awe; the apostles worked many signs and miracles. And all who shared the faith owned everything in common; they sold their goods and possessions and distributed the proceeds among themselves according to what each one needed. Each day, with one heart, they regularly went to the Temple but met in their houses for the breaking of bread; they shared their food gladly and generously".

We live in a society where few have everything and many have nothing. The gap between rich and poor is widening. The Church has not been able to change this situation to this day. There is still a big difference between rich and poor. It's a shame on humanity. Despite all efforts to bridge the gap between rich and poor, the Church has not yet been able to achieve these goals. The dream of an egalitarian and just society has not yet come true.

How did the early Christians manage to give everything, to share everything they needed for their lives? Karl Marx would have been happy. The early Christians could do this because they had a different orientation in life. After Easter, they could no longer amass immense wealth or possess as many worldly goods as possible. They had a more important goal, namely to meet Jesus Christ. They awaited the Parousia - the second coming of Christ in their own lifetime. Easter transformed these first Christians. If Jesus is the goal, then one has no choice but to give up all of the worldly things, goods and treasures in order to obtain the greatest treasure in life instead. The life of early Christians should inspire and create change for Christians living today. So that we no longer remain anchored in our worldly goods but look beyond to reach the eternal world.

## Lots of Joy

Joy! Joy is actually part of being a Christian. If you are a Christian, then you can laugh with me, laugh with God. Why not? Our God gave us joy - a joy that makes us happy.

Joy - that is a mood that people really need. When we are very stressed, when we work a lot, when we have to endure a lot of tension, then we long for joy. Joy is a gift from heaven. When I've slept well, when I've had a good meal with my best friend, with my partner, when I've had a good time with my children or my family, then I feel joy. Joy - it does not come from outside, but from within. Joy is a gift from God.

That is why the Bible says: *"Always be joyful, then, in the Lord; I repeat, be joyful"* (Phil 4:4).

We humans live with different problems, with different faces in our life. Right now we see people wearing masks on television or at a parade: for example, one is a lion, one is a pig or a cow. These are also signs of how we are inside: We also live with different masks in our lives. Sometimes I'm like a pig, sometimes like a cow, sometimes like a bird. So we live in great tension. That is a good thing. Why not? We are not angels. We still have time to be an angel. In heaven we can definitely become an angel. In this world we still live in tension between different masks with different roles and different problems. But we must not forget one thing: to have joy in spite of everything, joy, because God, no matter what I am, loves me, loves you. Do you notice that?

## Common Ground

I am sitting here next to my chickens, which are very peaceful. These are our happy chickens in Leimen. There are already some who live together quite peacefully. They are not afraid of me and I am not afraid of them. There is some unity between us.

In the Gospel according to John, Jesus prays: "May they all be one, just as, Father, you are in me and I am in you, so that they also may be in us, so that the world may believe it was you who sent me. I have given them the glory you gave to me, that they may be one as we are one" (Jn 17:21-22).

It's something we can really think about. Unity - who doesn't want unity? We have great globalization, we could really think: the unity of the world. We have the European Union, a symbol of the unity of more than 27 countries in Europe. We have the unity of pastoral care and the unity of the various associations and groups. We have the unity of families. It is not for nothing that people go to their relatives and friends. They visit each other regularly because they want unity. But there are also people who don't like unity.

Anselm Grün, a great Benedictine priest and spiritual writer of the Catholic Church in Germany, gives us a hint: "The path of unity is not dogmatic, but the path of unity is mystical." This unity is only perfect if we are one with God. I want to "put myself in" God and I want to unfold "in Him". Only if I am one with God, if i agree with God, then I am also ready to take the others into me. This is a wonderful message from Christianity, otherwise it would simply be humanistic, otherwise it would only be political, otherwise it would only be social. But religious unity is that we human beings should be united with one God, that we find our identity in God, as Jesus said: "I have made your name known to them and will continue to make it known, so that the love with which you loved me may be in them, and so that I may be in them."(Jn 17:26).It's a long way, isn't it? In a time in which individualization is increasing very strongly, in which the elbow mentality is increasing strongly, we should make sure that we ourselves feel the need to be fulfilled by others and by God.

## Magnet of Love

Love is like a magnet. It attracts people, makes it easy for them to meet each other and to create peace, happiness and unity among themselves. We have seen so many times how a small magnet can easily attract the piece of iron. Even large junks can be easily attracted with this small magnet and even carried with the help of the magnet. Such a little thing! And when I have two magnets that attract each other, it's incredibly difficult to separate them. Love is something like that too. You notice it yourself when you are in love. Or when you have given your love to someone, and if you have really felt this love in you, because we are basically created out of love. We live for love and also die in love. That's why we are people of love. And we hear about it in the Scriptures when Jesus comes by and says: "Come with me, forever, whether that is a Peter or a John or an Andreas and he calls out: You, Peter, you, John, you, Andrew, come with me!"

Yes, that is the love of God. The love for God is something that grabs us and tells us: "Yes, I need you!" What is interesting, however, is that God's love differs in some ways from many of the love experiences we have in our lives. This love attracts us and leaves us with our freedom. God is not someone who says: I need you right away! He knows we belong to him. That at some point we will unite our soul, our spirit with him. But he will never oppose our personal freedom. This magnet directs the piece of metal and gives it its freedom.

But God doesn't wait. He will say to each of us: "Come to me". Have you ever felt the call of God in your heart? Did you experience his love for you? Or have you ever felt drawn to him? If you ever feel something like this, just say, Oh God, I love you too! Then you will feel how you are united with him in this wonderful feeling. Do we want to try this?

## We are all Members of one Body

Every person is a universe. If we find components in our body that have actually existed since the Big Bang, then we are components of this universe. The whole thing is in me too. In other words, I am part of the whole. But I am also a whole. This is confirmed by quantum theory in physics, this is confirmed by psychology, and this is also confirmed by religion. We are all part of the whole.

Paul talks about what the church should be like. A church is a wonderful image for a body with many members. A head, then the shoulders, then the stomach, also legs, toes, fingers, they all belong together to form one body. The head, shoulders, ribs, legs, all the organs of this whole body are related to one another. One really depends on the other. If we imagine all of this without a head, what would it be like?

The head is also self-sufficient in itself. My fingers don't think - but the head thinks. My fingers are now reaching for the microphone. But the head cannot do that. Every organ has a specific task to perform, and if everything works properly without any problems, then the whole body, the whole person, is fine. Paul wants to tell us that. We are not separate from each other. All situations, all persons, all living beings, all belong to the one. With the emergence of our Christian religion, there is unity as we see and live it here. It doesn't work without unity. As we see it with this skeleton, everything belongs together.

## I wish you Love

Love is a word that is often used in a very inflationary way. There are many ways to try to love, from childhood to death, people love. We love as a child, as a mother and father, as a teenager, as a boyfriend, girlfriend, spouse, husband, wife, as an elderly person, grandma, grandpa. So there are different types of love, but what is interesting is that love still smells like a withered rose. But love still exists. All of life is there to learn how to really love. There are different attempts. There are different experiences that we have had in our life.

Even when I live alone, I love. I can't live without love either. So what could real love look like? And Paul tried to report it in his letter to the Corinthians. 1 Corinthians 13th chapter describes the different dimensions, aspects and properties of love. At the beginning Paul said: "Though I command languages both human and angelic - if I speak without love, I am no more than a gong booming or a cymbal clashing" (1 Cor 13:1).

Next he said, "And though I have the power of prophecy, to penetrate all mysteries and knowledge, and though I have all the faith necessary to move mountains - if I am without love, I am nothing."

Knowing and being intelligent would be of no use to a man who does not know how to love. All his knowledge would be crap. He even talks about giving away everything, including his own life, and notes that if he did so without a loving heart it would be NOTHING. There should also be love in giving and not bragging. Bragging is only for self-growth, to increase one's pride, status in society, and that has nothing to do with love for God and for one's neighbour.

"Though I should give away to the poor all I possess, and even give up my body to be burned, if I am without love, it will do me no good whatever. Love is always patient and kind; love is never jealous; love is not boastful or conceited, it is never rude and never seeks its own advantage, it does not take offence or store up grievances. Love does not rejoice at wrongdoing, but finds its joy in the truth"(1 Cor 13:3-6).

If we loved so much it would be heaven. But it is often the case that we use or abuse for our own benefit. That we expect more from the people we love than they already do. We are often not merciful. We cannot forgive. We even punish people by withdrawing our love.

True love is easy to accept. Christianity is a religion of love. From the time of Jesus until today, it has been teaching love. If we live the love of our religion, we will have fulfilled what our religious leader wanted to acoomplish. He was a man of love. That's what he was born for, that's what he lived for, and that's why he died and rose again on the cross.

## Love your Enemies

Have you ever had enemies in your life or do you currently have an enemy? Do you have someone you don't want to contact, someone you stay away from because he or she talked badly about you, stole something from your did something bad to you? There are probably always people we consider our enemies. In private and publicly, Nations become enemies; ethnic groups hate each other; people who think differently from us become enemies. When does someone become my enemy? If I treat another person badly and feel hostile towards him / her, then he / she becomes my bitter enemy, whom I may not want to forgive and also do not want to forget what he / she said to me or did to me. Jesus said: love your enemies. What did he mean by that?

I think he meant by declaring someone to be my enemy, I make myself small. When someone hurts me, I tell them, "even though you did this to me, I like you, I forgive you and I don't take it to heart. Then he cannot become my enemy. This is what Jesus means when he speaks of loving your enemies. Or when he says if someone asks you to do something, do it twice more. If we think like this, we are as holy as God, who is always forgiving and kind and loves all people, including sinners.

## Overarching religious Concepts

Religions have always been a sign of their own demarcation. In the history of religions, many have tried to explain that their own religion is the best and that others are worthless. To this day there have been many wars and acts of violence because people postulate that their own religion is the only true one. There are several ways to believe in and worship God, and each one follows the path in which he was born, grew up and has since practiced as his own religion in which he finds comfort and satisfaction. There is a concept of "inclusivism", which means that a religion can say, "I have the truth, but this fundamental truth is also found in all other religions. Therefore every religion is in a certain sense part of my religion."

The pluralistic religions like Hinduism say: Even if you are a Christian, you are also a Hindu, because Jesus Christ is not an opponent of Hinduism and his resurrection is tantamount to a new birth. The exclusivist trend, on the other hand, claims to be the only true religion, there is no other. She is convinced that I have to fight against all people who disagree with my religion or who accept it, the so-called unbelievers. All who do not belong to me and my religion are therefore against me.

The pluralistic belief unites all religions like a stew: one can be born a Christian, marry in a synagogue, be buried like a Buddhist; Everything is compatible. But there is something missing in everything: where is the  individual? The reading from the Old Testament says: My house has many rooms. It should be a house for the prayer of all people. Interesting. 2000 years ago it was the realization that every place of worship should be there for everyone, regardless of culture or religion. Man is important. Every religion can and should show its own depth, but never exclude it. And that would be a wonderful concept that we urgently need in our time.

## Use Talents correctly

Who are you? Who am I? Do you remember? You are a child of god! We are children of God because Jesus gave us this power. We are children of God! Today I am leading you to think: what can you do? Do you have talents? Do you enjoy doing something in particular? Or which gift have you received undeservedly: a talent or a charisma? The apostle Paul wrote the following wonderful text that I would like to read to you: "There are many different gifts, but it is always the same Spirit; there are many different ways of serving, but it is always the same Lord. There are many different forms of activity, but in everybody it is the same God who is at work in them all. The particular manifestation of the Spirit granted to each one is to be used for the general good. To one is given from the Spirit the gift of utterance expressing wisdom; to another the gift of utterance expressing knowledge, in accordance with the same Spirit; to another, faith, from the same Spirit; and to another, the gifts of healing, through this one Spirit; to another, the working of miracles; to another, prophecy; to another, the power of distinguishing spirits; to one, the gift of different tongues and to another, the interpretation of tongues. But at work in all these is one and the same Spirit, distributing them at will to each individual" (1Cor 12:4-11).

In other words, you and I have received one, and perhaps even more, gifts and charisms. They are all given by only one spirit.

Nowadays there are people who have more than just one job in their life. You do a job for five years. Then later, you try to learn something else. Then you do something else again or you don't just work for one employer. You change jobs. This is commonplace in today's society. People have different talents, different expectations, different challenges. But these challenges shape a person. However, we must not forget the following: We do all this through our individual talents, through study and through the knowledge we have gained in our lives. But the root of everything is the gift of the Spirit. One Spirit gives each of us what we need. Are we aware of this? Are you aware that you received your gifts and talents from this one spirit? Our gifts and talents have one goal: It's not about making myself more important, more popular or richer in any way, but about using these talents for others. They are designed to benefit other people. Many people, but one spirit, many people, many thoughts, but one God - One God, He brings us together. Maybe you have a thing or two that you want to use for others. Talk to someone! Find ways in which your gifts can unfold even further and bring joy and spiritual wealth to you and our society!

# 25. WHO, WHERE AND HOW ARE YOU?

*"For my house will be called a house of prayer for all peoples" (Is 56:6-7).*

## The World is a House for all People

To be honest, I am very sad to hear what is going on in this world right now: so many conflicts, so many wars, so many deaths. I was recently told by someone that the world may never have seen so many conflicts. It has been counted how many conflicts there are currently in this world, of which we know: There are over 400 conflicts in different countries on earth - small and large! Many conflicts are unknown to us, especially what is happening in African countries and the Middle East. And one wonders whether this world is really a house for all peoples. Is that so? Can we even have a world in which we can live comfortably? We only live in this world for a few years! Why do we destroy the others? Why is one or the other person not important to us, why do some even have to live as refugees? Is the world really a house for everyone? If this house is to stand, as God says in the vision, then the law must be kept and righteousness done (Is 56:1). Yes, every human being, every living being has the right to live, no matter where. I didn't choose to be born in India, in Tamil Nadu. But I was born there. Nor did any person choose to be born here or anywhere else. I am a citizen of the world, I am allowed to live in this world. If I work and contribute to the good of the country I live in, why should not I be ? I have the right to live. And that applies to everyone in this world. Obey the Law and Bring Justice! This is a clear invitation from the God of Jews and

Christians, but also from people of all other religions. I am ashamed when I keep hearing that religions cause division. It can be that religions are very "sensitive" in many things and wars arise as a result. But that's only superficial. In the background, the lust for power of many people - the lust for power of the politicians, the lust for power of the people who want everything for themselves - plays an important role. If we look closely at all of the wars, we find that they are about something other than religion itself. The faith of Christians clearly states that we should uphold human rights, develop the uniqueness of each individual, respect human dignity and bring justice to the whole world. There is no other way! Otherwise there is no religion! We can only be religious in this way. If we do that, this world will be a home for all people. The Church has already started doing it. Everyone is allowed to be here. All people flock to different places of pilgrimage in the Church because they just feel at home. If that is possible here, why not in politics? Why not in business? Obey the law and bring justice! If we do that, Heaven will be here with us.

## Beloved child of God

I want to ask you: who are you? When I ask such a question, you may say, "I am a teacher." "I'm an official." "I'm a construction worker." "I work in a large or small company." "I'm a social worker." "I'm a consultant." Or: "I am a politician. I determine a lot." "I am a priest, pastor, parish clerk." We'll say all of that. Perhaps we can also give the following answer: "I belong to a farming family." Or "I belong to a noble family." So I will always give an answer regarding my merit and the merit of my family. Who are you? Who are you? I take what I have or what my family did as a mark of identify. That's all? Who are you? Who are you? You are even more! You are than that more! This is the theme of the Gospel according to St. Luke (Lk 3: 15-16:

21- 22), in which Jesus is told what he is:"You are my Son; today have I fathered you"(Lk 3:22).There were also various questions and answers about himself in the life of Jesus. Pilate asked him: "Are you the king of the Jews"(Jn 18:33)? Or after a healing, an evil spirit said: "I know who you are: the Holy One of God"(Mk 1:24). Peter also said:" You are the Christ, the Son of the living God"(Mt 16:16). In all these conversations with people, Jesus gave an answer: "It is you who say that I am a king" (Jn 18:37),or "Be quiet!" (Mk 1:25). And: "Then he gave the disciples strict orders not to say to anyone that he was the Christ" (Mt 16:20). Only in this one case - at the Baptism of Jesus on the Jordan, Jesus did not say anything when he received this promise from His Father, you are my beloved Son.

This is what I want to share with you today: You are a beloved son, you are a beloved daughter of God! This is the greatest gift we can get as Christians. I am a beloved son of God, a beloved daughter of God. During Catholic baptism, the priest says: The white robe should be a sign for you that you were born again in baptism and that you have put on Christ. - Our winter landscape shows a different colour, a different cover is possible. Every Christian receives the white colour as clothing at baptism, as a sign of his new birth, as confirmation that he has become a child of God. Do you feel that who are you? You are a beloved son / daughter of God. A beautiful Sunday!

## Courage - Arrogance – Humility

Courage - arrogance - humility. These are words that can be viewed with clarity in the passage in Luke's Gospel (Lk 14:1-11). "Now it happened that on a Sabbath day he had gone to share a meal in the house of one of the leading Pharisees;

and they watched him closely. Now there in front of him was a man with dropsy, and Jesus addressed the lawyers and Pharisees with the words, 'Is it against the law to cure someone on the Sabbath? But they remained silent, so he took the man and cured him and sent him away. Then he said to them, 'Which of you here, if his son falls into a well, or his ox, will not pull him out on a Sabbath day without any hesitation?' And to this they could find no answer. He then told the guests a parable, because he had noticed how they vied for places of honour. He said this, 'When someone invites you to a wedding feast, do not take your seat in the place of honour. A more distinguished person than you may have been invited, and the person who invited you both may come and say, "Give up your place to this man." And then, to your embarrassment, you will have to go and take the lowest place. No; when you are a guest, make your way to the lowest place and sit there, so that, when your host comes, he may say, "My friend, move up higher." Then, everyone with you at the table will see you honoured. For everyone who raises himself up will be humbled, and the one who humbles himself will be raised up" (Lk 14:1-11).

The advice that Jesus gave his fellow guests and the host as part of the festive Sabbath meal was described as a parable by Luke the evangelist. Jesus indirectly admonished his disciples to behave correctly towards others. Here Jesus uses a familiar scene that provides insight into proper table etiquette to convey religious advice. Jesus' counsel came after seeing the manipulation of the guests who wanted to occupy the places of honour with selfish motives at the banquet. Such people were humiliated by the host when the person who was higher in their standing than the one who had taken the place of honour entered the banquet hall and the man who had taken that place before was asked to leave the place of honour to him to hand over to the arrived. Just then he would be forced to move to a lower place, which would put him to shame. At the same time, Jesus also pointed out that the person who had humbled himself and taken the lowest place would be rewarded. If this should be the most dignified . person, then he would be personally brought to the place of honour by the host. This would bring honour and fame to this man in the midst of the guests gathered there. So Jesus wants to show us that we should be humble.

Humility is bitter for most people. The philosopher Nietzsche says, "Humility is one of the dangerous, defamatory ideals behind which cowardice and weakness, i.e. forgiveness, hide in God." For Hitler, humility was the greatest evil of the German people. Humility is difficult for such people. But what is humility? Humility is the realization that I am not the one who is higher or superior, but that there is someone or something above me, i.e. God or other persons in office or in society. I should accept this truth without hesitation. In my own way, I can honour God or I am ready to give up the place to the really higher-ranking ones. Humility is the willingness to take the lowest place, it is something creative that I can give the other the place and at the same time feel that I am not losing anything. This would allow the humble person not to destroy himself with his pride and arrogance. The moment I am haughty or arrogant, I am sure to be discarded. Humility is great. Pope John XXIII also wrote: "My humble and now long life has developed like a knob under the sign of simplicity and purity. I don't mind acknowledging and repeating that I am nothing and that nothing is considered pure nothingness. The Lord made me to be born of poor parents and I remember my life to this day as it is". Humility, even if it's difficult, makes everything even easier, bigger. It is encouraging to note that our Pope

Francis, who met the leaders of the war-prone countries of Sudan that had signed a peace accord, urged the leaders to remain in peace. He asked them to do this in a very humble way. He asked them to address him as their brother and also asked them whole- heartedly to remain united and avoid war. He said there could be problems, but they could be solved by staying together in the office and not going to war. After saying this, the Pope bowed to each leader and kissed their feet, which no leader of the papal office had dared to do before. This is the greatest gesture of humility the Pope showed in front of so many bishops, cardinals and other dignitaries at the time. He then simply resembled Christ in his words and deeds. If he can, why can't we?

## Lazarus and the rich man - Concern for Others

Let us today reflect on the beautiful parable of Jesus, found in the Gospel according to St. Luke. It is about a poor man named Lazarus and a rich man. A well-known famous parable.

"There was a rich man who used to dress in purple and fine linen and feast magnificently every day. And at his gate there used to lie a poor man called Lazarus, covered with sores, who longed to fill himself with what fell from the rich man's table. Even dogs came and licked his sores. Now it happened that the poor man died and was carried away by the angels into Abraham's embrace. The rich man also died and was buried. 'In his torment in Hades he looked up and saw Abraham a long way off with Lazarus in his embrace. So he cried out, "Father Abraham, pity me and send Lazarus to dip the tip of his finger in water and cool my tongue, for I am in agony in these flames." Abraham said, "My son, remember that during your life you had your fill of good things, just as Lazarus his fill of bad. Now he is being comforted here while you are in agony. But that is not all: between us and you a great gulf has been fixed, to prevent those who want to cross from our side to yours or from your side to ours." 'So he said, "Father, I beg you then to send Lazarus to my father's house, since I have five brothers, to give them warning so that they do not come to this place of torment too." Abraham said, "They have Moses and the prophets, let them listen to them." The rich man replied, "Ah no, father Abraham, but if someone comes to them from the dead, they will repent." Then Abraham said to him, "If they will not listen either to Moses or to the prophets, they will not be convinced even if someone should rise from the dead." (Lk 16:19-31).The above parable teaches us all a beautiful lesson. When the rich man saw the story, he did no harm to poor Lazarus. He even allowed the poor man to eat the crumbs that fell from his table and he didn't mind. But when they both died, they were rewarded according to their lives on this earth. Although the rich man did no harm to poor Lazarus, he was sent into hellfire. The reason was that he did not care about his fellow human beings, who suffered miserably in his presence. Had he worried about the poor man?. He had enough to share with others, he could have shared some of his possessions, could have given the poor enough food and drink, and dressed him in such a way that he would be protected from the dogs that licked him. He could have lived a decent life because he had everything in abundance and nothing would have been lost for him if he had shared a small part of his enormous wealth. This attitude of the rich man drove him into hellfire. But Lazarus, who endured all the agony and pain, shame and inadequacy even for his basic needs, was rewarded in unimaginable ways. He enjoyed eternal bliss in Abraham's lap. Only now did the rich man realize his mistake. So he wanted Abraham to send someone from the dead to counsel his brothers who were following the same method of his earthly life. There, too, he did not get a positive answer because Abraham rightly pointed out the teachings available on earth through prophets and other elders to which they must heed and live the law and commandments. Some may think, "I am not harming anyone. I live my life in silence" This is not the right attitude. Failure to do good is sin.

Do not say: "I spend what is mine. I enjoy what is mine". It is not yours, it belongs to someone else "(St. Chrysostom).

## Immaturity

May I just ask you a question? How old are you? 14 or 16? 40 or 50? I ask because being over 15 or 18 also means a lot. For example, when you are 15 you can get your scooter license. But at 18 you can do anything and vote. Age is already an important thing in one's life. Every child is happy when they outgrow childhood The other and reach puberty. When you grow up you have more rights. One day a girl told me that she said to her mother: "I'll show you my rights!" Young adults want to show that they now have more rights - right is also associated with power. This is also the case in the church, for example. In the Catholic Church in particular there is a strong movement in which the laity want to have a greater say. There are various associations calling for this. In their opinion, laypeople should also be consulted in advance when appointing bishops and should also have a say in the election.

In the Gospel according to Matthew Jesus praised the little ones (Mt 11:25-30). He said in a prayer" I bless you, Father, Lord of heaven and of earth, for hiding these things from the learned and the clever and revealing them to little children". He praised the small, inconspicuous people. And he said that his message was actually for these little ones and not for the wise, not for the adults. The message of Jesus is especially for children and infants. We hear this, for example, when Jesus blesses the children. (cf. Lk 18:15- 17). Why are these infants and children so important to God and not to us? We want to show that we have experience. We believe that we are filled with wisdom and that we do not need any messages or advice from God or other elders. It is not so with children and infants. These children, these underage sons - are the ones who are spontaneous, who can absolutely trust, who enjoy every experience, no matter how small. They are the ones who are genuinely grateful because they know they are getting everything they may not deserve. These are people who really hear the message of God and are also enthusiastic about it. Children are dependent on someone, they are always open to any kind of news or event that happens around them and believe it the way they hear it. These children forgive and forget easily even if they are scolded or beaten by their parents or elders. The next moment they run to those who have hurt them. They are telling the truth because they don't know what to see or hear. There are also people in our churches who do not want to hear any message or listen to any piece of advice. They want power, they want to have a say. This shows that they are still immature in their beliefs. They don't even accept the teachings of Jesus. In contrast to the small children, who always live with a light heart, they burden themselves. This is why Jesus said in this gospel: "Come to me, all you who labour and are overburdened, and I will give you rest"(Mt 11:28). These inferior human beings are allowed to rest with God. And they also know where to rest.

Are you over 18? Or are you still "unfinished"? Then you are the people addressed in the above message.

## I realize my Problem

In our lives we often look the other way when we feel sorry for something or when we are faced with something terrible.

Especially when we see a dead animal or even a dead person, we have the urge to run away. We don't like to watch that. Because we feel uncomfortable. We say there are better things to see than such a terrible situation. But in our lives we still experience that there is something unpleasant somewhere, those problems that we somehow cannot get rid of. Likewise, there are our pains, our disabilities, our shortcomings, our illnesses, or our bad habits that we cannot easily overcome. The story of a young woman - once a young woman who had problems with being overweight went to a psychologist to express her uncomfortable feeling about being too fat. She said she wanted to reduce her body weight significantly. She also told the psychologist that despite her efforts to lose weight, she had not had any success so far. The psychologist tried to find out what was causing this problem. After long dialogues and conversations, the psychologist found out the reason for her obesity. Her father had been very brutal and aggressive in her childhood. The mother took the child and fled from the father and stayed away again and again. So mother and child were often left alone. The child (currently young woman) always remembered the brutality of the father and talked to his mother about it, and she was sorry for that. To calm the frightened child, the mother kept giving her candies to eat thus distracting her for the time being. As a result, over time, the girl learned to eat sweet to calm herself down and developed a habit of consuming more sweets. This habit stayed with her until she grew up into a young woman. She could never avoid it, because for a long time she had experienced that she could gain inner joy just by eating sweets.

Dear friends, this story also shows me that this woman had finally taken a closer look to find the cause of her problem. Through psychological treatment, the young woman realized that one can come to inner joy even without sweets, and because she understood that this desire for sweets was only sown into her consciousness by her mother.

In the Book of Numbers we find an interesting story. The Israelites who were on their way to Cannon left Mount Hur and made their way to the Red Sea. But they lost patience and complained about God and Moses throughout the journey. They mumbled that even if they had enough of everything, there wasn't proper food and not enough water. The Lord sent snakes to bite people, and many died. As a result, people came to Moses and pleaded that their sins be forgiven and that the serpents be removed from them. Moses prayed for the people. The Lord told Moses to make a seraph and attach it to a pole, and if someone who was bitten looked at him, he would recover. Moses did this as directed, and those who were bitten and looked at the bronze serpent were healed.

So there are definitely uncomfortable situations in our lives that we don't know how they came about. But we know we want to get away from it. There are also spiritual memories and experiences.

Jesus also says that the Son of Man is exalted and that all who look to the Son of Man will be saved. What does this analogy mean? Here I can recognize Jesus as crucified. Jesus hangs on the cross between heaven and earth and we can see how brutal people can be. We see that the brutality, the sins of one person can destroy another person, even though this person is God incarnate. When we look up to this crucified Jesus of Nazareth, we can reflect on our problems, illnesses, loneliness, or even the problems that other people can cause us, especially if they are cruel. This gives us some strength for our life. Healing can take place in our life. Not only is this a psychological process of rationally realizing what is causing the problem, but it is also about learning that Jesus, the Son of God, gives us the strength we need. Hence the cross is one of the most important symbols of our Christian life. Because we know, that Jesus, as an exalted man and as the Son of God, can help us.

Psychology can help me see where it's coming from. But where it goes next, the need for new strength - Jesus alone can help us. As Christians, we may wonder how we can identify our problems. And when we have recognized them, we can draw strength from Jesus, who is our Savior and Redeemer, who gave his life for us on the cross.

## I am There

Where are you, man? We sometimes hear this question in our family or with friends. Where are you? And sometimes the answer comes: I am there. God showed himself for the first time in the history of men. He said: "I am here." "I am Who I am" (Ex 3:14). Moses discovered God in the burning bush. He learned that through this burning bush he could see God himself. God asked him to take off his shoes, as the place he was standing was a holy ground, Moses prepared himself to meet the God who was calling him. He made Moses the liberator of the Israelites. Moses asked: "Who are you?" God replied: "I am who I am." (Ex 3:14). This was a breakthrough in the history of mankind in connection with its God. Until then, people had not known who or where God was. And here, for the first time, God says his name as "I am who I am". This is a wonderful term for philosophers and theologians. Nobody would just say "I am who I am". But there is a workable explanation here. The "I am who I am" God is a God who is forever present. He doesn't say he can't be there tomorrow. Yesterday he was here, today he is present and tomorrow he will be here and forever until the end of time he will be present. We should always try to experience the presence of God within us, in our midst, in our families and wherever we are and whatever we do. Even if we could rise and enter the clouds above, we can experience God. You will see that in your everyday life too. Whether we get up, whether we are at work, while enjoying, whether we are sad or simply tired, we cannot hide from God in any situation in life and He can be experienced in everything. This breakthrough from Moses is a great gift for all of us. God is always there. He is there for you and for me.

## Not me, but Christ lives in me

I no longer live, but Christ lives in me. A book by the author Christoph Koch was published with the title: "I am offline". In it, the author describes how you can live for a few weeks without a mobile phone, without the Internet, without SMS. I think you look at your smartphone a lot. One study found that people check their cell phones an average of 83 times a day. I am no longer alive, but Christ lives in me, wrote Paul two thousand years ago. Why is he writing this?

The cell phone and various other things keep us busy, and that means that we no longer lead our own lives. We are carried by different experiences, we are carried by different objects, we are carried by different emotions. This is what Paul meant when he said: I no longer alive. I mean everything that has occupied me. What Paul wants to convey to us in this text is a mystical experience. I no longer live, that is, I live completely freely, only with Jesus. In Christ. I can love, live, dance, be happy and do everything as if I were Jesus Christ myself.

Jesus Christ was spontaneous and divine. So if I too live so spontaneously and divinely, that is, in Christ, then I will become a different creature. I am no longer alive, but Christ lives in me. This is another reality, another spiritual reality that every human being can strive for. Paul did it. And what about us? We are often preoccupied with different things. We have trouble falling asleep. There are many people who cannot sleep at night. There are many people who live with their wounds and injuries every day and simply cannot forget or forgive. And in such a situation this sentence helps us: I no longer live, but Christ lives in me. In this way, Jesus Christ, who is really God for our world and for all of us, frees us from all our worries, pains and fears. Let us all be more secure in him, throw all of our burdens at his feet and live a life of liberation.

## Reconcile with Nature

The theme of last Sunday's liturgy was "Rogate", which means "Please". We and many European countries have a wonderful tradition of prayer processions. When I was still working on Lake Constance, we had a prayer parade once a week where people walked through nature, which is why this tradition is also called a hallway procession. Perhaps this tradition has become important again for us today. Such processions take place to ask for a good harvest, so that there will be no storms and damage, and to unite and be reconciled with God. Perhaps this tradition has become important again for us today. But agriculture today is no longer the same as it was 50-100 years ago. There are large corporations, a lot is automated, profit maximization is the most important thing, so often at the expense of nature. In spite of this, or precisely because of this, environmental awareness is greater today than it used to be. I am thinking of the "Friday for Future" movement or the significantly higher proportion of organic products available than before. People want to live with nature, live healthily, preserve nature. These processions are also intended for people to repent if they have done something against nature.

The corona virus is also part of nature. And it shows us that we haven't been good with nature, with our earth, for a long time. We depend on nature, it is our living space. And we now see that nature is more powerful than we think, and what the consequences of exploiting the earth and only thinking of our gain. Rethinking is more important than ever. We have to be aware of the great gift nature from God's hand and handle it carefully, otherwise it will only be to our disadvantage. It's not too late to apologize, to regret, to make amends. The processions usually take place 3 days before the feast of Ascension. We are allowed to be in nature, to be aware of it, and whether you believe in God or not, I invite you to come with us. And we thank our Creator for this great gift so that we can become one with nature and our God.

## What is Life

These days, I think a lot about life. Everything comes into life, people, plants, animals. They all want to live their lives. That is why we are fighting for every human life in these days of the Corona virus. But how can you live properly? Jesus said, "Whoever finds life loses it, whoever loses life for my sake, wins it". I have looked at various translations and I like the most the one which says: "Those who cling to their lives lose it / Whoever holds their life loses it". What does that mean? How can you say that you are not clinging to life? Everyone wants to live. I think it means that life is a movement, not a stagnation. If I want to live, I have to let it happen, let it grow, life is dynamic. If a child stayed crawling on the floor and didn't learn to get up and walk, their life wouldn't get very far. It would have no per-spective, it could not move, it could not experience anything new. That's why I understand life as movement. It goes on, it doesn't stop. "Whoever loses his life in my name wins it". I understand that Jesus is the measure of life, the alpha and the omega, the beginning and the end. But my life will not end in Jesus because He gives eternal life. They say if you want to fly you should leave everything that pulls you down. We were born to fly. High in the sky So don't hold onto anything, just let go, go on, especially with Jesus.

## Life is an encounter

Life is an encounter. Have you ever met people you don't want to see, people you don't want to have anything to do with? Or the experience of walking across the street when you noticed an unpleasant person was walking towards you? Have you ever used the excuse "very cleverly" to someone: I would have liked to see you, but somehow I don't have any free date or time at the moment? We have such encounters and experiences in our lives. In the Bible there is a beautiful story of two women who meet, Mary and Elizabeth (cf. Lk 1:39- 45). Two pregnant women come together. They have something in common: They both have a child. Both may have two different births, but these two different births have a common goal, which is to meet the kingdom of God. Mary and Elizabeth did not have any of reservation. Could I or do I have to see her or visit her?. They did not ask what do I learn from this gospel reading.

I may meet people when I "take" God with me, if I carry his goal within me and if I have His kingdom as my goal in my life. Then people are also good, even if they don't think like me, even if they don't have the flavour that I have. In the meeting of both women, a great thing happens. The women as well as the child in the womb of Elizabeth are filled with the Holy Spirit. The words spelt out by both women are precious, valuable. There is no envy, no pride - both are joyful. Presence of God is felt throughout Mary's stay with Elizabeth. So also all our encounters and meetings with people should be. When we meet anybody or visit anybody it should before the glory of God. People should feel the presence of God within us and in their hearts too. There should not be flattery or pride or arrogance or envy in our meetings with people. All differences in the name of colour, creed, caste, language and region should be set apart and pure love should be shared. Then that meeting would be of great value and experience like the visitation of Mary and Elizabeth in the New Testament. What are your talents There has been a lot of talk in the last few days about saving the euro. No Europe without the euro. A lot of banks nowadays try to advertise that they make a lot of returns, that money can be invested well, and so on. Savings books with one percent interest are a thing of the past! Lots of people want something more interesting. You are collecting money at high risk. They also want to buy securities and increase their holdings. They are right. We will hear something similar in the Gospel of Matthew (cf. Mt 25:14-30). It is about a rich man who distributes some money to three different servants and says:"It is like a man about to go abroad who summoned his servants and entrusted his property to them. To one he gave five talents, to another two, to a third one, each in proportion to his ability. Then he set out on his journey. The man who had received the five talents promptly went and traded with them and made five more. The man who had received two made two more in the same way. But the man who had received one went off and dug a hole in the ground and hid his master's money. Now a long time afterwards, the master of those servants came back and went through his accounts with them. The man who had received the five talents came forward bringing five more. "Sir," he said, "you entrusted me with five talents; here are five more that I have made." His master said to him, "Well done, good and trustworthy servant; you have

271

shown you are trustworthy in small things; I will trust you with greater; come and join in your master's happiness." Next the man with the two talents came forward. "Sir," he said, "you entrusted me with two talents; here are two more that I have made." His master said to him, "Well done, good and trustworthy servant; you have shown you are trustworthy in small things; I will trust you with greater; come and join in your master's happiness." Last came forward the man who had the single talent. "Sir," said he, "I had heard you were a hard man, reaping where you had not sown and gathering where you had not scattered; so I was afraid, and I went off and hid your talent in the ground. Here it is; it was yours, you have it back." But his master answered him, "You wicked and lazy servant! So you knew that I reap where I have not sown and gather where I have not scattered? Well then, you should have deposited my money with the bankers, and on my return I would have got my money back with interest. So now, take the talent from him and give it to the man who has the ten talents. For to everyone who has will be given more, and he will have more than enough; but anyone who has not, will be deprived even of what he has. As for this good-for-nothing servant, throw him into the darkness outside, where there will be weeping and grinding of teeth."

For all of us who want more interest and returns in this age, this may look strange. The third servant can be said to have done the right thing by at least not losing the money. After all, we don't need to take too much risk! But the Bible has a different view in telling us: The Lord is coming again! The Second Coming of Jesus Christ is a fixed program in the Bible. Jesus Christ lived 2000 years ago, he left, but will come again. We humans live in this provisional time of the kingdom of God. We are at a stage where we can see the Lord anytime He returns. We are waiting for the Lord and live with him in an exciting time! The Bible asks us how we behave during this time. Many of us in this world get on just fine with beautiful homes, cars, and insurance for our property. We have it all, but what we really need is the Bible: Are you ready for the Second Coming of Jesus Christ? Is what you have in this world all you have? This world is a transitory world. Only the return of Jesus Christ will bring us fulfillment. These two servants, who increased the talents entrusted to them, enjoyed the messianic return. They wanted to help make them more. This is also the case in our lives: if we wait for the coming of Jesus Christ, prepare for that coming so that we can bring more out of what we have received, then we are ready for the second coming of Jesus Christ. Everyone has talents in their own way to strengthen the faith. Can we do that?

# 26. WONDER WORKER – JESUS (MIRACLES)

*"…to another, the working of miracles; to another, prophecy; to another, the power of distinguishing spirits; to one, the gift of different tongues and to another, the interpretation of tongues" (1 Cor 12:10).*

## Miracles written in the Gospels

Jesus, God Incarnate, the Saviour of the world lived only for a short period of thirty three years on earth. During his life on earth, he had been a wonder worker, performing various types of miracles, which are countless, and they are amazing. He changed the lives of many people around him and in places he went. The four Gospels - Matthew, Mark, Luke and John are the documents consisting of the miracles performed by Jesus. What is given in the four gospels is only a tiny fraction of the innumerable wonders he had worked on earth. This is clearly mentioned in the Gospel according to John: "There was much else that Jesus did; if it were written down in detail, I do not suppose the world itself would hold all the books that would be written" (Jn21:25).

## Jesus performed seven types of miracles:

- feeding thousands of people in the wilderness
- casting out evil spirits
- healing disabilities like the blind, deaf, infirmed, injured and also curing various sicknesses, including leprosy
- changing water into wine - the first miracle during a wedding feast at Cana

- controlling the elements of nature - calming the storm, the waves of the rough sea

- allowing Peter and his companions to catch a huge catch of fish in a surprising way.

- raising people from the dead (this can also include his own resurrection)

Also we can see the Transfiguration of Jesus as a great miracle and also the Eucharist - changing bread and wine into His own Body and His Blood (till today during the Mass). The total number of miracles recorded in all the four Gospel comes to 37. When performing supernatural acts of love and power, He revealed his divine nature. Limitless compassion and his absolute authority over nature, death, evil spirits and sickness showed that he was the Son of God and the promised Messiah.

## Cure of the Woman with a Hemorrhage, the Daughter of Jairus raised to Life – explained

Mark's Gospel (Mk 5:21-43) we can see two miracles performed by Jesus are recorded in one cluster. If we just read them as two different miracles, two different deeds of Jesus without giving a little thought to the milieu in which they were done, what kind of laws, rules and regulations prevailed at that time, then they would remain just two mighty deeds of Jesus. But keeping in mind the Jewish background of that time, if they are read and understood, the miracles would reveal the revolutionary spirit in Jesus.

The story of healing the woman with hemorrhage (Mk 5:25-34) is inserted into that of the raising of the daughter of Jairus (Mk 5:21-24, 35-43).

Now let's imagine the scene. Jesus had just crossed the Sea of Galilee and was on the shore of the lake. Large crowds crowded to approach Jesus. Synagogue President Jairus approached Jesus, fell on his knees, and pleaded with Jesus to heal his only 12-year-old daughter who was seriously ill.

Jesus agreed and just started going to his house with him to heal the girl. The crowd pressed on Jesus. Something else happened then. A woman who had been bleeding for 12 years and who firmly believed that Jesus alone could heal her came there too. When she saw the crowd, she thought that she didn't even have to see him or be touched by Jesus, but that it would be enough if she had the opportunity to touch the clothes of Jesus. Fortunately, she was able to. She touched the cloak of Jesus walking behind him. Immediately she could feel the miraculous healing. Jesus too became aware of the power that was going out of him. This power is seen as a physical emanation that heals. So Jesus asked, "Who touched my clothes?" The disciples said, "You see the crowd pressing you, but then how can you ask who touched my clothes?" Startled, the healed woman stepped forward and explained her illness and her touching the clothes of Jesus and the miraculous healing of her illness she experienced as a result of it. Jesus called her "daughter" and said her faith had healed her. While this was happening, the journey was interrupted by Jesus following Jairus to his house to heal the little girl. He was stopped. In the meantime, some people came out of Jairus' house to tell him about his daughter's death and to stop bothering Jesus. But Jesus told Jairus to "believe" and went to Jairus' house. There he took only Peter, John and James with him and went into the room in which the girl was lying. He sent the crying people out of the room. He allowed the girl's parents to stick with it, then took the girl's hand and said

"Talithakum". It's an Aramaic word, the language Jesus spoke at the time. That means "little girl, I tell you to get up". The girl got up and began to walk.

## Now let's analyze the whole incident:

The first miracle happened to a woman who was bleeding. Women with such bleeding illnesses shouldn't mingle with other people. They were considered unclean. As long as the bleeding problem persisted, she had to be separated from the others. The disease was not just a matter of shame, but also of legally unclean as described in Lev 15:25-27. In Lev 15:28-30 we see:" Once she is cured of her discharge, she will allow seven days to go by; after that she will be clean. On the eighth day she will take two turtledoves or two young pigeons and bring them to the priest at the entrance to the Tent of Meeting. The priest will offer one of them as a sacrifice for sin and the other as a burnt offering. And in this way the priest will perform the rite of expiation for her before Yahweh for the discharge which made her unclean."

Of course, the woman knew this strict law very well. Even if she had stuck to it so far, this time she forgot everything. She had only one goal - she wanted to be healed. The only person who could do that was just Jesus - that was their deep faith. As the saying goes: Need knows no law, she forgot the law, and her body touched many people as she pushed through the crowd to reach Jesus and touch his clothes. By touching Jesus' clothes, she also defiled Jesus. She thought it would all end secretly. But Jesus made the issue public. Jesus did not do it to be known for his miracle work. But he wanted to break the unnecessary law that made women suffer separation, shame, loneliness and also made them mentally ill. Bleeding has something to do with the body. There is nothing sinful in it to be punished. Interestingly, all of these things were experienced not only by ordinary people, but also by the president of the synagogue, who had to strictly obey the law and was also the one who enforced the law and made sure that it was properly implemented. When Jairus knew what had happened, he did not complain, so as not to judge Jesus or the woman for making the entire atmosphere "unclean". For him, too, "the unclean Jesus" was the only source of hope during this time to heal his only daughter or even to raise her from the dead.

Strictly speaking, after the healing of this woman, Jesus and his disciples should have followed the purifying ritual of separation until evening and then had a bath, cleaned their clothes and made the prescribed sacrifice, in order to return to normal life. The woman who broke the law should have been convicted and punished. But none of this happened.

The law also forbade every priest (rabbi) to enter the house of a deceased / they were forbidden to touch the corpse (Lv 21:1). The synagogue president knew this law. But he took Jesus into his house, where his daughter's body was lying. Jesus touched the body and the girl rose. Now we can see that many laws have been broken. Both the woman with the blood flow and the synagogue board of directors are clear examples of how Jesus simply broke the so-called laws that no one dared question. Neither Jesus nor the people involved, i.e. the women who were healed, nor Jairus, the president of the synagogue. Everyone ignored the rules, regulations, laws, rituals prescribed by society. Jesus was their only hope. They all had a firm belief in Jesus and their faith gave them what they wanted.

**Lazarus come Out**

"When he had said this, he cried in a loud voice, 'Lazarus,

come out!" (Jn 11:43). There was even a very loud cry: Lazarus, come out! - a mighty voice with strength! The voice came from a man who was to be extradited in Jerusalem a few days later and barbarically killed on the cross on Calvary, and he is our Lord and Savior Jesus Christ. From this man came this mighty voice: Lazarus, come out! Why is he doing this? For whom?

There is a saying that everyone has a dead body in their basement. Yes, that's right! I myself have many corpses in my basement. Maybe you too: a broken marriage, an unfulfilled career, a dream never materialized, small or large injuries to friendships, or a word or two that hurt me. We somehow lock everything away, we may have "crammed" everything into a "basement" of our life and then simply locked it up; maybe we built a great wall around everything. Everyone has their corpses in the basement. If that is the case, if I know as a person that I will die one day, but do not know when death will come and I will have to live with this fear, then it is important that someone says: Lazarus, come out! A powerful voice that wants to give new life, a new way. (Jn 11:1-45). A powerful voice gives everyone new life. I cannot and should not start without the past, but with what I have been up to now. Lazarus, who has been lying dead in the grave for four days, is a prototype for all of us. When Jesus said: "Take the stone away" (cf. Jn 11:39), they even said, "Lord, by now he will smell" (Jn 11:39). In this situation, too, comes this powerful voice of God that wants to give life. He gives the new life. If that happens to Lazarus, then it is also possible for me today, in the year 2021. This is a voice with power that gives me confidence and a future life. But even before his death, Jesus wants to show us his divinity, his authority over death. Through the Gospel text we, who live with the corpses in our cellars, can identify with this deceased Lazarus. Jesus' word can open our basement and make everything come alive by destroying all of our past things. We can all live fresh lives again. Perhaps we will find meaning for the experiences we have that will enable us to live, to lead a whole new life.

# 27. WORD OF GOD

*"His cloak was soaked in blood. He is known by the name, The Word of God." (Rev 19:13).*

## The Power of Hearing

You know the power of hearing, the power of words, from personal experience. They also say: go in my ear - stay in my head. We hear thousands of words every day, on the radio, on television, at work, in the family. Yes, a word has a lot of power. The Old Testament also says that "God said, let there be light, and there was light (Gen 1:3). Jesus said, "I am Truth and Life" (Jn 14:6). He is the word and that word is always truth. Words are always wonderful, The sense hearing is very important to us. And that is why God always speaks to his people, in the past and now. When the Israelites heard the Word of God at that time, there was no paper to write it down. Everything was passed on orally until King Solomon later wrote everything down. This Word of God is an important force element for us today. Not just in the church, but for everyone in their daily life. That is why the Pope has proclaimed 2020 the year of the Wrd of God. The healing and sanctifying Word of God will come to all people and remain with them. It is often said that the Catholic Church has little to do with the Bible. This is wrong. The liturgy is based on the Word of God: texts from the Old and New Testaments and the Gospel are read and preached in every Mass. I would therefore like to invite you to reflect on the power that you can gain from the Word of God.

## Listening And Speaking

Speaking and listening - how important is this for our life! Have you ever seen a person who has hearing disability? A person who can neither hear nor speak? It is a severe handicap. Such a disabled person cannot perceive a lot in our world. I recently had a baby baptism. Both parents of the child were deaf. I tried sign language to help them understand what baptism is. Especially during baptism there is a rite in which the priest or deacon touches the ear and mouth of the recipient and says: 'Ephphata' - Open yourself! And this word Ephphata - Open yourself! - comes from the Gospel of Mark (cf. Mk 7:31-37).

There was a deaf person who was brought to Jesus. Jesus took this deaf man away from the crowd and touched his mouth with his own saliva. He sighed and said: Ephphata! 'Open up'! (Mk 7:34). Jesus touched him with his own saliva. Saliva is very personal. Healing was very important to Jesus. He is God incarnate, and that God touches a deaf man with his saliva and says Ephphata! Open up! Why is it important for God that his people hear and speak? Hearing is important for our communication. It is said that hearing is one of the most important things we need to live. Speaking is just as important. But do we all really hear? Sometimes we don't hear. But we love to talk. Sometimes we use vain words in our conversations that are inappropriate for a particular situation. Instead, however, we often don't talk when we should influence something important or relevant. That is why Klemens Nodewald wrote in a sermon: "Listening to God, listen to what he wants to tell you! Take the legitimate concerns of your fellow human beings! Listen to their unspoken pleas! Take their laments, their words of sorrow, their please for help! Hear their somewhat described apology from their words – and that they will reconcile with your want! Listen to the hidden praise! The hidden rebuke, the hinted disappointment! Listen to warnings and where people care about you because they love you!

Listen consciously to the voice of your heart again and again! Hear when God calls you!" And referring to the speech, he said: "Don't be cowardly where you need to talk! Say a clear yes or no! Pray, thank you, please! Trust yourself! Take your opinion, testify to your faith! Be an advocate! Acknowledge the good, the effort, Talk, relieve! Confess your mistakes, weaknesses, failures! Inspire, convince, warn! Say yes to God and His will!" All who can hear and speak are capable of doing more. The Gospel tells me personally that I should hear more, speak even more, and remain silent even more.

Goethe once said: "You only see what you know." When we go to a church or a museum and see a lot of things, we don't really understand everything. But just when someone comes and interprets or explains it, then we will probably understand a little more about it. In seeing there is a certain growth, a process, because I don't see everything I see. When we live with people, especially in married life or in a partnership, at some point after many, many years you learn what you didn't know about the other before. We are actually born blind. We can't see everything. We read that in the Gospel of John (Jn 9:1-41). It is about a blind man who is healed by Jesus. That's part of the narrative. The other is that the Pharisees do not believe in healing. Therefore, they are blind. There are three different stages in which this blindness is described. This will probably help us a lot when we go to a church for a bite play and celebrate a certain feast or participate in the worship. There are various Sacraments such as baptism, the Eucharist, confirmation that we celebrate as a community and also other kinds of worship, popular devotions etc., all are various acts of the Spirit. Do we understand everything? Very often we hurt people because we did not understand them; because we only saw what we already know.

285

This might be an occasion for us to change and open ourselves, or to open our hearts and humbly say that we do not understand everything we see.

## Two ears, one Mouth. Listen!

Do you hear me? Hello Hello? I thought at first that you might not hear me, but now I've realized that you can hear me. This week we think about listening. Listen. It is interesting that in our body there are some organs in pairs. Sometimes you wonder why you need two of the same organ. I don't want to teach anatomy, I'd rather stick with a double sense organ. Namely with our ears. Why do we have two ears and only one mouth? We also have two eyes, but speaking and listening are linked. The two ears only have one task, namely to hear. In contrast to the one mouth with which you can do a lot: talk, taste, eat, bite, lick and much more. So why did God give us two ears? Maybe we can become a more listening people.

A young man was taken to a temple by his mother, who was completely normal at that time. His name was Samuel. He stayed in the temple with the priest who lived there, whose name was Eli. One night Samuel heard the words: "Samuel, Samuel!" After Samuel heard this, he went to Eli and asked if he had called him. The priest said, "no". Samuel went back to bed and heard the call again. "Samuel, Samuel!" Again he went to Eli, and again he came back and went to sleep. The third time Eli came up with the idea that Samuel had heard something completely different. Maybe he had heard his inner voice, or even the voice of God. Then Eli realized that the Lord had called the boy. Eli said to Samuel: "Go, lie down. When he calls you, answer and speak, Lord; for your servant hears. He went and lay down in his place. Then the Lord came and called as before: "Samuel! Samuel!". Samuel replied: "Speak, Yahweh; for your servant is listening" (1 Sam 3:10). Samuel later became a great prophet and a Judge.

Our whole life is a great field of listening. Do we really hear what's coming from our hearts? Do we hear the voice of God especially in this time of the corona pandemic, when there are more and more restrictions, lockdowns, panic, loss of human life and livelihoods?. We can hardly visit other people and talk to them. But this is a wonderful opportunity for us to hear the unspoken words of our fellow human beings in their suffering and pain. To hear what God wants to tell us. What God expects from us. What God wants to communicate to other people through us at this crucial time.

There is so much guilt, so much sin, so much filth in this world because people don't listen to each other. If people could hear about the longings, the pain, the anger, the disappointment, but also the joy of other people, a lot could be changed.

## The Camel through the Eye of the Needle

Can the camel go through this eye of a needle? The whole time I thought about how the camel could go through this eye of the needle. Now let's show how big or how small this eye is so that the camel can try to go through this little hole. In the Gospel according to Mark there is a narrative, wherein a rich man met Jesus and entered into a dialogue with Him. "He was setting out on a journey when a man ran up, knelt before him and put this question to him, 'Good master, what must I do to inherit eternal life?' Jesus said to him, 'Why do you call me good? No one is good but God alone. You know the commandments: You shall not kill; You shall not commit adultery; You shall not steal; You shall not give false witness; You shall not defraud; Honour your father and mother.' And he said to him, 'Master, I have kept all these since my earliest days.' Jesus looked steadily at him and he was filled with love for him, and he said, 'You need to do one thing more. Go and sell what you own and give the money to the poor, and you will have treasure in heaven; then come, follow me.' But his face fell at these words and he went away sad, for he was a man of great wealth. Jesus looked round and said to his disciples, 'How hard it is for those who have riches to enter the kingdom of God!' The disciples were astounded by these words, but Jesus insisted, 'My children,' he said to them, 'how hard it is to enter the kingdom of God. It is easier for a camel to pass through the eye of a needle than for someone rich to enter the kingdom of God" (Mk 10:17-25).

The disciples were amazed about the answer of Jesus, because the statement of Jesus was in contrast to their mental make up. In the Old Testament wealth and material goods were considered a sign of God's favour (Job 1:10, Ps 128:1-2, Is 3:10). The words of Jesus in the above narrative provoke astonishment among the disciples because of their apparent contradiction of the Old Testament concept. Since wealth, power and merit generate false authority, Jesus rejects them utterly as a claim to enter the Kingdom. Achievement of salvation is beyond human capability and depends solely on the goodness of God who offers salvation as a gift (Mk 10:27). The rich man, who wanted to keep everything to himself and who thought himself to be the center of the world and who thought everyone else was unimportant, thought he was so important that he didn't care about the rest of the world. He saw the world as a slave and wanted to enrich himself in it and have eternal life. The Old Testament concept was that only observance of the laws and commandments would bring salvation to the people. For Jesus, that was a completely wrong concept, and that's why Jesus said: "It is easier for a camel to pass through the eye of a needle than for someone rich to enter the kingdom of God". If the above saying of Jesus applies to you in any way, then as a sincere follower of Christ you must seek to change your ways. When God has blessed someone with tremendous wealth, it is not only for selfish purposes, but it should be shared with those in need. That we make it available for the benefit of the little ones, the inconspicuous, the sick and the needy. Then we become the heirs to inherit the kingdom of God. The attachment to possessions, wealth and power is always an obstacle to entering the kingdom of God.

## Refugees in the Bible

The refugee issue has become one of the most important issues. I'm bringing you to the Bible now. The Bible is a book that has many stories about refugees. Flight and displacement were an important theme in the Bible.

Starting with Abraham, who has to leave the country, or for example Moses as a political refugee or later Joseph or Naomi. In the Bible, we meet a number of refugees who had to leave the country because different situations made life in their own country very difficult for them.

We also find many refugees in the New Testament, starting with Jesus, who had to leave the country as a small baby with his parents Joseph and Mary. Or later, when the Christians had to leave the country because of their faith and then lived scattered in the surrounding countries. The Bible is a book in which we can read such stories. But there is a very important reference to the very first escape, namely the fictional story of Adam and Eve, who had to leave the country or paradise and settle down on earth like refugees. But Paul is rightly mentioning where our real home lies. It is the kingdom of God, it is the Eternal world that we have to long for and reach there. Our home is in heaven. For attaining salvation or to inherit the kingdom of God, we have to listen to the Word of God, listen to His will and obey them and live up to the expectation of God. For Jesus himself has said to us: "In all truth I tell you, whoever listens to my words, and believes in the one who sent me, has eternal life; without being brought to judgement such a person has passed from death to life" (Jn 5:24).

## 28. X-RAY EYES OF GOD

*"Where shall I go to escape your spirit? Where shall I flee from your presence?" (Ps 139:7).*

### Can you Hide?

Often times, people think that whatever sins and crimes they commit in the dark, when alone, no one knows about it. Of course, with CCTV cameras and other modern devices in telecommunications technology, it becomes difficult to hide anything today. But even modern techniques often fail. There is only one technology at work - that has worked, that works and that will work until the end of time. And these are the eyes of God Almighty. Scripture says: "The eyes of Yahweh are everywhere: observing the wicked and the good" (Pro 15:3). He is omniscient, omnipotent and omnipresent. Nothing can be hidden from Him. Even after becoming well aware of this fact, the hide and seek of man continues from the time of creation to this moment all around the world. We can just look at a few examples:

God created Adam and Eve. our first parents in his own image (Gen 1:26) and made them live male and female in the garden of Eden. He gave them all freedom, but made one condition for them: they should not eat the fruit of the tree of the knowledge of good and bad (Gen 2:16). But tempted by the serpent, they ate the forbidden fruit, thus disregarding the Creator's commandment. The moment they ate this fruit, their eyes were opened and they found that they were naked. They were running and hiding from the Lord among the trees in the garden when they heard the sound of the Lord in the garden (Gen 3:1-8). Could they hide there forever? No, it wasn't possible. The Lord, who knows everything, caught them and ultimately they were driven from His presence (Gn 3:23- 24). Out of the behavior of Adam and Eve, sin was born = the sin of disobedience and greed.

Cain and Abel were the sons of our first parents, Adam and Eve. Cain became a tiller of land and Abel became a shepherd. Both of them went to offer sacrifices to the Lord. Cain brought as offering fruit of the soil and Abel brought the best firstling of the flock. The Lord, while accepting the offering of Able, rejected that of Cain's. Cain became angry. The anger and fury mounted in the heart of Cain who went to the extent of committing a murder - murdering his own brother. The thoughts of Cain were fully known to the Lord. Cain could not hide his anger and violent thoughts from the Lord's eyes. So God came to him and advised him to drop the idea of killing his brother. He warned him that sin was a demon lurking at the door. But Cain did not listen to the Lord and took his brother into the field where no one could see them, and there killed Abel. Thus, through Cain, the sin of murder was born on earth. The Lord, in whose eyes nothing could be hidden, learned of Cain's sin. He asked Cain, "Where is your brother Abel?" Forgetting the power of the Lord, Cain lied, "I don't know. Am I my brother's keeper?" The Lord then pointed out to Cain what he had done to his brother (Gen 4:3-11).

Saul. It's an interesting story about a man who hid from the people. The Lord had to reveal to the people where he was hiding. The Israelites, after being freed from the slavery of Egypt and settled, felt the need for a king to rule over them like the rulers in their neighbourhood. Neither God nor Samuel, the judge and prophet of the time, liked the idea of the people. But the people insisted that a king should rule over them. Finally, the Lord accepted her request and told Samuel to anoint a person from all the tribes of Israel to be king. The tribe of

Benjamin was selected. The tribe of Benjamin consisted of many clans. Among the clans, the clan of Matri was chosen, and from among them Saul, the son of Kish, was chosen. But Saul wasn't there. Everyone was looking for Saul, but no one could see him. They asked the Lord whether Saul was there or not. The Lord had to come to help. He revealed the place where Saul was hiding. The Lord said: "He is hiding in the luggage". Then they ran over there and brought him. Samuel anointed Saul as the first king of the monarchy to rule the Israelites (1 Sam 10:17-24). Such are the eyes of the Lord. Nothing can escape his presence and his gaze. So the psalmist exclaims: "Where shall I go to escape your spirit? Where shall I flee from your presence? If I scale the heavens you are there, if I lie flat in Sheol, there you are". -"Even darkness to you is not dark, and night is as clear as the day" (Ps 139:7-8, 12).

## Jesus' Sermon

In His Sermon on the Mount, Jesus gave some tips about the ways to please God and be rewarded by Him instead of just receiving temporary rewards from people. He said that people must take care to do righteous deeds, such as providing help, secretly and unnoticed by other people around them; otherwise, they will not receive a reward from their Heavenly Father. So when giving alms, they are not allowed to blow the trumpet, as hypocrites do in synagogues and in the streets to gain the praise of others. People who do such things will get their reward (from fellow human beings). He instructed that anyone who wants to give alms should do so that even their left hand does not know what their right hand is doing. So the giving of alms should be hidden (hidden from other people). And the Heavenly Father, who is watching this, will reward the secret giver (Mt 6:1-4). As Christians who follow His principles,

293

these instructions should be followed by us, and we should not advertise alms giving for reward by praising and glorifying them by those around them. Jesus also said: "For nothing is hidden but it will be made clear, nothing secret but it will be made known and brought to light" (Lk 8:17).

# 29. YOUTH

*"Remember your Creator while you are still young" (Ecc 12:1).*

## Defining Youth

Young men and women are great and they are the most significant part of the people in the Church and in society. Without the youth, work in church and society would be in vain. From a church perspective alone, their potential in the church exceeds the level of human calculations. Adolescence, is the critical transition phase of an individual as he goes through the rites of passage from childhood to adulthood. Adolescents are those members of humanity who are too old to be children and too inexperienced to be adults. Many of them are of the stature of men and the demeanour of boys; they have women's bodies but girls' ideas. Whatever definitions we may give for youth, they are insufficient, since youth is a complex interplay of physical, mental, emotional and social factors that affect the whole personality.

The word youth means a period of freshness, vigour, spirit. that are the characteristic of a young person. To define the characteristics of youth, there are some general perspectives - physical characteristics, mental characteristics, emotional characteristics, social characteristics, and the spiritual life.

Physical: At this age, girls and boys experience various physical changes. It is a transition period from childhood to youth. Both boys and girls experience many changes in their bodies. Their voices change too, especially with boys. These physical changes have psychological effects on youth. They

295

may feel uncomfortable, embarrassed, and sometimes unsatisfied with the way they look.

Mental: The mental power of adolescence in the early stages unfolds quickly with an awakening of self- awareness and an increased desire for knowledge. The adolescent love to read, learn many things, and talk. They come on intellectual fronts; they have many dreams and ideas, their thinking skills and their judgment grow enormously. They are now trying to explore the world; they are finding their ambitions, they are looking to a bright future and they are conquering the vast fields that lie before them. They are influenced by the opinions of others, especially their friends and peers, and they also see certain personalities such as politicians or film heroes as their role models.

Emotional: Youth is a time of the search for personal identity. The youngsters are inundated with questions about themselves: "Who am I?", "Where am I going?" and so on. Emotions are the only way that adolescents can express the frustration they are going through due to changes in their physical and mental makeup. These emotions include pride, shame, love, hate, discouragement, fear, anger, joy, bitterness, etc. They are suddenly happier and suddenly they are upset and even angry. But young people are also often thrown into a dilemma by the different conditions that their home, society, their peers and the church place on them.

Social: This means that people live together as a group in a situation that requires interaction with one another. Family members are in good social community when there is mutual love, acceptance, understanding, and security. Since love is the basis for acceptance, the youngsters look for new friends. They gradually shift their loyalty from their parents to their peers, they long for more independence and want to belong to a group. For their recreation, they play online games and everyone wants to take part in them at the same time. They need friends with whom to confide in, exchange ideas, share things, and go to specific places. Their lives begin to narrow and deepen, but in the sense of expanding their employment, home life, worship and service to humanity.

Spiritual: In the spiritual dimension, you would like to ask various questions to those who teach you spirituality, God, faith, etc. The questions are often asked in such a way that even teachers find it difficult to give an adequate and convincing answer. But if the youth get the right answer and understanding and guidance, then they will definitely answer the call of the Spirit and dedicate themselves to serving God and humanity. That only happens in adolescence.

## What does the Bible say about Youth?

*"Young man, enjoy yourself while you are young, make the most of the days of your youth, follow the prompting and desire of heart and eye, but remember, God will call you to account for everything."* (Ecc 11:9). "So that Christ may live in your hearts through faith, and then, planted in love and built on love, with all God's holy people you will have the strength to grasp the breadth and the length, the height and the depth" (Eph 3:17-18).

The following verses explain the concept of youthhood:

## Old Testament

- "The pride of the young is their strength, the ornament of the old, grey hairs" (Pro 20:29).

- "His bones used to be full of youthful vigour: and there it lies, in the dust with him, now!" (Job 20:11)

- "His flesh will recover its childhood freshness, he will return to the days of his youth" (Job 33:25).

- "For you are my hope, Lord, my trust, Yahweh, since boyhood" (Ps 71:5).

  "When the wrath of God attacked them, slaughtering their strongest men, laying low the flower of Israel" (Ps 78:31).

- "He contents you with good things all your life, renews your youth like an eagle's" (Ps 103:5).

- "May our sons be like plants growing tall from their earliest days, our daughters like pillars carved fit for a palace" (Ps 144:12).

- "Youths grow tired and weary, the young stumble and fall" (Is 40:30).

- "Yahweh is good to those who trust him, to all who search for him. It is good to wait in silence for Yahweh to save. It is good for someone to bear the yoke from a young age" (Lam 3:25-27).

## New Testament

· "In the same way, younger people, be subject to the elders. Humility towards one another must be the garment you all wear constantly, because God opposes the proud but accords his favour to the humble" (1 Pet 5:6).

· "If a widow has children or grandchildren, they are to learn first of all to do their duty to their own families and repay their debt to their parents, because this is what pleases God" (1 Tim 5:4).

· "Turn away from the passions of youth, concentrate on uprightness, faith, love and peace, in union with all those who call on the Lord with a pure heart" (2 Tim 2:22).

· "Let no one disregard you because you are young, but be an example to all the believers in the way you speak and behave, and in your love, your faith and your purity" (1 Tim 4:12).

Youth in the Bible:

Since there are many young men and women who have acted courageously and accomplished heroic deeds in the Bible, we can get to know some of them and try to use their lives as models for our lives. We want to briefly introduce ourselves to the four personalities from the Old and New Testaments, who were young men and women and who stood up for their convictions until the very end, who achieved great things and are still the best role models for humanity today.

Old Testament personalities: Joseph, son of Jacob, David, The slave girl in the palace of Naaman and Prophet Daniel and his friends.

New Testament personalities: John the Baptist, Mary mother of Jesus, Jesus and Paul.

## Old Testament

Joseph (son of Jacob) (Gen 37: 21-28, 39-41): Joseph was the beloved son of Jacob and God gave him the gift of interpreting dreams. Since Joseph's dream interpretation tasted bitter to his brothers, they were angry with him and wanted to get him out of the way. But the Lord was always with him and had other plans for him. They planned to sell Joseph to the Ishmaelites who were walking by while they ate after throwing Joseph into a dry well. Meanwhile, some Midianites who passed by the same way pulled Joseph out of the well and sold him to Potiphar, one of the Pharaoh's officials and the commander of the guard in Egypt. So Joseph was brought to Egypt. God was with him and he gave him wisdom and intelligence and so he gained the confidence of Potiphar. He became the personal assistant of Potiphar and was also made in charge of the household. Joseph as a youth was beautiful and Potiphar's wife wanted to have illegal relationship with Joseph. But Joseph did not yield to the temptation. But Potiphar's wife becoming angry with Joseph falsely charged Joseph that he was trying to seduce her. Joseph was arrested. He was innocent; but he suffered injustice because he was righteous before God. He did not commit a serious sin for not accepting the illegal wishes of Potiphar's wife. But God's grace rested on him. He could interpret the dreams of the two prisoners who were with him in prison. At an appropriate time, when Pharaoh was having some dreams, the prisoner remembered him having had an opportunity to meet Joseph and his precise interpretation of the dreams. He informed the Pharaoh and Joseph interpreted the dreams of the Pharaoh in a very convincing and perfect manner. Thus Joseph was not only released from prison but also he was raised to a higher position as the Governor of Egypt. As per the interpretation of Joseph, there was a famine throughout the world. But in Egypt there was enough stock of food. Joseph could bring his father and brothers during the years of famine to Egypt. Thus Joseph created a great history. He came as a slave, as a single individual into the land of Egypt. Then he had a family of his own in the land of Egypt. Then when he brought all his brothers and their families along with his father, it grew up into a community settled down in Egypt. They increased and multiplied in Egypt. With the passage of time, they became slaves. But when they were liberated under the leadership of Moses, they became a nation to leave the country. It is a big evolution from a single man to a nation.

In Joseph we see many noble qualities: The determination not to sin, faith in God, sincere and hardworking young man gaining the confidence of the authorities and proper utilization of the God given special talents and gifts. He stands as an exemplary youth - and many can surely take him as their role model.

David was the son of Jesse, who was from Bethlehem in Judah. Jesse had 8 sons of which three were working in the army of Saul. David was the youngest. David was looking after the flock of his father at Bethlehem and also serving Saul. At that time Philistines brought their forces for battle at Judah and camped between Socoh and Azekah. Saul and Israelites gathered and camped in the Vale of the Terebinth. Goliath of Gathcame from Philistine camp and he challenged Saul that if anyone who could kill him, they would surrender and become vassals to Saul and serve him. One particular day when David went to give food to his brothers, he saw the Israelites and Philistines drew up opposite each other in battle. While David was talking with his brothers, Goliath came and challenged as before. David wanted to fight with Goliath. Saul tried to prevent him from fighting with Goliath because he was very young. David had confidence in himself and a deep faith in God. He said "The Lord, who delivered me from the claws of the lion and the bear, will also keep me safe from the clutches of this Philistine". Saul said to David "God the Lord will be with you". David took five smooth stones and with a staff in his hand he went to meet Goliath the Philistine. Goliath was sarcastic of David and of God of Israel and said to him that he would give the flesh of David to birds of the air and beasts of the field. David told him that he came in the name of the Lord of hosts, the God of armies of Israel who he had insulted. The Philistine then moved to hit David. David ran towards him quickly, he put his hands into his bag, took out a stone, hurled it with the sling and hit on the forehead of Goliath. David struck the Philistine without a sword.(1 Sam 17:50)

In David we see a young man filled with faith in God. He was a brave warrior. For winning over the giant like Philistine he put his entire trust on God and without sword or any other bigger weapons, he killed the mighty person with five pebbles. Youth can learn from him the bravery and firm faith in God.

The Maid (slave girl) in Naaman's house: Naaman was the army commander to the king of Aram. He enjoyed his master's respect and favour and Yahweh granted victory to Aramaeans. But he suffered leprosy. He brought a slave girl while he went for war into Israelites territory. She became the servant of Naaman's wife. That girl was a believer in Yahweh. Though she was a slave, she wanted her master to be cured of the disease leprosy he was suffering. So she boldly approached the wife of Naaman and told her that there was a Prophet of Samaria, who would cure the disease of Naaman, her master. Naaman went to king of Aram and told about that. King gave a letter to the king of Israel for helping Naaman to meet the Prophet and get cured of his disease.He went to the King of Israel and presented the letter. Though the king initially became angry and tore his clothes, Elisha the prophet sent messengers to the king and asked him to send Naaman to him. Naaman went there expecting the prophet would come and meet him, touch him and cure him. But the prophet instructed Naaman to take a bathe in the river Jordan. Naaman got angry. But his servants pacified and convinced him and asked him to bathe in River Jordan. Finally Naaman was cured of his leprosy (2 Kgs 5:16). Naaman not only was cured of his leprosy but also he became the believer of Yahweh and proclaimed "Now I know that there is no God anywhere on earth except in Israel".

The girl who advised Naaman's wife was only a slave. Back then, slaves were never allowed to talk to their masters or mistresses about such things. Her life was in danger when the girl spoke of her master's illness and a way to be cured. But she was brave enough to speak about it because she believed in God and was sure that Yahweh would heal her Master.

She appeared to be a young evangelist. Through them the mighty general of the king of Aram was able to find out about Yahweh and began to believe in him. The growth of the Church is in the hands of the youth alone. Young people should be deeply rooted in their faith in Jesus and also have the courage to speak about the Lord, to whom they profess and believe in Him, for whom this slave girl is an example.

Daniel and his friends: When Jehoiakim was reigning the kingdom of Judah, Nebuchadnezzar king of Babylon marched on Jerusalem and besieged it. Jehoiakim was defeated. Daniel and his friends were brought as slaves to the king's court because Ashpenaz the chief eunuch of the king was ordered to bring a few perfect youth of royal and noble descent. They should have good appearance and versed in every branch of wisdom. So he brought Daniel, Hananiah, Mishael and Azariah the four young men of king's expectation. But they were differently named by the chiefe unuch: Daniel as Belteshazzar, Hananiah as Shadrach, Mishael as Meshck and Azariah as Abed-Nego. They learnt everything but they kept up their Judaic customs and beliefs. Daniel had the gift of interpreting every kind of vision and dream. The king found the four youth excelled in knowledge and wisdom. Daniel was in the Royal Court until the first year of King Cyrus. Daniel was interpreting the visions of King Nebuchadnezzar without fear and hesitation. Nebuchadnezzar made a golden statue after the 3-23rd year of the Babylonian captivity. All people including Jews were ordered to worship the statue. But Daniel and his friends did not worship that statue. Some Chaldeans maliciously accused the Jews and told king Nebuchadnezzar, that Daniel and his friends did not worship as per the order of the King. So the king arrested Shadrach, Meshach and Abed Nego, bound and threw them into the burning fiery furnace. They walked in the heart of the flames, praising God and blessing Him. As the king and his men were watching, they could see four men. All the four men were walking free, untouched by the fire. The fourth man looked like a child of God (the angel), Nebuchadnezzar was astonished and approached the mouth of the fiery furnace and called out the three to come out. They came out as intact as they went it. Even their clothes were untouched by fire. Nebuchadnezzar accepted the God of Shadrach, Meshach and Abed-Nego. He declared that no one should speak against the God of Israel. Also in the later instance when Daniel was put into the lions pit, the beast did not harm Daniel. Again it was another great moment for the king to declare his faith in Yahweh the God of Israel.

The faith of the four youth is amazing. Though they were serving a king of different religious background, the four did not give up their own faith and their own obedience to their own commandments and laws. This tells us that we should also develop such kind of faith and also be convinced of our own way of living, our faith, our worship.

## New Testament

John the Baptist: He was the forerunner of Jesus Christ. He was the one who introduced Jesus to the people. He was baptizing the people with water and preaching to the people and trying to make them to repent for their sins and be reconciled. He lived in the wilderness. On seeing his deeds and hearing his words, people thought that he was the

Messiah, of whom the people were expecting for thousands of years. At one point, people even asked him whether he was the Messiah. Though John the Baptist had a very good opportunity to grab the situation and proclaim in public that He was the Messiah, sent by God, whom people were expecting, he did not do so. He honestly declined and pointed to Jesus and announced that Jesus was the Messiah. He was bold enough to question even those in authority. He pointed out the sin of King Herod because he had illegal contact with his brother's wife Herodias. For this courageous act, John was behind the bars and finally was beheaded (Mt 14:6-12).

John the Baptist teaches us honesty and bravery. He teaches the need to question the authority.

<u>Mary, mother of Jesus:</u> Mother Mary was a very simple and humble young girl from Nazareth. While she was betrothed to Joseph, the messenger of the Lord (angel Gabriel) was sent to her to announce the birth of Jesus when she was still a virgin. It was an unexpected situation in Maria's life. But at that moment she understood the will of God, she did not hesitate. She immediately gave her consent, even though she was well aware of the consequences she could have in male-dominated society. She immediately gave her consent. She gave her FIAT on the spot. But she did not give this in a state of the resilient instrument, only to nod her head at anything. She knew what it meant, and she was free and brave enough to give her consent. Mary was also very helpful. She travelled to the hill country of Judea (Ain Karim) to visit her relative Elizabeth, who had become pregnant in old age, and stayed with her for 3 months. She had the courage to go as far as Calvary, and there she witnessed the death and burial of his son. Despite her young age, she already had a strong mental strength to endure all kinds of shame and vehement criticism. Mother Mary

is the greatest role model for people of all ages and all walks of life. She has multidimensional virtues and was an exemplary woman. She was a compassionate mother, an obedient wife (of the Holy Family), a woman full of grace and love for God, a thoughtful person about everything that had happened in her life, and thus learned the will of God every moment of her life. She was a courageous woman who withstood all humiliation, shame and pain all her life, a woman who enjoyed inner freedom; always happy in the presence of the Divine Redeemer in the form of their own Son.

Jesus: He was the Son of God, the second person of the Holy Trinity. God sent the Messiah, the Redeemer of the world. He was the one who actually belonged in heaven, but who came to earth following the will of God. He took the form of a human and, like all of us, was in the womb and born of the Virgin Mary. During his earthly life, he has faced difficulties and problems since birth. He was born in a sheepfold / cowshed, which is an unimaginable emergency for a normal birth. He was placed in a manger. When Herod wanted to kill Jesus, he had to be brought to Egypt with Mary and his parents Joseph. They stayed there until they were called back. He obeyed and lived with Joseph and Mary until he was 30 years old. After that He left his house and began his Ministry, preaching the Kingdom of God and performed miracles. During his public ministry he was ridiculed, mocked, criticized by the Pharisees, Scribes and Sadducees. Though he was the God incarnate, he endured everything. But his teachings were authoritative. He was not afraid to point out the mistakes and atrocities of those in authority and the religious heads who were cheating people and burdening their lives. He was called a glutton, a possessed etc. In the end he was given the capital punishment of crucifixion. Till the end He was obedient to the Will of the Father. He is the only one who rose from the dead and left empty the tomb in which he was buried. In all his life he had never tried to accumulate wealth, he never wanted to get names and fame from people. He was full of love and compassion. His teachings are valued to this day, even by people of other faiths. He was only 33 when gave up his breath on the cross. The cross, previously seen as an instrument of shame and punishment, was made to the great symbol of Christians and Christianity. A symbol of victory and sacrifice.

Jesus was a youth. As a youth he roamed about the streets of Galilee, Capernaum, Cana, Bethany etc., meeting people. He did not wait for the people to come to Him but he went in search of people to comfort and console them and to cure their diseases and disabilities, to raise them from the dead. He is the role model for all of us. He has to be followed by all of us, especially youth for his patience, for his leadership qualities, and how he marched towards His goal in the midst of sarcasm and mockery. That is to be imitated by youth if they want to achieve their goals in their lives in the midst of various hurdles, blocks and barriers.

Paul: A learned person, fluent in Hebrew and Greek, deeply rooted in the faith of His God Yahweh and monotheism. He initially opposed Christ and Christianity. He did not understand Jesus fully. He was thinking very high of himself for his educational qualifications, for his staunch belief in his God, for the perfect adherence to the Jewish laws, customs etc. But once he was called by Jesus on the road to Damascus, there was no turning back in Paul's old life. He was a zealous missionary, who took Christianity outside the borders of Palestine and globalized the religion. He established many churches and he is also known as the 13 th disciple of Jesus and as the second founder of Christianity. The first one was

Jesus Christ. After learning the message of Christ and found his faith in Him, he began to regard as superfluous everything that had previously been important to him for his pride and reputation. He lived and served only for Christ. He worked with the pagans and brought them to Christianity. He wrote 13 letters to various churches that he founded, and these letters make up about 50% of the New Testament. He was martyred for believing in Jesus. From Paul youth should learn diligent efforts to achieve goals. If there is a good change in life, the youth should hold on to this change and try to improve on this level even more and to become perfect people in life, like Paul, who, despite many difficult and problematic situations, never returns to his old age life returned. He suffered many tortures for Christ's sake. But his love for Christ never decreased, but increased day by day, which enabled him to give his life for Jesus, who had called him to serve him.

# 30. ZEAL

*"For I am eaten up with zeal for your house, and insults directed against you fall on me" (Ps 69:9).*

## Zeal

Generally all languages have letters of their own. There is a first letter and at the end there is a last letter of that language. The Holy Bible was written in three different languages: Aramaic, Hebrew and Greek. Aramaic and Hebrew have 22 letters each and Greek has 24 letters. Most of the Old Testament was written in Hebrew in a few places the language used was Aramaic. For example some parts in the Book of Prophet Daniel 1:1-2:3, 8:12-12:13 are in Aramaic. Also the text of Dan 3:24-90 - about the three young men, the story of Susanna's virtue (Ch. 13) and the story of Bel and the Dragon Ch. 14are in Greek. The whole New Testament was written in Greek. In the last book of the Holy Bible, in the last chapter of the book of Revelations, we find the Lord saying: "I am the Alpha and the Omega, the First and the Last, the Beginning and the End" (Rev 22:13).The words Alpha and Omega are respectively the first and the last letters of the alphabets in Greek language. So too in this book "The Speech of a Stutter", written in English, which has 26 letters. The topics are arranged in alphabetical order of the English language, beginning with the letter "A" - for the chapter Abba Father and the last chapter of the book is titled with the last letter of the alphabet of English language "Z". The little is given as "Zeal" (The English word has Greek origin. And the word Alphabet is derived from the first two Greek letters: Alpha and Beta).

The word zeal means enthusiasm. As Christians, our zeal and passion should be directed towards Christ and his words; we should also have the ultimate goal of living a life that reflects the values of Christ. Jesus selected apostles and disciples and trained them for about 3 years. He always encouraged their zeal to work for the kingdom of God and to preach the good news. In the Gospel of Matthew, a chapter, namely chapter 10, is dedicated to the commissioning and sending out of the disciples. Not only did Jesus give the rules and regulations, but he also told what they should take and what they should not take, how to proceed, etc., including the following persecutions and the rewards that were waiting for their zealous efforts. This kind of encouragement and training from time to time enabled his disciples to work zealously for Christ and His values and words, and they were brave enough to give their lives for Him.

In the Scriptures, in both the Testaments, we find various personalities burning with the zeal for the Lord and they bear all kinds of tortures for the sake of the One in whom they have their belief.

"For I am eaten up with zeal for your house, and insults directed against you fall on me. I mortify myself with fasting, and find myself insulted for it" (Ps 69:9-10).

## The Dialogue between Prophet Isaiah and Yahweh

· Is 63:7-64:11 is in the form of a collective supplicatory Psalm, particularly Ps 44, 89, and parts of Lamentations. These two spoke about the destruction of Jerusalem city and Jerusalem Temple in 587 BC. The memory of the catastrophe was still fresh. This poem dates from the beginning of the Exile. The appeal to past history 63:7-14 conforms to Deuteronomic theology: God punishes his rebellious people, then He is the

One who rescues them. Is 63:11-14 evoke God's great saving act, the deliverance from Egypt as the earnest of salvation to come, but the actual supplication of the prophet Isaiah begins with 63:15.He said: "Look down from heaven and see from your holy and glorious dwelling. Where is your zeal and your might? Are your deepest feelings, your mercy to me, to be restrained? After all, you are our Father" (Is 63:15-16).

<u>2 Peter 3:1-16</u> — When Peter wrote the letter to the believers, they were frustrated with the Second Coming of Christ. During the Ascension, the angels told the waiting people that Jesus would return soon (Ac 1:10-11). So they believed that He would return in their lifetime. Paul also wrote about it to various churches. So there was a common belief and expectation of the Second Coming - the Parousia would take place in its generation itself. As it was delayed, some people started promoting that the Second Coming was a false doctrine. So there was division, conflict and disagreement among believers. With this in mind, Peter just wanted his people to live righteously and be ready to meet and welcome Christ at all times of his coming. He also wrote: "The Lord is not being slow in carrying out his promises, as some people think he is; rather is he being patient with you, wanting nobody to be lost and everybody to be brought to repentance." Finally he wanted to tell the people: "So then, my dear friends, while you are wait-ing, do your best to live blameless and unsullied lives so that he will find you at peace" (2 Pet 3:14).

So let all of us preserve our zeal for the Lord and work zealously for the building up of His Kingdom on earth.

Let us all hold on to our belief in Him and live His words and values and bear witness to Christ till He will come again.

Let us say with Paul:

"I have fought the good fight to the end; I have run the race to the finish; I have kept the faith; all there is to come for me now is the crown of uprightness which the Lord, the upright judge, will give to me on that Day; and not only to me but to all those who have longed for his appearing." (2 Tim 4:7-8).

References:

New Jerusalem Bible, online

https://www.bibliacatolica.com.br/new-jerusalem-bible/

Kathpedia.com

http://www.kathpedia.com/index.php?title=Englische Bibelabk%C3%BCrzungen